A Shared Truth

Latinx and Latin American Profiles
Frederick Luis Aldama, Editor

A

The Theater of
Lagartijas Tiradas al Sol
Julie Ann Ward

Shared Truth

UNIVERSITY OF PITTSBURGH PRESS

Published by the University of Pittsburgh Press, Pittsburgh, Pa., 15260
Copyright © 2019, University of Pittsburgh Press
All rights reserved
Manufactured in the United States of America
Printed on acid-free paper
10 9 8 7 6 5 4 3 2 1

Cataloging-in-Publication data is available from the Library of Congress

ISBN 13: 978-0-8229-6588-6
ISBN 10: 0-8229-6588-7

Cover photo: Gorka Bravo for Donostia Kultura, dFERIA 2018, licensed under CC BY-SA 2.0
Cover design: Alex Wolfe

This book is dedicated to the memory of
══ *Margarita Urías Hermosillo* ══

Una verdad compartida, es otro tipo de justicia.

A shared truth, is another kind of justice.

——————————————— Tita Gutiérrez

Contents

Julie Ann Ward has written an engaging, in-depth study on Lagartijas Tiradas al Sol, one of the most prominent theater groups in Mexico today, which has gained international acclaim due to the way its repertoire addresses urgent questions regarding the representation of history, memory, and truth. Lagartijas's artistic directors and main actors are Gabino Rodríguez and Luisa Pardo, whose work can be placed within current trends of documentary theater and the "theater of the real." Their work that interweaves archival research, apocryphal memories, and fictional accounts problematizes mainstream narratives of historical truth, especially regarding Mexican history and current political struggles.

Documentary theater in Mexico has known a recent boom, coinciding with the "war against drug trafficking" that was announced by former president Felipe Calderón in 2007. This Washington-aided policy led to the use of Mexican military and paramilitary forces to hunt down leaders of the drug cartels, in an attempt to dismantle widespread criminal organizations around the country. The policy was, however, tragically flawed, as the capturing or killing of one drug lord only resulted in his replacement. It also became more and more evident that different police forces around the country, as well as many city mayors, state governors, and businessmen were associated with the criminal organizations. Meanwhile, between 2006 and 2011, the United States (by means of the Arizona Field Office and the US Bureau of Alcohol, Tobacco, Firearms and Explosives) promoted Operation Fast and Furious, which allowed the illegal sale of over 2,000 weapons across the border to Mexican drug cartels, in the hopes of tracking them and capturing high-level criminals. The operation failed, as the agents were unable to track the majority of these weapons, ultimately reinforcing criminal organizations south of the border. The number of people killed during this drug war—most of them "collateral damage"—is staggering, today nearing between 200,000 and 300,000, plus over 40,000 people who have been forcefully "disappeared," and nearly 2 million displaced, virtual refugees within their own country. We are talking of numbers that surpass the war of the Balkans during the 1990s and the Iraq wars.

This unofficial civil war has deeply affected all levels of Mexican society, paralyzing and silencing many with fear, something that doubtless is in the interest of the powers that be in this scenario of what Achille Mbembe has identified as necropolitics. But hundreds of thousands refuse to stay silent; activists and grassroots organizations have responded to this scenario of violence with vigorous public demonstrations, which involve artists, journalists, students and teachers of all levels. Examples of this include the mobilization led by poet Javier Sicilia, the #YoSoy132 movement, and the massive demonstrations to demand justice for the families of the forty-three students who were "disappeared" in the town of Ayotzinapa, Guerrero, back in 2014.

What is the place of the performing arts in all this? Critic Luz Emilia Aguilar Zinser wrote that it is possible to find Mexican theater groups that are creating public spaces for person-to-person interaction that facilitates the sharing of testimonies, strategies of caring, and affective complicity in the midst of the catastrophe. Most of these projects cross the boundaries between theater and visual arts, fiction and the real, resorting to ethnographic, historiographical, and archival research strategies, in what critic Ileana Diéguez has described as *escenarios liminales* (liminal performances), and Rubén Ortiz calls *la escena expandida* (the expanded scene). For Diéguez, this kind of performance is crucial not so much because of its aesthetic innovations, but because of its ability to procure a *communitas chamánica*, or healing sense of solidarity, empowering artists and activists to work with their audiences to explore possibilities of resistance. Other notable theater groups in Mexico working today in this vein are: Teatro Ojo, Teatro Línea de Sombra, Colectivo Campo de Ruinas, Microscopía Teatro, Murmurante Laboratorio Escénico, Teatro Para el Fin del Mundo, and La Comuna.

The emergence of documentary theater in Mexico also coincided with the double commemorations that took place in 2010: the bicentennial of the beginning of the War of Independence, and the centennial of the Mexican Revolution. As Ward demonstrates in this book, Lagartijas Tiradas al Sol used theater to critically engage with the narratives of revolution and resistance, with its 2010 project *La rebeldía*, which focused on the guerrilla movements of the 1970s. In the performance *El rumor del incendio*, Luisa Pardo embodied her guerrilla mother, as a self-reflexive gesture to ask how her current generation relates to the past, especially through questions such as: "How can a critical view of the past transform the future? What struggles have we inherited? What does rebellion mean in the twenty-first century? How do we engage in dissident acts today? How do we build a better country?" which can be read in the performance's statement.[1]

These are questions that interest not only Mexican audiences: young people worldwide today are asking what their role in history is, how to resist inflammatory discourses of violence and hatred. That is why I believe Ward's book is a necessary contribution to theater and performance studies in the United States and other English-speaking countries. This volume not only helps fill the void of full-length studies available in English on contemporary theater in Mexico but also illuminates the way performing arts today provide a scenario for playing out urgent questions regarding the representation of history and truth.

Antonio Prieto-Stambaugh

=== **Acknowledgments**

This book taught me that writing is an act of generosity and collaboration. When I first saw a play by Lagartijas Tiradas al Sol, as a graduate student in Mexico City, I wrote a comment on their blog asking for more information. Luisa Pardo, Gabino Rodríguez, and Paco Barreira opened their door, their tequila, and their work to me. Over the years I have had the good fortune to get to know more members of the company: Mariana Villegas, Carlos Gamboa, and Sergio López Vigueras. Their creativity and kindness are the reason for this book.

At the University of Pittsburgh Press, I am especially grateful to Frederick Aldama, who believed in and championed this project unwaveringly. He taught me the true definition of collegiality. I thank Josh Shanholtzer for his patient support as this book grew into itself. The anonymous reviewers helped me to find focus and direction, and I appreciate their labor.

Thank you to Ileana Diéguez, for working as the first adviser on this project. Thank you for seeing me as a person, beyond my project, and giving me the exact advice I needed at the exact moment I needed it.

The University of California Institute for Mexico and the United States in Riverside, California, was a soft landing spot where I could work out the first inklings of this book. Thank you to Wendy DeBoer, my fairy godmother, for creating time and space where there had been none for me to work and think. Thank you to Andrea Kaus for your stunning photographs. Thank you to Exequiel Ezcurra and Irene Dotson for making my residency in Riverside possible and so very meaningful.

I thank Antonio Prieto Stambaugh for his kind and constructive way of building up the field and his colleagues. Thank you for writing a beautiful foreword and for your support.

At the University of Oklahoma, many colleagues and friends have taught me to just keep writing and helped me navigate the publishing world. I appreciate Nancy LaGreca for teaching me how to connect with publishers. I thank Michele Eodice for her invaluable work fostering a community of writers on campus, and for introducing me to my writing buddies: Sandy Tarabochia, Angela Urick, Kristy Brugar, and Anne Hyde. You all keep me running and I am so grateful for your friendship.

My online goal-setting group is a never-ending well of support and encouragement. I am lucky to enjoy the friendship of Julia Chang, Manuel Cuellar, Krista Brune, and Ashley Brock.

Susan Drouilhet has been there every step of the way. Thank you so very much for telling me to write the book I wanted to write. Here it is!

Finally, my dear family has been a source of unending love. Joey Albin inspires me to write honestly and to take risks, nourishes me when I am spent, and makes my life beautiful. Laura Lee Crandall, Matt Crandall, Avi, Evan, and Levi, Teri Pennington, David Pennington, Dennis Ward, Pat Ward, Kathryn Albin, Bobby Albin, Erin Albin, Courtney Glazener, Justin Glazener, and Amelia: you give me space to be myself and I love you so much.

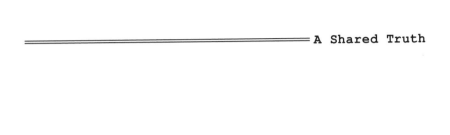A Shared Truth

══Introduction

In 2003 two university students in Mexico City joined forces to create something that was uniquely theirs. Today Luisa Pardo and Gabino Rodríguez, founding members of the theater collective Lagartijas Tiradas al Sol (Lizards Lounging in the Sun), continue to make theatrical art that transcends generic and national boundaries. The collective has grown to include many more members, including actors, videographers, graphic artists, and lighting and sound experts, and is now one of the leading sources for homegrown, unique theater in Mexico. Its work has a strong connection to reality, staging national history and autobiography, testimonies and family stories. Lagartijas is still based in Mexico City, though it performs its work all over the world.

Another Kind of Justice

This book focuses on Lagartijas Tiradas al Sol and how it engages with the genre of theater of the real. Theater of the real is defined by theater scholar Carol Martin as "a wide range of theater practices and styles that recycle reality, whether that reality is personal, social, political, or historical" (*Theatre of the Real* 5). Lagartijas's work is a shining example of theater of the real, as it persistently stages reality, in the forms of intimate personal stories, the histories of social movements and national politics, and inherited family stories. This study addresses this relationship between stage representation and political and private life. In this book, the work of Lagartijas Tiradas al Sol is a case study that illustrates how the theater offers a forum to present alternatives to official histories and rewrite the traditions of family and personal histories in the Mexican context. The theater's claims to veracity are often in opposition to those versions of history that erase or pardon state violence. In a sociopolitical moment in which facts are under fire, the theatrical space has positioned itself as a source of and repository for the real. I look at three levels of

history—personal, family, and national—and analyze how theater of the real engages each of them to create a sense of reality that goes beyond the documentary
to invoke a bodily truth. This book shows how the contemporary stage serves as a
site for re-creating, questioning, and subverting traditional discourses of the real,
such as history, journalism, and official governmental sources.

Lagartijas joins a long tradition of documentary theater in Mexico. Very soon
after Peter Weiss's *The Investigation* was produced in East and West Germany, Latin American theater practitioners found his verbatim form to be a useful one for
representing history and current events, especially in political situations in which
more traditional sources for such news were controlled by oppressive authorities
or censored. In classical documentary plays, the playtext is made up of or based on
the verbatim text of source materials, such as court transcripts. Documentary theater emerged onto the Mexican scene in 1968 with *Pueblo rechazado* (A rejected
people), Vicente Leñero's theatrical portrayal of a monk's use of psychoanalysis at
a monastery in Cuernavaca, Mexico, and his consequent excommunication from
the Catholic Church. It premiered October 15, 1968, in the Teatro Xola in Mexico City, only thirteen days after the massacre of student protestors by military
and police in the Plaza de las Tres Culturas in the Tlatelolco district of the city.
The furor of the student movement, its violent repression, and the intensity of the
Olympic Games and its international witnesses combined to create a critical moment for the foundation of Latin American documentary theater. Hugo Salcedo
attributes Leñero's pioneering move toward the documentary to the writer's voca-
tion and passion for journalism.[1] Though *Pueblo rechazado*'s ties to the documentary are at times tenuous, its influence on later practitioners—who would study
Bertolt Brecht, Erwin Piscator, and Weiss more closely and focus on testimony as
their primary source—is unquestionable. Leñero would continue in the documentary genre throughout his career as a playwright, with works such as *Compañero*
(Comrade, 1970), a biography of Che Guevara; *El juicio* (The trial, 1972), based
on the trial of León Toral and "La madre Conchita," two Cristeros found guilty
of assassinating President Álvaro Obregón; *Los hijos de Sánchez* (The children of
Sanchez, 1972) based on the ethnographic work of the same name by Oscar Lewis;
and several more. Leñero's influence on contemporary Mexican theater is undeni-
ably vital; his numerous disciples include Víctor Hugo Rascón Banda, and fellow
northerner Humberto Robles. Rascón Banda assumed the mantle of documentary
dramaturgy with plays like *Los ilegales* (The illegals, 1979), *La fiera del Ajusco* (The
beast of the Ajusco, 1985) and *Homicidio calificado* (Murder in the first degree,
1994);[2] he examines national myth in historical plays like *La Malinche* (1998);
explores testimonial theater with *Sazón de mujer* (Taste of a woman), 2001); and
participates in the documentary mode with, for example, *La mujer que cayó del cielo*
(The woman who fell from the sky, 1999). Salcedo (102) and Armando Partida

Tayzan (82) note Rascón Banda's innovative use of the theater as an agent for social change that implicates the spectator. Important contributions to documentary theater in Mexico also come from the playwright and author Sabina Berman,
whose plays *Rompecabezas* (The puzzle, 1981) and *Herejía* (Heresy, 1983) portray
national historical events in a humorous light. As Stuart Day points out, "Berman
combines the power of humor with the strong tradition of Mexican documentary
theater, eschewing the misguided fear of many practitioners of this subgenre that
laughter diminishes social commitment. . . . Yet the unique combination of documentary theater and humor (irony, parody) is one of Berman's most significant
contributions to Mexican art" (*Outside Theater* 132). Indeed, the playfulness of
Berman's work can be seen in Lagartijas's documentary pieces as well.

Other Latin American roots for contemporary theater of the real include August Boal's *Teatro Jornal*, founded in 1971 in São Paulo, Brazil, which attempted to
demystify the supposed objectivity of journalism, make the theater more popular,
and demonstrate that theater can be practiced by nonartists (Boal 58). It is Boal's
first objective that is of interest for this study; by staging the real, many of the plays
I examine subvert the idea of reality and the possibility of ever representing the
"real." The possibility of defining or narrating reality, however, has been rendered
risible by postmodernity, which, as Jean-François Lyotard defines it in *The Postmodern Condition*, is a crisis of narratives, and incredulity toward metanarratives
that explain the world. In other parts of the region, while the document may not
have had the primacy it finds in traditional documentary theater, the real continued to be a source of dramatic inspiration. Boal's work resonated with practitioners
Enrique Buenaventura and his Teatro Experimental de Cali, in Colombia; Alan
Bolt's Nixtayolero, in Nicaragua, and Cuba's Teatro Escambray, which attempted
to effect social change through theater (Versényi 159–73). Companies like Grupo
Cultural Yuyachkani, for example, in Peru and Mapa Teatro in Colombia participated throughout the latter part of the twentieth century in the tendency to stage
reality. In the second half of the twentieth century, leading into the twenty-first,
Ana María Vallejo de la Ossa points out, theater in Latin America has privileged
the place of the body and renounced fiction, features that in turn have changed
the way that theatrical texts are generated (53–54). In late twentieth-century theater, Mexican performance practitioners like the Teatro de Ciertos Habitantes and
Jesusa Rodríguez, along with many other Latin American collectives, preferred
a devised theater method that also puts the performer's body at the forefront.[3]
Twenty-first century theater practitioners—like Humberto Robles, Lagartijas,
Teatro Línea de Sombra, and Teatro Ojo—draw on the strong tradition of performance in Mexico, with its emphasis on the body and the political, to experiment
with the representation of reality, revealing the problems with asking audiences to
both believe and disbelieve.

Methodology

My approach to Lagartijas's work has been shaped by pragmatic limitations as well as theoretical influences. I first came across its work in 2010, when I saw *El rumor del incendio* (The rumor of the fire) at the national university in Mexico City. The play mixes autobiography, biography, family history, and national history in a documentary drama that follows Pardo's mother through the latter half of the twentieth century, citing important international and national events throughout. I included the play on my doctoral exam on autobiographical discourse in Latin America, and discovered that the idea of playing one's parent onstage was gaining in popularity in the region, in plays like Lola Arias's *Mi vida después* (My life after, 2008). I wrote my doctoral dissertation on auto/biographical theater in Latin America, and now take this opportunity to zoom in on the trajectory of Lagartijas. Its work has evolved over the past seven years, and its influence in Mexico and internationally has grown as well.

While I was able to attend *El rumor del incendio* and other plays while living in Mexico City, the ephemeral nature of theatrical performance makes it impossible in some cases to access documentation of performances that I was not able to attend personally. In those cases, especially for the earliest plays in Lagartijas's repertoire (*Noviembre* [November], *Pía*, *Esta es la historia de un niño que creció y todavía se acuerda de algunas cosas* [This is the story of a boy who grew up and still remembers some things], and *En el mismo barco* [In the same boat], I have relied on the company's generosity and its own documentation of its work. For the four plays mentioned here, I have had access to the playtext, photographs, and sometimes video clips of performances. Additionally, I have interviewed the company with regard to these early plays, though it is more reticent about the incipient works that predate its more characteristic productions. In these cases my work must be categorized as largely literary analysis, reading the dramatic text and analyzing its relationship to other texts and its sociohistorical context. I also rely heavily on reviews in the popular press, where available. Fortunately, I have had the opportunity to attend productions of several of Lagartijas's plays since discovering them in 2010, both in Mexico City and in forums in the United States (*El rumor del incendio*, *Asalto al agua transparente* [Assault on clear water], *Montserrat*, *Se rompen las olas* [The waves break], *Tijuana*, *Santiago Amoukalli*, *Este cuerpo mío* [This body of mine], and *Elisa*). In these cases, photographs, my notes and impressions, access to the playtext, and interviews have been my primary sources for research. In addition, the ability to see more than one presentation of a given play has allowed me to gauge audience responses.

Finally, for some plays I have only had access to video recordings of productions (*Está escrita en sus campos* [It is written in the fields], *Veracruz, nos estamos deforestando o cómo extrañar Xalapa* [Veracruz, we are deforesting ourselves or how to miss Xalapa]). As time goes on, the company has begun documenting its work and archiving it, making my work as a researcher much easier. This has also enabled me to go back and review plays I attended in person, or see how a given play has evolved over time. The various formats in which the plays and information about them exist, then, include:

playtexts,
video recordings,
live performances,
performer interviews,
critical reviews,
scholarly articles,
audio recordings;
photographs; and
extratheatrical publications, including books published by
the company to accompany its plays.

All these formats enrich our understanding of Lagartijas's trajectory and its relationship to other theater troupes in Mexico, Latin America, and the world. It is important, however, to keep track of what the object of study is in any given case when drawing conclusions about Lagartijas's work. For this reason, throughout this study I have, where possible, referred to the playtext when reproducing dialogue, while I may refer to live performances or video recordings to discuss the other legible signs of the theater such as lighting, blocking, gesture, makeup, costumes, or sound effects.

The significance of these other elements cannot be overemphasized. Indeed, in this book I argue that it is the unique aspects of the theater that make it an apt space for re-creating, communicating, and storing knowledge about reality. The requirement of the simultaneous presence of bodies sets theater apart from film and television, narrative, or graphic arts. It is only in the moment of performance that real meaning-making occurs, and that is precisely why the theater is so powerfully positioned, in the digital age, to challenge hegemonic discourses and traditional notions of what is real. For this reason, my analysis always focuses on the performance of the text, even though I use the text to reproduce quotations here, for the sake of consistency and clarity.

Overview of Chapters

This book is organized in chronological order, to show the development of several of the most significant characteristics of Lagartijas's theater: auto/biography, family, and nation. Chapter 1, "Enacting the Collective," traces Lagartijas's creative process to the devised theater or collective creation that became especially popular in Latin America in the 1960s. It shows how the personal, intimate biographies presented in plays are reflective of collective processes, such as national history and family relationships. I examine the play *Asalto al agua transparente* (and, briefly, the early plays *Esta es la historia de un niño que creció y todavía se acuerda de algunas cosas, Catalina*, and *En el mismo barco*), linking its development through collective creation and its emphasis on collectivity as a subject matter, as well as the auto/biographical impulse that begins to emerge with these plays.

In chapter 2, "Unfolding Genealogy," I analyze the cycle *La invención de nuestros padres* (The invention of our parents), which was created retroactively to encompass three independent plays, all produced by Lagartijas: *El rumor del incendio, Montserrat* (by Gabino Rodríguez), and *Se rompen las olas* (by Mariana Villegas). These three plays exemplify the aesthetic and political preoccupations that most readily define Lagartijas's work. They are documentary dramas that emphasize the display of "proof" in the form of legal documents and personal effects, privilege the interaction between corporal performance and digital technology as a means for theatrical communication, and focus on the relationships and breaches between generations with an eye to national events.

Chapter 3, "Falling Out of History," looks at the play *Derretiré con un cerillo la nieve de un volcán* (I shall melt a volcano's snowcap with a match) alongside the cycle *La democracia en México* (Democracy in Mexico), which began with the return of the Mexican Partido de la Revolución Institucional (Institutional Revolutionary Party; PRI) to the presidency in Mexico after a twelve-year hiatus. While the company retains its focus on personal stories and family relationships, the national becomes an urgent question as it seeks to use the theater to understand political processes in Mexico. The project is not only dramatic; it is investigative. This shift toward theater as research supports my observation that the theater, not only in the hands of Lagartijas but throughout Latin America, is being promoted and used as a source for discourses of reality.

Finally, chapter 4, "Loosening the Bounds of Theater" follows the company as its various members venture separately into the world, always linked to the collective through the loose confederation of Lagartijas. The company's most recent works are often unipersonal monologues mixed with video and digital sound effects and demonstrate a heightened urgency when it comes to Mexican political realities. Whereas its earlier works were characterized as theater or scenic documentaries, it has begun to label certain creations as lectures, emphasizing the real nature of the subject matter. In this chapter I also situate Lagartijas within the constellation of Latin American theater of the real, to show that it is not an exception but rather an exemplary figure among a growing trend toward representing reality onstage in Latin America.

With this book, my desire is to make visible the important contributions that artists like Lagartijas Tiradas al Sol are making to the world theater scene. Additionally, I propose, by shining a light on their work, that looking to the arts, especially the art of presence, the theater, will provide comfort and truth in times when facts and reality seem to be under fire. The title of this book, *A Shared Truth*, refers to this promise of solace. Theater implies a communion, the ritual sharing between actor and spectator, that can only exist through the simultaneous gathering of bodies and souls.

Presenting Lagartijas Tiradas al Sol

Lagartijas Tiradas al Sol, a theater company from Mexico City founded by Luisa Pardo and Gabino Rodríguez in 2003, is at the forefront of twenty-first-century documentary theater in Mexico.[4] Its plays—like *Asalto al agua transparente* (2006), which stages a history of water in the Valley of Mexico, or *Catalina* (2009), which documents a past love affair of Rodríguez—display an affinity for staging the real. In *El rumor del incendio* (2010), the personal and collective come together, as Pardo's mother's biography is intertwined with national history. While its plays dance on the line between fiction and nonfiction, including fantastic elements alongside historical evidence, its inclusion in the documentary genre is questionable. Some critics have come to call this kind of production "theater of the real," an umbrella term that encompasses any theatrical performance that attempts to portray reality, in some form or other. The term is useful for understanding the work of Lagartijas Tiradas al Sol as well as many other Latin American theater practitioners, who push the boundaries of the documentary genre, testing the limits of what theater can do. By inserting reality into the theatrical, the genre allows the stage to become a space for resisting official discourse, offering alternative versions of history, and cocreating, with the audience, new understandings of what is real.

Studies such as Carol Martin's *Theatre of the Real* (2013) or the 2006 special issue of *TDR/The Drama Review* devoted to theater of the real aim to define the genre as well as to theorize the relationship between theater and reality. While theater of the real has seen a surge in popularity throughout the world, with an increasing number of examples over the past two decades, critics have consistently overlooked Latin American productions.[5] Aside from Martin's inclusion of a fragment of Argentine dramatist Vivi Tellas's staging of her mother and her aunt (*Mi mamá y mi tía*) in *Dramaturgy of the Real on the World Stage*, theater scholars in the North, who are not specifically Latin Americanists, have virtually ignored the region's vibrant production of drama. As far as critical attention to Lagartijas Tiradas al Sol goes, the bulk of documentation has taken place in student theses (including my own doctoral dissertation), indicating that the scholarly dialogue about Lagartijas forms part of the newest wave of theater criticism.[6] This book, focusing entirely on Lagartijas's theatrical production, is my contribution toward a greater understanding of contemporary Mexican theater and how it fits into theatrical traditions in Latin America, the Americas, and the world. As the company takes its place in the contemporary canon, studies like this one will be useful for students, teachers, and enthusiasts who want to learn about Lagartijas's history and theater of the real.

The publication of this book signals the seriousness with which Lagartijas's work is received. Indeed, the group is invited to festivals all over the world, often winning festival prizes,[7] and scholars have begun to turn their attention to its unique blend of theatricality and documentary that challenges traditional notions of what the theater is supposed to do. *El rumor del incendio,* its 2010 play focusing on the guerrillas in mid-twentieth-century Mexico and actor/director Pardo's mother's biography, has received the bulk of critical attention. My own article and accompanying interview in *Latin American Theatre Today* (see Appendix B for the translation of the interview into English), along with an article that situates Lagartijas's 2013 play *Montserrat,* published in *Theatre Journal* in 2017, joins studies by Tim Compton (2006, 2013), Lina J. Morales Chacana, Antonio Prieto Stambaugh and Martha Toriz Proenza, Paulina Sabugal Paz (2017), and Hugo Salcedo.[8]

This study documents the work of Lagartijas in order to situate its contributions to the dramatic field within the larger context of Mexican, Latin American, and global theatrical traditions. I offer a complete vision of the company's oeuvre, from the earliest productions of its founders as theater students at the Universidad Nacional Autónoma de México (National Autonomous University of Mexico, UNAM) Centro Universitario de Teatro (University Theater Center, CUT) to its more recent contributions to international theater. The purpose of this study is to hold up Lagartijas's work as an example of how theater of the real transforms the stage into a site for making meaning of reality. Though the book's conclusions apply to Latin American theater of the real in general, I limit my analysis to Lagartijas's work as a case study. This focus allows me to engage with a body of work in its entirety; the plays work together as a system that supports each work's claims of reality. The company's construction of a style, and its insistence on reality throughout its trajectory, is also a characteristic of other examples of theater of the real that tend to appear in series or cycles.[9] By limiting this study to Lagartijas, both general trends of theater of the real and particularities of contemporary Mexican experience come to light. In the final chapter, however, I examine how the specific relates to the general, with a discussion of how Lagartijas's star fits into the constellation of Latin American theater of the real. In this chapter I will focus on how the individual, the family, and the nation are all implicated in the representation of the real, and how the theater itself reveals the limits of its own representational capacity.

The Political and the Personal

One of Lagartijas's innovations to documentary theater is its documentation of the extremely personal and its use of autobiographical performance, tying the actors to the characters they play. Whereas previous works—like Rascón Banda's aforementioned *La Malinche*, Wilberto Cantón's *Nocturno a Rosario* (Nocturne for Rosario, 1957), or Sabina Berman's *Rompecabezas* (1981)—include psychological portraits of historical figures of international importance, Lagartijas focuses on autobiography in its works, shortening the distance between the staged and the subject. At the same time, it elevates the ordinary individual to the level of national poets and political leaders. In early works this autobiographical tendency appears as intertextuality; the scripts are based on literary texts that provide a summary of the artist's education: a staged, autobiographical *Künstlerroman*. References to high and popular culture combine with fictionalized and real accounts of the actors' lives to form the bud of what will later flower into full-fledged autobiographical and documentary theater. For example, its first production as a company, *Esta es la historia de un niño que creció y todavía se acuerda de algunas cosas* (2003), draws on texts by authors like Charles Bukowski, John Kennedy Toole, Paul Auster, Fabio Morábito, and Larry Tremblay to examine how we remember childhood. *Pía* (2005), characterized as an in memoriam by the company, also compiles texts by various authors to construct a play about human intimacy that memorializes a late friend of Rodríguez. *Noviembre* (2005) portrays a sixteen-year-old protagonist whose mother has just died, and draws on Pardo's biographical experience of her mother's death as well as texts by other authors, directors, and Pardo's own brother. These earliest texts were produced when Pardo and Rodríguez were students at the UNAM.

On leaving the confines of the university, frustrated by the institutional structure, Lagartijas set out to create documentary theater that addressed Mexican realities created through collective coproduction rather than relying on single-authored texts. Debra A. Castillo points out that while Latin American devised theater or *creación colectiva* "recognize[s] a heritage that includes inspiration in and dialogue with projects like the US-based Bread and Puppets (1963), Living Theater (1947), and Teatro Campesino (1965), it would not be difficult to argue that in the Southern Hemisphere this kind of work took on a prominence it never achieved in the North" (63). Though the hemispheric division proposed by Castillo would separate Mexico from South America, the linguistic and cultural separations create analogous divisions between the United States and Mexico. Devised theater in Mexico is also prominent and, until recently, has gone largely unnoticed by Anglophone critics in the north. Lagartijas is no exception; beginning with *Asalto al agua transparente*, its commitment to collective creation and an emphasis on historical documentation comes to the fore. The focus on family relationships that began in *Noviembre* continues throughout the company's trajectory, including its next play, *En el mismo barco* (2007), which takes a generational perspective to explore the political ideals and individual desires of a group of young people.[10] *En el mismo barco* serves as a bridge between the parallel emphases on the collective and the generational in Lagartijas's works.[11]

Other important preoccupations present throughout the company's trajectory include the representation of reality through the documentary mode as well as through staging intimate, auto/biographical dramas.[12] This focus on the intimate is particularly present in *Catalina*, the reenactment of a romantic breakup and its aftermath. The play provides evidence such as music, photographs, text messages, e-mails, and video to reenact the end of a relationship, applying documentary methodology to the intimate realm. In *El rumor del incendio* (2010), the personal and collective combine to create an auto/biographical family drama, with twentieth-century Mexican history as its backdrop. This play forms a trilogy called *La invención de nuestros padres* along with *Se rompen las olas* (2012) and *Montserrat* (2012). The former is a re-creation of the protagonist's conception, tied to the 1985 earthquake in Mexico City; the latter is a false documentary that effectively revives the protagonist's late mother through the power of desire and fiction. This last play tests the limits of the documentary mode, turning it against itself and creating a falsehood. The playful gesture is a serious theoretical proposal, and continues in *Derretiré con un cerillo la nieve de un volcán* (2013), a history of the PRI. The group's most recent project, *La democracia en México* is an ambitious series of plays, with one planned production per Mexican state. So far there are four: *Tijuana*, *Veracruz*, *Santiago Amoukalli*, and *Distrito Federal*, each named for a location. Every play in the series portrays an aspect of democracy in contemporary Mexico, fifty years after the publication of Pablo González Casanova's sociological study *La democracia en México* (1965). Lagartijas uses the stage to portray the most intimate details of personal lives, to re-create family bonds, and to make sense of the nation.

Lagartijas, from the beginning, has been concerned with resisting the tendency toward imported, translated theater. As Rodríguez said in an interview in 2010, "There's something a little impersonal about the idea of playing Hamlet. In some ways it could be me, it could be another actor, and we liked the idea of doing plays that could only be cast with those people. That couldn't be other people."[13] Pardo added, "To think that we are indispensable, that it's really something of our own. In contemporary culture, a topic I've been thinking about, everything is disposable and everything is alien and everything is temporary. . . . We aren't bureaucrats of the theater, we aren't theater *maquiladoras*, but rather we are very conscious of the personal aspect of theater" (Ward, "Entrevista" 141–42).[14] For Lagartijas, then, the personal is a way to resist the commodification of theater and art in general. National theaters in Latin America only broke from Spanish influence in the early twentieth century, beginning to use local accents and dialects and portray issues of national import on the stage; Lagartijas shows the intensification of this impulse a century later. It rejects imported plays and translated texts to the extent of only staging plays it has devised itself. These plays may be highly intertextual, lifting passages from novels, essays, and poems, but they are given new meaning when remixed into the world of a Lagartijas play. Beyond the push for including local content onstage, here that content is localized down to the person, so that Lagartijas's plays resist any adaptation whatsoever.[15]

While Lagartijas is inspired by diverse artists from all over the world and tends to remix its heroes' work in its playtexts, the result is always original and personal. Its unwavering preoccupation with staging real life relies on its dedication to the crafts of writing, directing, and acting; its do-it-yourself aesthetic is supported by its attention to the technical details of the theater. The success of Lagartijas's trajectory is, in my view, a result of its making meaning of reality through theatricality.

My reading of these plays draws on performance studies's critical efforts to parse theater of the real and properly situate the text vis-à-vis performance. In their introduction to the concept of *theatricality* in performance theory, Tracy Davis and Thomas Postlewait trace society's mistrust of the theater, from ancient Greece to the present, citing condemnations of its "illusory, deceptive, exaggerated, artificial, or affected" (4) character. Marvin Carlson, meanwhile, notes how the field of performance studies itself has seen theatricality as suspect, associating the term "primarily with formal, traditional and formally structured operations, potentially or actually opposed to the unrestricted and more authentic impulses of life itself" ("Resistance" 242). This tension between authenticity and structure hearkens back to Elinor Fuchs's essay on the importance of the text within theatrical performances of the 1980s, "Presence and the Revenge of Writing." What she calls "a new kind of textuality" (165) challenges the theater's "enterprise of spontaneous speech with its logocentric claims to origination, authority, authenticity—in short, Presence" (172). Twenty-first-century discussions of theater of the real parallel the twentieth-century debate over the authenticity of spontaneous speech and the unreliability of edited writing. Liz Tomlin aptly points out that "there is a tension at the heart of twenty-first century verbatim practice and reception that is the result of seemingly irreconcilable conflict between, on the one hand, the drive for political change that necessitates both a relationship with the 'real' world and an ideological commitment to a particular political discourse, and, on the other, a philosophical skepticism of the 'real' world, and a consequent discrediting of truth claims or ethical imperatives that seek to distinguish any one narrative as authoritative" (120).

In a more recent contribution to the discussion, Carlson reminds us of the question of mimesis in theater: "What challenges to representation and to mimesis arise from the fact that the dramatic artist, unlike the painter, utilizes material from the real world to create his art?" (*Shattering Hamlet's Mirror* 5). Because audiences know better than to trust even so-called reality, documentary plays become treatises on the nature of documentary theater. Indeed, the theater has recently focused on representing the real, even in the face of antitheatrical prejudice (although critics like Carlson argue that using real material "has been a defining characteristic of theatre from its very beginnings" [17]). The tension between reality and theatricality is like the tension between speech and writing that Fuchs examines. As reality itself is recognized as theatrical, the ritual presence that theater offers can be considered a more reliable source for facts than other discourses more traditionally associated with reality, as the next section elaborates.

The Real on Stage

The question of how to categorize Lagartijas's theater is one that comes up almost immediately on discussion of their work. Is it documentary theater? Much of its work relies on documentary evidence and includes re-creating histories that have long gone unreported. These stories may be personal, such as Rodríguez's reconstruction of a breakup in *Catalina*, or national, such as the aftermath of the massacre at Tlatelolco in *El rumor del incendio*.[16] At the same time, though, its later work has stretched the documentary genre to its limits, by using falsified evidence or claiming that real evidence was falsified. Perhaps auto/biographical theater is a better term, then? The *unipersonal* movement in postdictatorial Argentina is an example of a parallel genre,[17] and Lagartijas's works, especially those whose titles are proper names like *Catalina* and *Montserrat*, seem to fit within this framework. Its documentary projects, however, like *Asalto al agua transparente*, *El rumor del incendio*, and the *Democracia en México* series, escape the bounds of the auto/biographical through the company's ambitious attempts at documenting national history. Politics and social movements are always linked to the quotidian in the plays, because they are enacted by real people with real lives, but loom larger than they would in a traditional auto/biographical focus. The works, then, are both auto/biographical and documentary, but the sum is greater than the parts.

Carol Martin's theater of the real is an apt term for categorizing Lagartijas's work because it is broad enough to include the company's various approaches. With origins in the documentary theater of the 1960s, Martin has characterized the international, post–9/11 dramatic phenomenon, which insists on its own relationship to reality, as "theater of the real." Though some might argue that this definition is so broad that it loses usefulness, I find it to be a worthwhile category, particularly because the plays I examine here insist, in various ways, on the reality of the events they portray. Martin defines the genre as including those types of theater that "claim a relationship to reality" (*Theatre of the Real* 5). The broad reach of

Martin's terminology allows for encompassing the work of Lagartijas, which defies more specific definitions. It indeed lifts verbatim from legal texts, works of fiction, interviews, and diaries, and reenacts historical events, combining this content with its autobiographical experiences and the biographies of its family members to create truly innovative, moving works of theater.

Martin summarizes the questions that theater of the real poses: "What does it mean to be an instrument of memory and of history? In what ways is performance embodied kinesthetic historiography, and what end does this serve? What is the relationship between individual stories and the grand narrative of history? Is using the imagination an assault on historical accuracy?" (*Theatre of the Real* 11). Indeed, Lagartijas's productions grapple with these issues. The company's members explicitly ask about the responsibilities of a generation to uphold the revolutionary values of the ones that came before; they not only invoke but represent and embody their late parents onstage; they painstakingly force the viewer to see the workings of history played out, in and on the bodies of real individuals; and they use documentary evidence to spin lies in the service of greater truths.

Many spectators accustomed to the documentary mode not only expect a faithful representation of reality onstage but also know how to look for the cracks in the facade, those moments where the work reveals its own mechanisms and therefore inspires a questioning of the very possibility of rendering the real in the theater. Lagartijas plays directly into these expectations, regularly mixing fantasy and reality, complete with documentary evidence supporting the fiction. Audiences that have not been exposed, however, to this kind of work in the theater might expect a more direct relationship between what is staged and "what really happened." Indeed, many audience members and even festival promoters have sincerely taken Lagartijas's works at face value, never imagining that what is presented as documentary might be completely falsified, as is often the case. In a special online issue of the journal *Foundations of Science*, editors Frederik Le Roy and Robrecht Vanderbeeken ponder documentary aesthetics and touch on this very problem. They write, "Too many people still see the production of documentary as a self-evident aesthetic strategy, premised on the belief that, with the help of indexical media such as film or photography, a simple depiction of facts is all it takes to access the real world that surrounds us" (2). They attribute this state of affairs to the lack of a clear definition of documentary and argue that "the documentary opens up an intermediary space between fiction and reality" (2), likening the documentarian's craft to Hayden White's account of historians' creation of literary narratives. Documentary, then, is not the opposite of fiction. Rather, it is the aesthetic construction of a representation of reality. Jenn Stephenson provides a helpful explanation for what theater of the real is doing, if not representing reality: "Emphasis placed on the material real in this genre operates not to stake claims to the absolute authenticity of original experience, but rather draw attention to these real-world foundations so as to interrogate the processes of 'creating' reality" ("Winning" 215). Undoing the opposition fiction/documentary is essential to approaching Lagartijas's works, as well as that of many other of its contemporaries in Latin America. Determining which details are factual and which are fabricated might keep a person busy; it is in examining the reality that is constructed onstage, however, and analyzing how it creates meaning that the real contribution of contemporary Latin American artists will be illuminated.

Lagartijas's earliest works flirt with the real, relying heavily on the devised theater or collaborative creation model and source texts that are more artistic than informative. As it moves into more autobiographical works like *Catalina* and *Noviembre* the collective nature is not lost, but its romance with the real is made official, a constant element of its theatrical production. With *Asalto al agua transparente* and *El rumor del incendio*, national history and historiography take center stage; *Montserrat* and *Derretiré con un cerillo la nieve de un volcán* question the possibility of ever representing the real, while proposing that theater can transmit realities that documents alone cannot reveal. Lagartijas is not alone among Mexican theater practitioners in its obsession with staging the specific and the real—indeed, Teatro Ojo, Teatro Línea de Sombra, Pendiente Teatro, Compañía Opcional, and Gabriel Yépez, among others, practice what Yépez calls the collective creation of relationships (81). These artists point out the strong relationships between reality and the theater, and question the expectations of spectators to create new relationships with what is presented onstage.

While the aforementioned companies will be fruitful sources for future investigations into Mexican theater of the real, this book focuses entirely on the works of Lagartijas Tiradas al Sol because of its particular relationships to the self, the family, and the national, as well as its strong connection to the traditional stage. Its shows are all scripted and rehearsed, and take place in more or less traditional theatrical spaces. Audiences are under no illusions about the fact that what they are seeing is drama. While it incorporates elements of improvisation, such as changing between characters and scenes fluidly without warning, and cinema, by playing film reels and providing soundtracks to its plays, it generally does not create site-specific plays or spontaneous performances. It is an excellent case study for interpreting the role of the theater, with its combination of text and body, repetition and simultaneity, in the construction of self, family, and nation in Latin America.

Family Documentary

The notion of staging the real, is of course, not a new one. Besides the obvious long tradition of history plays, the documentary genre is concerned with not only providing a theatrical version of real events but also documenting them with evidence given onstage in the form of photographs, official or legal documents, and a link between the script and verbatim transcripts or interviews. Beginning in the 1960s, with Augusto Boal's *Teatro Jornal* (Newspaper theater) and Vicente Leñero's 1968 documentary play *Pueblo rechazado*, political reality entered the theater as the dramatic representation of real events in Latin America. In the latter half of the twentieth century, theater of the real made up an important contingent of Latin American drama, most notably in the form of documentary and testimonial theater.

In the twenty-first century, political reality combines with personal history in plays that explore the relationship between the individual and society, personal versus national trauma, and the (im)possibilities of artistically representing the real. The newest representations of this reality-based theater in Latin America are still tied to a text, as in documentary theater. I consider Lagartijas's plays, examined in this volume, as going beyond the text, however, and therefore beyond the term "documentary," because they offer up the body alongside the document as evidence. In fact, the plays' meaning-making possibilities rest upon the audience's understanding that what is presented is not fiction. Whether via photographic and documentary evidence displayed on the stage, references to historical events, or through paratextual means, such as newspaper reports and reviews, and information in the program, the plays insist on their realness. In particular, the autobiographical representation of all the performers I examine is a gesture against dramatic adaptation, the reproduction of a play script, and rather an insistence on the unique and wholly real nature of their lives. By playing themselves and their parents, contemporary actors reinforce and surpass the text as currency of the real. Jose António Sánchez points out that recent interest in the real in scenic practice intends not to demonstrate the possibility of presenting the real, without any construction, but rather to show that incorporating formal composition or fiction does not necessarily obscure the real (Sánchez 16).

Several scholars have taken up the question of representing the real in Latin American cultural production, and I draw on their work to describe Lagartijas's plays. Performance studies scholar Ileana Diéguez cites the inclusion of research as a primary function of the artistic creation in contemporary performance practices, observing that the "artists become documentarians and witness-bearers to the pain of others" (*artistas devienen documentadores y testimoniantes del dolor de los demás*) ("La práctica artística" 77). Indeed, the works of Lagartijas bear witness to the pain of a generation, and its own pain, by documenting it and, I would add, re-creating it onstage. Meanwhile, in the collection *Corporalidades escénicas*, edited by Elka Fediuk and Antonio Prieto Stambaugh, several authors comment on the representation of violence on the contemporary Latin American stage. Óscar Armando García writes that the character's staged corporality is the source of solutions for how to represent violence theatrically. The violated body onstage results in the complicity of the audience as well as the blurring of the lines between spectacle and spectator (García 175–76). Prieto Stambaugh himself describes how memory is embodied (*corporizada*) in testimonial and confessional theater and performance. Prieto Stambaugh notes that explicit embodiment is not a guarantee of being in the presence of "the truth."[18] He writes that what is actually demonstrated is that the body is traversed by discourses and ideologies, that the personal is always collective, that the reality of our bodies, of our personal histories, and of official history depend on interpretation, as well as on the re-presentation given to them (207). These ideas are essential to understanding Lagartijas's proposal, as it plays with the truth, with memory, with embodiment and, of course, with various versions of history. In this book, I focus not only on the testimonial and auto/biographical quality of the representation of memory, but also on how, in Latin American theater and in Lagartijas's work in particular, the idea of family, and the insertion of the self into a generational network, emerges as a way of understanding the nation.

In reference to this performance of archival research, Carol Martin states, "Adherence to an archive makes documentary theater appear closer to actuality than fiction. The archive is concrete, historically situated, and relatively permanent; it is material and lasting while theatrical representation is intangible and ephemeral" ("Bodies of Evidence" 19). While Martin refers principally to English-language plays, the works I study show less adherence to or reverence for the archive as signifier for reality. This trend might be rooted in the inherent distrust in the archive from a postcolonial standpoint; indeed, in Mexico and several other Latin American countries the archive is a technology inherited from the colonial period, its disciplinary uses reapplied by twentieth-century authoritarian governments. Lagartijas veers away from the documentary genre in this sense; rather than adhering to an archive, it performs it. In her seminal work *The Archive and the Repertoire*, Diana Taylor advocates for the reexamination of "expressive, embodied culture, ... shifting the focus from written to embodied culture, from the discursive to the performatic" (16). She argues that the rift between practices of knowledge after the colonization of the Americas is "between the *archive* of supposedly enduring materials (i.e., texts, documents, buildings, bones) and the so-called ephemeral *repertoire* of embodied practice/knowledge (i.e., spoken language, dance, sports ritual)" (19). In many of Lagartijas's plays the archive is physically present, often in the form of stacks of paper, official certifications, or video footage, but the actors are clearly mediating its contents. On the stage the actors take control of the archive; while the documents they present may seem to be unchanging, the very nature of the theater as a representational art questions the archive's permanence and, therefore, its authority. It is precisely the visible manipulation of the concrete archive in Lagartijas's plays that gives weight to the ephemeral theatrical performance.

In this way, Lagartijas performs dramatic magic. By bringing the archive into live theater, the company "decenters the historic role of writing introduced by the Conquest" as Taylor suggests that "performance, as an embodied praxis and episteme" (*Archive* 17), can do. Performance, in combination with the archive, is a way of knowing, a way of remembering. Lagartijas performs the words of the archive, reading aloud the documents that make up national, family, and personal history onstage. The actors perform genealogy, playing their parents or re-creating their lives; they play themselves explicitly as the children of real human beings. The lives of their parents are reconstructed through the manipulation of the archive. *El rumor del incendio*, for example, relies heavily on archival research and interviews, with the character at the center of the play being reconstructed as though she were an unknown historical figure and not, as she is in reality, the mother of the actor playing her. At the same time, through their copresence with the audience, the actors conjure up the dead, allowing their beloved family members and political enemies alike to inhabit their bodies for the moment of the play. In so doing, they transcend the truth of verifiable fact and can communicate and re-create a reality even deeper than the documentary. Through its special brand of family documentary, Lagartijas personalizes the national and collectivizes the individual.

Magic Acts

Lagartijas uses a series of techniques to transform the theater into a space of ritual in which it conjures up the spirits of ancestors and rewrites national history. Its use of documentary evidence, projection of audiovisual materials, and embodiment of real people onstage is like alchemy: these ordinary elements mix together to create a new element, much more valuable than the sum of its parts. The materials Lagartijas finds in the archives are the bureaucratic leftovers of officialdom such as arrest reports, laws, and interview transcripts. They are what one would expect when approaching history from the archival angle: so many stacks of paper. In the same way, the audiovisual footage it uses is sometimes original, archival footage; other times it is video it has contrived itself. Either way, without context, the footage is lifeless. The philosopher's stone, in this case, that which brings the paper and film to life, is Presence. Taylor's repertoire, which also "requires presence,"[19] is a source of information; an embodied means for passing down knowledge and adding to it.

The auto/biographical nature of Lagartijas's plays adds the capital P to presence—thus not only transmitting cultural memory, but claiming, by the very act of being *here*, to be the one who experienced the events portrayed. In the inaugural edition of the *Revista Brasileira de Estudos da Presença* (Brazilian review of studies on presence), Gilberto Icle defines Studies on Presence as the self-referential study of performative practices, and moves on to the more difficult question of defining presence itself. Icle acknowledges that the term "presence" is often used in the theater to define a certain je ne sais quoi in reference to a quality of acting that escapes language (16). Finally, Icle arrives at a definition of Studies on Presence as "a specific form of analysis [that] attempts to emphasize the dimension of present-ness, of tangibility and of *materiality* that such practices possess, insofar as they are corporeal practices par excellence. Therefore, Studies on Presence are articulated . . . around the objective of avoiding interpretation as the only and exclusive access to the truth and to knowledge"[20] (Icle 19). While I am analyzing the work of others, not my own performance work as Icle's self-referentiality indicates, the principle of Presence as a way of knowing is significant for this study. In Lagartijas's work, the actor's body becomes an archive; the actor is simultaneously witness and pro-tagonist. I capitalize the term Presence here to emphasize its almost sacred, mag-ical power within Lagartijas's particular brand of documentary theater. It is the co-Presence of spectator and actor that gives the documentary evidence—stacks of paper and projected footage—meaning.

This is not to say that Presence belongs exclusively to Lagartijas. On the con-trary, documentary theater has long depended on the intimacy of the dramatic space and the interaction between the various participants to create meaning. In his theorization of the earliest examples of what we now call documentary theater (which he termed "epic"), Bertolt Brecht rails against what he calls the "old (magic) way" (188) of representation, where the audience goes into a trance and identifies completely with the simulation onstage. Rather, the actor "no longer has to per-suade the audience that it is the author's character and not himself that is standing on the stage, so also he need not pretend that the events taking place on the stage have never been rehearsed" (194). The interaction that Brecht proposes, and that Lagartijas exemplifies, is not the magic of the spell or the trance—it is the magic of communion. In epic theater, spectators are invited to partake of the real along with the actor. They are permitted behind the veils and curtains that separate the magic of the theater—the body—from the ordinary. And the magic is that the ordinary is what is special. Flesh, blood, bone, voice: it is humanity and shared time and space that make the theater capable of creating something out of nothing.

As Martin concludes in "Bodies of Evidence," bodily presence transcends questions of reality and truth: "What is real and what is true are not necessarily the same. A text can be fictional yet true. A text can be nonfictional yet untrue. Documentary theater is an imperfect answer that needs our obsessive analytical attention especially since, in ways unlike any other form of theater, it claims to have bodies of evidence" (24). In Lagartijas's works, the bodies onstage are often the ones that have lived through the events being portrayed, or have inherited the memories from their close relatives, embodied in the plays. The archive comes to life with the help of the philosopher's stone: the body that lived through it.

The magicians also constantly assert their own power in their theatrical concoctions. They keep audiences on the edge of knowledge, unsure what is real and what is contrived. Jenn Stephenson, examining recent Canadian autobiographical drama, points out that "for audience members, who are phenomenological witnesses to the live performance, so much is given to apprehension, but an equal, if not greater amount is withheld. Every detail, multiplying to infinity, begs a veridical confirmation, which will always be beyond my reach. The striving audience of nonfiction is mired in doubt" ("Winning" 217). Indeed, this withholding of confirmation and resulting doubt is part of what brings the audience into interaction with the play and actors. By mixing the "real" archival materials with materials they have edited or created from scratch, Lagartijas asks spectators to participate actively in parsing what they are seeing. Brecht's directive to shake audiences out of their trance so that they might judge and therefore change the injustices that have come to seem normal in society is present at the core of Lagartijas's plays. By presenting evidence that could be created by the theater group alongside evidence that most Mexican spectators will recognize, like the national constitution or footage of famous presidential addresses, the troupe asks audiences to ponder what is real, what we mean when we deem something trustworthy, and how best to communicate that reality.

This magic matters because it represents a new possibility for engaging with reality in a world that can seem overwhelmingly predetermined. As sovereign power and disciplinary measures impose norms that are so ingrained as to seem inevitable, the theater opens up as a space for reclaiming lived experience as a reliable source of truth. When Lagartijas revives a long-dead family member as a character onstage to connect its own experiences with the past and its individual lives with national history, spectators must decide what to believe. They must look critically at the evidence presented onstage and decipher the supposed veracity of documents and evidence, recognizing all the while that these pieces all form part of a constructed play. As the documentary evidence, imposing in piles of papers and unassailable film reels and legalese, is shown to be, if not untrustworthy, then at least worthy of questioning, the alternative and complementary source of reality presented is that of lived experience, transmitted through the copresence of bodies in a single time and space.

Chapter 1

Enacting the Collective

The alchemy that happens onstage during Lagartijas's plays also depends on a particular series of lenses through which the company examines reality. These perspectives often overlap, sometimes bringing certain things into focus, other times taking a wider view, always looking at *what happened*. They allow for both an internal vision—of memory, experience, inheritance—and an external one, which examines the world from the position of *I*. These lenses are the national, the generational or familial, and the individual or self. As Lagartijas's theater has increasingly become more overtly political, more explicitly focused on Mexican history and society, it has also become intensely personal and intimate. The personal generates affects that respond and provoke greater emotional reactions to the political.

While the distinction between reality and theatricality might seem natural, it is actually a highly contested issue in terms of theories of representation. By representing one's "real" family in a theatrical space, a play not only bends the rules of drama, creating a new pact between spectator and play in which audience members can expect to see a re-creation of "real" events. By placing the family in the realm of theatricality, it also challenges notions of family as a stable category, questioning genetics, culture, and relationships as determinants of identity by reminding us that family roles are performative. When adult children play both their parents and themselves, the symbolic structure of the family is deconstructed. The desire to be unique in an age of mass consumption melds with a desire for family connection in contemporary Latin American theater of the real. It is hardly surprising that a search for individual meaning would lead to a search for ancestral roots, even more so in political contexts like those of present-day Mexico. It is important to note the effects on family and individual life that collective, national trauma has had in Latin American society, and in Mexico in particular. This generational split, marked by kidnapping, torture, disappearance, and death in the worst cases, is a recurring theme in contemporary Latin American theater of the real.

Rather than understanding the theater as a separate space dedicated to fiction, and everything outside of the theater as reality, I prefer Liz Tomlin's take on reality's incursion into the theatrical mode, which considers postmodernity's mistrust of the idea of objective reality: "The conviction that we are, to some degree or another, now living in a simulacrum, conjoined with the widespread discrediting of grand narratives, has brought about an ultimate collapse of the boundaries between the fictional and the real that once formed the basis of dramatic theatre's mimetic representational apparatus" (Tomlin 35). It is not my task here, then, to parse the definition of reality, precisely marking off its borders. Rather, it is sufficient to make evident that these borders are disputed.

Of particular interest is that the audiences of the plays analyzed in this book do seem to agree on an understanding of what they consider to be "real." In various examples, I will share anecdotes of audiences that swallowed fictional stories presented by Lagartijas, hook, line, and sinker. Even its 2016 play *Santiago Amoukalli*, which opens with a voice-over declaring it to be a fiction about events that never happened to people who are not alive, has been considered by some European audiences to be fully auto/biographical and documentary, or *real*. The auto/biographical mode, which transmits verifiable facts about a person who has lived or is alive, does not allow for the complete razing of boundaries between fiction and reality. In the wake of postmodernity, which has toppled grand narratives and systematic ways of understanding the world, it might seem surprising that anyone would care whether theater of the real is *really* real. However, the stakes are high in the plays I analyze here. If the actors starring in autobiographical plays are not who they claim to be, if their parents are not who they say they are, if the historical events they describe and reenact did not really happen, then the plays' meaning-making apparatus fails. Theater of the real depends on a pact with the audience that accepts the verifiable, factual nature of a play's content even as that acceptance necessarily leads to doubt. While subjective experience cannot always be verified, practitioners and audiences generally agree that what an auto/biography recounts is real, and bald-faced lies are not pardoned by pleading postmodernity. In this chapter I focus on how the ideas of the collective and the auto/biographical influence the work of the troupe, particularly in its early plays: *Asalto al agua transparente*, *En el mismo barco*, and *Catalina*.

Staging the Real

In 2001, an especially significant undertaking by renowned Argentine director Vivi Tellas became the catalyst for the Latin American phenomenon of auto/biographical and biographical dramatic representation. Tellas, artistic director of Buenos Aires's municipal Teatro Sarmiento at the time, called for playwrights to submit what she called *biodramas*, plays about real, living Argentines. Tellas asked, "In a disposable world, what are our lives, our experiences, our time worth?" (Brownell). Her preoccupation with the disposable nature of globalized culture provides a clue as to the reason for the surge in auto/biographical theater.

Tellas's *Archivos* (Archives) project inspired a regional trend toward auto/biographical theater of the real, by staging the director's family members and other real, nonactor Argentines, playing themselves. Her subsequent call for proposals of biodramas, plays about real, living Argentines, inspired Argentine director Lola Arias's incredibly popular *Mi vida después* (My life after, 2009), in which six actors born during the Argentine military dictatorship re-create their parents' lives, acting as their stunt doubles. Arias was criticized for adapting the play to the Chilean context years later with new actors in *El año en que nací* (The year I was born, 2012), due to the extremely personal nature of the original and the actors' role in cocreating the script (Ward and Arias). This issue did not affect Arias's success, however. The play was so successful that Peruvian theater practitioners Sebastián Rubio and Claudia Tangoa created their own version, *1980/2000: El tiempo que heredé* (1980/2000: The time I inherited, 2013), based on the Peruvian armed internal conflict of the late twentieth century and casting the adult children of major players in national events. This series of plays inspires rich discussions on techniques that convince audiences of a play's "reality," generational conflict, and the ethics of representing the real. All these plays involve parents and children, themes that are also strong in works by Lagartijas. The works also feature auto/biographical, onstage self-representation, requiring a unique cast and precluding any possibility of adaptation, a focus on the relationship between generations (parents and children), and an insistence on the "real" nature of their content, requiring a pact formed between audience and play that resists the usual expectations of falsity typically accompanying theatricality. The works of Lagartijas Tiradas al Sol are representative of theater of the real in Latin America in that they offer the theater as an alternative discourse of the real, where the self, the family, and the nation are defined.

National History

The history of Mexico plays a prominent role in many of Lagartijas's plays. In one of its earliest productions, *Asalto al agua transparente*, the mythical foundation of the ancient Mexican city of Tenochtitlán, modern-day Mexico City, is juxtaposed with the story of interior migration from more rural areas to Mexico City. The play quotes essential national texts from Miguel León-Portilla's *Visión de los vencidos* (The broken spears), based on Aztec accounts of the Spanish conquest, along with accounts of the modern history of overpopulation and its environmental effects.

Asalto al agua transparente proposes a long view of Mexican history, nothing new to nationalist discourses that traditionally rely on the country's indigenous roots as a narrative thread.[1] In this case, however, the mythical foundation of the city on the lake is presented as a fool's errand and the litany of drainage efforts, floods, and droughts that follow it through the centuries up to the present day are evidence of national folly. The nation is summed up and documented onstage as a people's relationship to water.

Such a preoccupation with portraying national history is not unique to Lagartijas; rather it is a feature of many examples of Latin American theater of the real. The aforementioned plays *Mi vida después*, *El año en que nací*, and *Proyecto 1980/2000* are representative of a generation's desire to engage with the recent past throughout the Latin American region. In *Proyecto C'úndua* (C'úndua project, 2000–2003), Colombia's Mapa Teatro shares these plays' urgent desire for and impossibility of the re-creation of the national past. Grupo Cultural Yuyachkani's *Antígona* (Antigone) shines light on the complicated relationship between surviving family members and those who fought and died in Peru's internal conflict.[2] The group's *El último ensayo* (The last rehearsal, 2009) reveals the utility of biography for intertwining the personal and the political in national history. Cia. Teatro Documentário, of Brazil, also explores the connections of the past and family with *Terra de Deitados* (Land of the lying, 2016), a project that takes place in cemeteries and stages local people recalling their long lives.

Lagartijas Tiradas al Sol's trajectory is exemplary of this trend toward reflecting on national history in the theater. While Mexican history has long been of concern to Mexican playwrights,[3] the focus on the documentary and the proposal that what is being staged should be considered a reflection of reality, are more recent developments. Works like Lagartijas's *Asalto al agua transparente*, *El rumor del incendio*, *Derretiré con un cerillo la nieve de un volcán*, those included in the project *La democracia en México*, and the collaborative binational work *Pancho Villa from a Safe Distance* (2016) all grapple with the representation of the nation, using the unique space of the stage to question the narratives that define the state. The collective's obsession with presenting national history alongside extremely personal narratives of loss and love has intensified over the years. Lagartijas's insistence on questioning official versions of history through the very act of representing them onstage is an excellent example of theater of the real's function throughout the region.

In Lagartijas's earliest works, however, the nation is not quite as explicit. In *Esta es la historia de un niño que creció y todavía se acuerda de algunas cosas* (2003), a short play that revolves around the protagonist's first kiss, the Mexican peso crisis provides the backdrop for an otherwise innocent, almost clichéd, teenage love story. While the protagonist works up the courage to ask his crush to the movies, his unemployed father rages. In *Pía* (2005) the company deals with the death of Rodríguez's friend onstage, and *Noviembre* (2005), based on the death of Luisa's mother, is much more intimate and seemingly disjointed from any specific nation's history. This theme of the nation, which has come to be one of the company's most characteristic elements, was only germinating in its early works. It was below the ground, taking form and growing before finally coming forth green and alive with plays like *Asalto al agua transparente* (2006). The company's focus, however, on autobiography and collective creation laid the groundwork, planting the seeds for the blossoming of its later works portraying national events.

For example, in *Esta es la historia de un niño*, we can trace the way that the seemingly simple story about an ordinary teenager's first kiss contains echoes of the multiple versions of national history that will later obsess the collective. David, the protagonist, offhandedly refers to the rains of the so-called crisis, saying, "I remember in particular the rains of the crisis. There was no money but there was a lot of rain" (1).[4] David goes on to describe the frustration of the unemployed, "failures in the time of failure" (2),[5] imprisoned in their homes because of the rain, going crazy, and having terrible fights with their wives. The crisis, which goes unnamed in the play but refers to the Mexican peso crisis of 1994–95,[6] serves as a touchstone that subtly grounds the coming-of-age story in economic reality. This is only a hint of the connection to national reality that will emerge in later works, however.

In *El rumor del incendio*, for instance, the touchstone lies further back in time, in the 1960s, when the guerrilla movements of the Mexican countryside shared space in the national imaginary with the 1968 Olympics and the infamous massacre of student protesters in the Plaza de las Tres Culturas in Tlatelolco.[7] Lagartijas brings the Mexican 1960s and 1970s to life by using video footage of presidential addresses, reading from the Mexican Constitution, and reciting historical facts onstage in a dramatic collage with an effect similar to that of sifting through government archives. At the same time, the play brings in recognizable cultural artifacts like music and clothing, with a stylized choreography that popularly accompanies Luis Miguel's 1990 hit "Será que no me amas."[8] All this is overlaid with narration of guerrilla activity in the state of Guerrero, emphasizing the juxtaposition of the celebrity playground of Acapulco against the extreme poverty of the growing peasant movements in the surrounding area. The national is constantly at the forefront of the play while the protagonist, Comandante Margarita, functions as a narrative thread, tying the collective events together at the level of the personal.

The techniques Lagartijas uses to portray national history in *El rumor del incendio* run throughout its oeuvre. It uses documentary video footage of historical events in its plays, sometimes running in the background and other times catching the attention of the actors onstage who stop to watch along with the audience.

In addition to the audiovisual footage, the technique of rapid-fire recitation of chronological facts plays prominently in many of its works; this method makes it impossible for those unfamiliar with Mexican history to follow, while creating a community of those who do recognize the rote-recited dates. Finally, the subject matter of so many of its plays clings fiercely to the idea of Mexico, especially contemporary Mexico. These effects insist on the importance of knowing and shaping national history.

While Lagartijas's obsession with and execution of staging national history are interesting and commendable, its contribution to Mexican culture at large is also significant. "Post-truth" has emerged as the description of the current political age, as though reality were an event with a before and after: the 2016 Oxford Dictionaries International Word of the Year was "post-truth," while the Society for the German Language selected "postfaktisch" as its 2016 Word of the Year ("Dealing with Post-Truth Politics"). In the 2016 US political election, a campaign based on falsehoods and half-truths has succeeded, even though the reality of the popular vote, laws governing conflicts of interest, and plain facts would lead one to expect its downfall. This post-truth phenomenon is not limited to US politics; indeed, in Mexico, where the current president's campaign began years before it legally should have thanks to promotion by a powerful television conglomerate, including his highly publicized marriage to one of its soap-opera stars, the concept of *truth* is precarious. Mexico is among the world's most dangerous places to be a reporter: it ranked sixth on the Committee to Protect Journalists 2017 impunity index, with twenty-one journalists killed with complete impunity during the past decade (Witchel). Freedom House ranks Mexico's press freedom status as "Not Free" and summarizes, "Mexico is one of the world's most dangerous places for journalists and media workers. Most murders and other violent attacks are not punished, leading to an expectation of impunity, and journalists face extreme editorial pressure—including credible threats of violence—from criminal organizations and corrupt authorities. Governmental mechanisms to protect journalists are hampered by bureaucratic rivalries, lack of resources, and inadequate training" (Freedom House). In addition to the violence and impunity faced by journalists in Mexico, reporters and other media workers face an unfavorable legal landscape as well: "Nearly a third of Mexico's states retain criminal defamation laws, and high-profile civil suits continued to be filed against journalists during 2016. In May, the Supreme Court upheld provisions of a 2014 telecommunications law that grant the government extensive access to users' communications data, which civil society groups had criticized as a threat to privacy and freedom of expression" (Freedom House).

The organization Article 19 reports that under Peña Nieto's presidency, every

year has been more violent than the one before. In 2017 the organization count-
ed 507 aggressions, including twelve murders and one forced disappearance. As I
write, Mexico is on the verge of a new presidency. Article 19 warns that "the current government, but also whoever attempts to govern in the future, must face the
consequences of the 1,986 aggressions perpetrated in five years; with the ravages of violence and impunity that prevail in the majority of these aggressions, that
mark the most violent presidential term, up to now, against the press in the recent
history of this country" ("Democracia simulada").[9] As the press faces threats to its
ability to freely and independently investigate and report on real events affecting
the lives of citizens, the need for a forum in which experiences can be recorded and
held up as examples is urgent. Mexican documentary theater has positioned itself
over the past half century as just such a forum. Mexican documentary theater, by
presenting documentary and autobiographical evidence onstage, has emerged as
an alternative source for reality in the face of unreliability and a lack of transparency from other sources traditionally associated with objective facts.[10]

Lagartijas Tiradas al Sol stages Mexican national history in almost all of its
plays, with varying degrees of protagonism. In every case, though, bringing the
official version of the nation's past to the stage allows audiences to question traditional narratives. At the same time, by juxtaposing the intimate against the broad
backdrop of the collective, Lagartijas reminds us that, while the state is powerful
and often an abstract concept, the nation is made up of real, live people with Presence. As these individuals try to make sense of their place in the world, the themes
of family relationships, to which I turn now, are an important framework for positioning the individual within national society.

The Generational

As I have mentioned, there are several twenty-first-century examples of Latin
American theater practitioners who focus on representing real family relationships
in auto/biographical plays. Given the fact that, in the second half of the twentieth
century, many Latin American countries were caught up in US efforts to promote
democracy and destroy (or impede) communism during the Cold War, it is well-
known that politics in many Latin American nations were marked by authoritarian
dictatorships and state violence.[11] It is in this context that the innovative concept
of theater of the real emerges throughout Latin America. Why is this concept of
parental biographying and self-representation on the stage gaining ground just
now and in this particular region? The shared legacy of Operation Condor and
its devastating effects on the populations of many South American countries is
an obvious possibility, which coincides with Mexico's own dirty war (see *Informe*

Histórico) and "perfect dictatorship" along with its reception of exiles from Argentina, Brazil, Chile, and Uruguay.[12] The massacres and forced disappearances associated with all these political processes leave behind a cultural field in which traumatic memory and postmemory are at the forefront. These memories are in search of a concept, a way to be framed or staged. Theater of the real, especially that which biographies the parent and the self, is a concept that is ripe for the picking, so to speak. The stage becomes a source of truth and reconciliation where, perhaps, official attempts to get at the truth and reconcile the population are not always successful.

The importance of family as a metaphor for dealing with these national traumas in Latin American theater is well-documented. Jean Graham Jones notes, "In contemporary Western theater, a common synecdochic stand-in for the social structure has been the family. In plays considered to be naturalistic as well as those seen as avant-garde, the family unit has frequently been placed upon the stage for analysis as such or as a microcosmic substitute for society in general. . . . During the [Argentine] dictatorship's early years, and well after, family dynamics functioned as a metaphor for multilevel power relations" (28). This tendency is also observable in postdictatorial Argentina and throughout the Latin American region. Sharon Magnarelli's study of Mexican and Argentine plays from the second half of the twentieth century finds a divide between naturalistic plays presenting the disintegration of a traditional nuclear family unit and postmodern plays that begin after the disintegration. Magnarelli classifies this disintegration as "a typically postmodern gesture" (20), and it is important to note that these postmodern plays also roughly coincide with the postdictatorial context of Argentina and the neoliberal era in Mexico, coinciding with the introduction of NAFTA in 1994. The critic shows that these postmodern plays "underscore the contingency of the family unit," but that "while the traditional family may no longer be a presence on the stage, its specter definitively lives on" (21). This specter, the remaining memory of the family that could—or perhaps should—be, is alive and well in twenty-first-century theater of the real in Latin America. By engaging with documentary techniques and experimenting with staging auto/biography and testimonial, Lagartijas and other theater practitioners are grappling with the phantom of family, after its disintegration by death, estrangement, and state violence.

The generation of postmemory, then, is compelled to find ways to connect to the previous generation. When absence is the common denominator, substitution is a plausible, if not satisfactory, impulse for resolving the problem of generational loss. In each of the aforementioned plays, the actors play both themselves and their parents. They step in for the absent characters, who are actual, historical people, creating a narrative for them, giving them gestures, costumes, and facial expressions, and developing a connection between the past and the present. They do not, however, attempt to lose themselves in the character. They maintain a separate identity as "child" though the boundaries between parent and child are shown to be fluid as the actors move between the two roles at will. In the process of constructing the parent, these actors construct a role that might have been taken from them, that of son or daughter.

Given the trend of staging family as a metaphor for society, it is key to understand that Lagartijas's work follows this tradition and also builds on it. Its works, which re-create family bonds and revive late parents, do not only symbolize the nation. They also, through their intimacy and their insistence on their own reality, create new bonds with the audience. This pact, which transcends the usual contract between the silent, passive audience member and the lively actors onstage, produces affective bonds within the theater while it undoes or at least subverts traditional family ties. By understanding the theater as a collective work of art, created between cast members, crew, *and spectators*, we can see how what Teresa Brennan calls "the transmission of affect" takes place during a performance. She writes, "The transmission of affect was once common knowledge; the concept faded from the history of scientific explanation as the individual, especially the biologically determined individual, came to the fore" (2). By staging individuals as members of a generation or connected to family members, Lagartijas's plays allow for the relationships between characters to spill over and include audiences in the collective created through art. As Lagartijas and other theater practitioners in Latin America emphasize staging real-life parent-child relationships, playing the generation that came before them, they make sense of the past through the dramatic process. By embodying their parents onstage, they reveal the constructed nature of the family even as they construct a family, creating continuity between generations and filling in gaps.

Beginning in its earliest works, with *Noviembre*, Lagartijas has shown its affinity for engaging the theatrical space to represent and process familial loss. The play, loosely based on the death of Luisa Pardo's mother, is a scripted, fictional piece. The emotion, grief, and mother-daughter relationship that the play portrays, however, foreshadow the same themes that would come to fruition in the documentary play *El rumor del incendio*, a biography of Pardo's mother, Margarita Urías Hermosillo. Similarly, in *Montserrat*, Gabino Rodríguez creates a fictional version of his mother's life, an alternate reality in which, rather than dying of cancer when he was a young boy, she actually disappeared to Costa Rica, where she lives in hiding to this day. This play, while an imaginative representation of a false reality, a desire, uses the techniques of documentary, such as projected video footage, and the demonstration of diary excerpts, photographs, letters, and official death certificates.

These plays, along with *Se rompen las olas* form a trilogy titled *La invención de nuestros padres*. While *El rumor del incendio* premiered in 2010 independently, and *Montserrat* followed in 2013, when collective member Mariana Villegas developed *Se rompen las olas* in 2014, an auto/biographical play about her own conception and birth, the three plays were retroactively collected and presented as a series. Indeed, the series title emphasizes the constructed nature of any biographical play, but particularly these re-creations of the previous generation. The company "invents" its own parents by making them into characters and writing them into scripts. At the same time, the title of the series could also be read as referring to an invention dreamed up by the parents themselves; perhaps their children are their "invention." In *El rumor del incendio*, Lagartijas "invents" Comandante Margarita, and the play juxtaposes her biography, including her early political awakening, participation in guerrilla movements, and later life as a social organizer and intellectual, against national events like the assault on the Madera Barracks in 1965, the death of Lucio Cabañas in 1974, and the kidnapping of President Echeverría's father-in-law in the same year. The play invents Margarita as it reconstructs her life not from the point of view of her daughter, who plays her character, but rather through documentary evidence and interviews. In *Montserrat*, the titular character, Rodríguez's mother, is the parent who is invented. Though she died of cancer at a young age, so that Rodríguez has no memories of her, he invents a wild goose chase that ends in a dream of a reunion with his mother, who he says has been living in hiding in Costa Rica. Finally, in *Se rompen las olas*, Villegas necessarily invents her parents, as the majority of the play's scenes take place before she was born, when her parents were lovers. The play revolves around her father's absence in her life, climaxing with the deaths of his first wife and child in the 1985 earthquake that devastated Mexico City and the staging of an imagined family photo populated by stuffed animals and dolls. In each play, the parents are fictionalized characters, but they are based on real people, as evidenced by photographs, birth and death certificates, diary entries, and the memories of their children. The plays, then, are demonstrations of how the archive can be used to reconstruct a life, and of how it can be used to manipulate the truth. The lines between theatricality and reality are blurred, pointing to the possibility of questioning reality itself, as the real people are presented as inextricably linked to the individuals who stage them.

The Individual

In addition to portraying national and family history, Lagartijas also participates in the contemporary obsession with self-representation. In today's cultural production, the self has undoubtedly taken center stage. Sidonie Smith and Julia Watson document the proliferation of the autobiographical in literature, the arts, and pop culture. Between the so-called memoir boom, the persistence of the diary and confessional modes (Smith and Watson 128), and the emergence of autofiction, social media, first-person autobiographical audio shows, webcam confessionals, the graphic memoir, oral history, and the privileging of the autobiographical in performance, visual arts, film, video, and drama (Smith and Watson 167–91), the constructed, performed self is having a heyday. In 2004, Emily Nussbaum attributed a generation's embrace of online journaling to "multiple roots, from Ricki Lake to the memoir boom to the A.A. confessional, not to mention 13 seasons of 'The Real World.'" The theater takes part in this celebration of autobiographical production, taking advantage of the actor's autobiographied body, offering it up as the proof of a play's veracity. Spectators bear witness to the actor's testimony, even while the constructed nature of theater casts doubt on the possibility of ever representing reality. Philippe Lejeune's famous autobiographical pact is especially helpful for defining autobiography. For the purposes of analyzing theater, I must depart from his definition, which assumes narrative prose as its subject: "Retrospective prose narrative written by a real person concerning [their] own existence, where the focus is [their] individual life, in particular the story of [their] personality" ("Autobiographical Pact" 4). While Lagartijas's works examined here have at least some elements of the definition, they clearly do not adhere to all of them. Instead, portraying autobiography onstage—privileging the role of the individual—reveals problems with a basic assumption of this definition. That assumption is that the individual personality can be contained in one unified narrative. The collective nature of theater necessitates a departure from Lejeune's tripartite biographied subject: the historical person, the author, and the narrator. In the case of Lagartijas, and many other contemporary theater practitioners, collective creation involves the participation of various people, including directors, videographers, actors, stage managers and crew, dramaturges, and, of course, the audience.

In a more recent reflection, however, Lejeune posits: "There is no set 'I' that remains identical throughout the history of humankind and simply expresses itself differently depending on the tools at hand. In this case, it is the tool that shapes the craftsman" ("Autobiography" 248). He concludes with optimism: "Autobiography uses the resources put at its disposal by all other literary forms and no longer clings to the classical unifying narrative.... Could it be that our 'accelerated' world has found the forms demanded by our new 'narrative identities,' be they paper or electronic?" (257). This estimation again focuses on narrative autobiography, but it rings true within autobiographical theater and performance as well. In fact, theater is an especially fruitful forum for challenging the "classical unifying narrative." For one thing, it is an inherently collective space, requiring the interaction of several agents, and the multiple viewpoints represented by audience members and actors themselves challenge the idea of a singular self at the center of the story. Auto/biographical representation in the theater allows for an understanding of the life story as a collective endeavor rather than the work of a lone individual. This type of dramatic representation positions the theatrical work as one among many sources of truth. Furthermore, by insisting on the reality of portrayed events, auto/biographical plays ask the theatergoer to accept the "true" nature of the content and, simultaneously, the fiction of the theater. The actor, by playing the role of him- or herself, creates an autobiography through the signs of the theater: voice, gesture, language, and so on. However, the director and author (often one and the same person) play the part of biographer by arranging the actor's words and designing his or her activity onstage. By placing the biographied actor onstage, the plays ask the spectator to believe that his or her version of the truth is, in some way, unmediated. The fact that the onstage body is the same one that experienced the presented events gives the production immediacy and a sense of being "true." At the same time, however, the theatrical apparatus as a whole forces audiences to recognize the hand that directors and authors have in relaying that "truth." Similarly, spectators must recognize the collaboration that occurs in any theatrical production between the various crew members, actors, director, and the audience itself. The very nature of the theater precludes the possibility of an unmediated autobiography that so tantalizes the audience.

Lagartijas participates in this trend of emphasizing the self through its innovative use of auto/biography onstage. It regularly includes verifiable auto/biographical information in its plays, and its characters often share a name with the actors who play them. Lagartijas's work is in the vanguard of contemporary auto/biographical theater in Mexico, especially with plays like *Montserrat*, which stretch the limits of the genre and question whether it can include autofiction, dreams, and wishes as part of an auto/biography.[13] This impulse to create alternative versions of the self is exemplary of international trends in autobiographical theater. Jenn Stephenson argues that "autobiography is a uniquely powerful political act. Rather than impossibly documenting the backward-looking narrative of one's life, autobiography is . . . an evolving process of self-creation and transformation. Through the invocation of performative power, it is possible to remake one's identity and write a new future or magically even a new past" (*Performing Autobiography* 4). Indeed, by bringing the autobiography to the stage, Lagartijas and other theater practitioners reveal the political act of declaring one's own identity and, in the process, shaping that identity. The unique contribution of Lagartijas is the way the company interweaves national and family history into its self-constructing autobiographies. This trend, I find, is particularly strong in Latin America, and Lagartijas's work is exemplary among the region's theatrical productions. This trend is also what sets contemporary Latin American theater of the real apart from the twentieth-century tradition of documentary theater in the region.

As I mention above, documentary theater and a fascination with staging national history are nothing new in Mexican drama. A focus on family relationships, as well, is not a departure from the obsessions of realist theater. It is by combining these elements, juxtaposing the national with family histories, and bringing documentary methods to family drama, that contemporary theater of the real innovates the meaning-making enterprise of the stage. In addition, by portraying the intimate and autobiographical, documenting not just any family but the actor's own family, the mix becomes truly heady. Tracing national history through the generations to its manifestation in personal experience gives the theater of Lagartijas an immediacy and significance that is new. The combination of the elements of national history, documentary, family drama, and auto/biography bolsters the plays' claims to reality. Where one might see the chinks in the armor of officialdom, doubting accepted versions of historical events, memories fill in the cracks, patching them with personal details that seem irrefutable in their intimacy. Where multiple versions of a family story are portrayed, giving the lie to the anecdote, documentation is provided to verify that *something* happened, even if the details are fuzzy.

I have chosen Lagartijas Tiradas al Sol as a case study for this twenty-first-century blend of theatrical genres because of its expert use of techniques and international critical acclaim. Its mastery of the documentary genre takes it to its extremes, at times filling the stage with accumulating piles of paper, and Lagartijas's boldness in presenting autobiographical and family history is admirable. In a theater scene that is often dominated by large media corporations staging translated Broadway plays, a situation occurring not only in Mexico but also in several Latin American countries, Lagartijas persists in elevating the ordinary and insists on independence.[14]

Lagartijas Tiradas al Sol's theater, exemplifying a regional trend, boldly proposes that the theater is a reliable source of truth. Through its representation of personal, family, and national history, it questions traditional discourses of reality and offers up the theatrical space as an alternative venue for both collecting and sharing knowledge. The company, exemplifying trends throughout Latin America, takes advantage of the theater's essential element of copresence to transmit truths that go beyond the documentary. Rather, it invites spectators to participate in the coconstruction of alternatives to official versions of history. The act is a political one—by bringing the archive onto the stage and interrogating it publicly, it is an agent in the creation of meaning in an often-chaotic political landscape. This challenge, coming from the stage, attempts to unmask authoritarian visions of history and to democratize reality. Its work is a seductive invitation to bask in the warmth of the truth.

Collective Creation

Lagartijas Tiradas al Sol, while made up at its core by Luisa Pardo and Gabino Rodríguez, is a somewhat nebulous constellation of associated contributors. According to Pardo, members of the collective label their personal work as belonging to the collective, and the collective pitches in on the individual works by its members (Pardo and Rodríguez Personal Interview). The company defines itself as "a squad of artists convened by Luisa Pardo and Gabino Rodríguez. Founded in 2003, we develop projects as a mechanism for linking work and life, to erase borders. Our work seeks to give sense, articulate, dislocate, and unravel what everyday practice merges and overlooks. Nothing to do with entertainment, this is a space for thinking" (Lagartijas Tiradas al Sol "Lagartijas Tiradas al Sol").[15] In its fifteen years of "erasing borders," the company has grown to include the participation of Francisco "Paco" Barreiro, an actor who joined the company in 2005; Mariana Villegas, an actor who joined in 2007; Carlos Gamboa, videographer; light designer Sergio López Vigueras; audio and graphic designer and researcher Juan Leduc; film director and videographer Yulene Olaizola; set and costume designer Úrsula Lascurain; actor Hoze Meléndez; actor and playwright Carlos López Tavera; light designer Marcela Flores; multimedia designer Emiliano Leyva; actor Harold Torres; designer Juanpablo Avendaño; and actor César Ríos Legaspi.

Lagartijas Tiradas al Sol joins other Mexican theater companies that grapple with what it means to be a political subject in the contemporary context. For example, Mexico City–based Teatro Ojo, composed of Héctor Bourges, Karla Rodríguez, Patricio Villarreal, Laura Furlan, Gisela Cortés y Emanuel Bourge, works with theater that spills beyond the stage, crossing into the realm of performance art and collective exposition. Its subject matter is, as is that of Lagartijas, Mexican national history including moments of state violence and popular resistance, such as the 1968 student movement and the 2012 presidential elections, with a focus on the real through the use of nonactors and documentary evidence.[16] Another company, director Jorge A. Vargas's Teatro Línea de Sombra, founded in Monterrey and now located in Mexico City, also seeks to blend theater with visual arts, music, and video. Its multimedia approach is similar to that of Lagartijas, and the companies shared a residency at El Milagro theater in 2017. Its projects also focus on the guerrilla and student movements of the 1960s and on human rights. Other important aspects of recent Mexican theater have been the representation of violence. Playwright Edgar Chías explores bodily violence in his *Ternura suite* (Tenderness suite, 2011), explicitly connecting the very real violence onstage to the war on drugs ravaging twenty-first-century Mexico. Antonio Prieto Stambaugh points out the relationship between the confessional play and gender-based violence, mentioning Mayan director, playwright, and actor Petrona de la Cruz Cruz's auto-biographical work *Dulces y amargos sueños* (Sweet and bitter dreams, 2013) and art-ist Ema Villanueva's 2000 performance piece *Have You Raped?* (212–19). He goes on to analyze what he calls *teatro personal,* "personal theater," affirming that the personal lives of playwrights and actors were not fodder for plays until relatively recently (219), citing works by the company La Rendija and by Gerardo Trejoluna as examples of how memory is embodied onstage in recent Mexican plays.

These contemporary works, which forefront auto/biographical content as well as collective creation, form part of a longer tradition in Latin America. In the 1960s and 1970s "collective creation theater" (*teatro de creación colectiva*) in Chile proposed a change in attitude toward the monstrosities of the dictatorship, in-spired by the manifestos of North American groups like the Living Theatre, Bread and Puppet Theater, the Teatro Campesino, and the San Francisco Mime Troupe (Sutcliffe). The penchant for collaborative devised theater is, according to Attilio Favorini, a characteristic of documentary theater in general. Indeed, he points out, the early examples of the Living Newspapers "characteristically relied on research teams of writers, revisers, and editors to compose text-privileged productions, which nevertheless were irregularly attributed in playbills and other publications" (98). Favorini ascribes the affinity between collective creation and the documen-tary mode to cultural forces like collective memory, object relations psychology, communitarian values, and the "motivation to give voice to the voiceless" (98). Favorini traces the history of documentary theater from early Soviet manifesta-tions through Piscator and the Federal Theater Project in the United States, the Tectonic Theater Project's *The Laramie Project* and postcolonial documentary the-ater in Canada, Australia, and South Africa, showing how collective creation has been an important aspect of the genre throughout and inherent to documentary theater's political proposal: "The spectacle of an acting company working as a tight unit from script creation through performance is metonymic of a working society, and it also yields the advantage of grouping the theatre company with other essen-tial providers in the community. Finally, collective creation preserves the often contradictory multivocality inherent in historic events, content to offer reasonable truths rather than an author/itative truth" (109). Collective devised theater, then, is rooted in a long tradition of collaboration within documentary theater.

In her study *Creación colectiva: El legado de Enrique Buenaventura* (Collective creation: the legacy of Enrique Buenaventura), Beatriz Rizk proposes, as the title indicates, tracing the practice of collective creation back to pioneering Colombi-an theater director Enrique Buenaventura. Along with Jacqueline Vidal, in 1970,

Buenaventura published the "Esquema general del método de trabajo colectivo del TEC [Teatro Experimental de Cali]" (General outline of the method of collective work of the TEC [Experimental Theater of Cali]). Even further back into the past, Rizk traces the idea of a theatrical methodology based on collective creation to the Provincetown Players of Massachusetts (founded in 1915) and the Living Newspapers of the Federal Theatre Project (1935–39), which are often mentioned in discussions of the history of documentary theater (Rizk 112). The link between the presentation of the real and collective creation continues to this day, as we see in the works of Lagartijas. Rizk also notes that the practice begins to appear in Latin America in 1963 with the Guatemalan playwright Manuel Galich and, in 1966, the TEC's adaptation of *Ubu Roi* (113). After the publication of Buenaventura and Vidal's methodology, Colombian groups like Teatro Acción, La Mama de Bogotá, and La Candelaria began to produce collective works in the 1970s. The tendency spread throughout Latin America in the 1970s and 1980s: in Cuba, Teatro Escambray; in Argentina, Libre Teatro Libre de Córdoba; in Brazil the Teatro Arena de São Paulo; in Chile, the Aleph group and the ICTUS; in Venezuela, Rajatabla; in Peru, Cuatrotablas and Yuyachkani (114–15). Rizk chalks up the explosion of the method throughout the region in a relatively short amount of time to its politics: "That feeling that the world could be changeable and that collective work was the way, along with the zeal for staging problems that concern everyone, for establishing direct communication with a public with whom one wants to have an exchange in a dialectic sense—although in practice many times this was done with an openly pedagogical intention—is the basis of the success of the collective creation method" (119).[17] These idealistic and democratic sentiments are still present in the work of Lagartijas and others, and their methods offer an alternative to the hierarchy of commercial theater.

In the manifesto on collective creation, Buenaventura and Vidal point out two important aspects for its practice: "(1) The training of the group members and the elaboration of the artistic product. (2) The relationship with the audience that can no longer be 'free' cannot be a relationship of 'market supply and demand'" (Rizk 137–38).[18] Therefore, the collective itself becomes of utmost importance, flattening the theatrical hierarchy that deifies the playwright and director and enslaves the actors to the text. Rather, in collective creation, the director becomes "the one who can see the totality during *all* of the work. Their work is not that of simple coordinator, given that the totality is not the sum of the parts, is not quantitative but rather qualitative. Their work within the new division of labor not only has not diminished, but rather has become more rich and profound; what has been lost in authority has been gained in creativity" (Rizk 173).[19] This same operation occurs, according to Buenaventura and Vidal, with the development of the text and the role of the playwright. The values of collective creation, in which the parts are greater than the whole and hierarchies give way to greater opportunities for creative expression, are evident in Lagartijas's works.

In addition to the democratizing values of collective creation, the auto/biographical genre has also influenced Lagartijas's work. At the same time that it emphasizes the group, by working collectively, its pieces also forefront the importance of the individual by focusing on auto/biography. Staging a life story, insisting on its reality and importance, works in tandem with the collective. This may seem counterintuitive; shouldn't collective creation promote the good of the group over the whims of an individual? Rather, the marriage of the collective and the individual is the democratization of the representation of the real. The theater is only possible through cooperation—the spectators must show up; the crew must work the light and sound boards; the actors must perform. All these agents must come together in order for a single life story to be made manifest. The performance of collectivity, then, reveals the interconnectedness and interdependence of each individual.

This interconnectedness can be found in the origins of auto/biography. Smith and Watson trace the history of the definition of the autobiography genre. The general term "life writing" is said to involve life as the subject of writing, rather predictably. Placing the life narrative against biography, they conclude that in biography scholars document and interpret from an external point of view, while a life narrative is "simultaneously externalized and internalized" (5). By this they mean that the life narrative must be written during the subject's life, while death is not definitive for the biography; that life narrative draws on the personal archive while biography uses historical documents, interviews, family archives and in fact rarely uses personal memories; and that life narrative is usually written in the first-person while biography usually takes third-person narration (Smith and Watson 6–7).

Finally, Smith and Watson point out that in contemporary practice life narrative and biography are often blended, through embedding versions of a family member's life within a personal narrative, or entwining the case history of a patient with self-analysis (7). Such understandings of auto/biography are useful for studying auto/biographical representation in theater, too. In the case of self-representation, the play, as the autobiography, must be produced and performed during the subject's lifetime in order for the subject to act onstage.[20] That first-person perspective carries over from narrative auto/biography to auto/biographical theater, and would point to a definition of authorship that includes the self-representing actor/subject/character. I see this system as parallel to that of autobiography versus biography for documentary theater, in which those plays that feature actors who play themselves onstage are categorized as auto/biographical and those in which actors play others as biographical; each of these categories comes with its implications of authorship that call for recognizing the actor's role in creation and authorship. However, the fact is that plays are rarely the singlehanded creation of one author. Even when an actor plays himself onstage, the script has often been developed through interviews between the director and actor, and, as we have seen, the director often takes a strong editorial role in the creation process.

This brings us to the *testimonio* genre, in which such issues come to the forefront. In order to glean what we may from the criticism on *testimonio* to inform our understanding of the multiple subjectivities represented in auto/biographical theater, I look to John Beverley's thoughtful definition of the genre: "By *testimonio* I mean a novel or novella-length narrative in book or pamphlet (that is, printed as opposed to acoustic) form, told in the first person by a narrator who is also the real protagonist or witness of the events he or she recounts, and whose unit of narration is usually a 'life' or a significant life experience" (*Testimonio* 45). Obviously, the plays dealt with here are not novels, and their archival and reportorial natures make them both printed (the script) and acoustic and visual (the performance). However, the contents of these plays are the first-person accounts of life experiences by the real protagonist or witness of the events recounted. As Beverley points out, *testimonio* doesn't exactly have an identifiable "author" in the Renaissance sense of someone having an authorial intention ("Anatomía" 12). Rather, the *testimonio* employs what Miguel Barnet calls a *compilador* or *gestor*, "somewhat on the model of the film producer" (Beverley, *Testimonio* 35). This model, based on collaboration, challenges the figure of the "'great writer' . . . so evident by contrast in the narrative of the Boom" ("Anatomía" 13).[21] In this way, especially in plays with a clear political memory, the *testimonio* genre gives us insight into the relationship between *gestor* or *compilador* and the witness. Theoretical work on *testimonio* has often focused on the relationship between the protagonist, or witness, and the interviewer who, with varying degrees of intervention, takes dictation.

One of the most important political implications of this iconoclastic genre is, according to George Yúdice, the fact that the intellectual cedes his privilege as enunciator to the subaltern subject (212). When contrasted with what David William Foster calls "documentary narrative," the *testimonio* stands by giving voice to the witness. In the case of documentary narrative, an established author novelizes a true story, and the resulting book is often classified as nonfiction.[22] While, in Foster's words, documentary narrative "overtly involve[s] the difficulties of narrating a segment of Latin American reality" (42), *testimonio*'s process of direct transcription, with little or no editing, displays those difficulties while effacing the compiler rather than putting the author at the forefront. In documentary theater, there are several possible configurations for the compiler-witness relationship. The most common is also most like *testimonio*: the director or company interviews witnesses, transcribes their reactions, and presents them verbatim, albeit mediated through an actor's body, onstage. In Lagartijas's auto/biographical plays, this relationship becomes more hidden and complex due to the presence of the witness onstage; that is, the onstage actor's body is also the witness's body. The mediation that occurs between the events experienced by the actor-witness and the conveyance of these events by the same actor-witness is partially concealed by the fact that witness and actor are one and the same. As in the case of *testimonio*, the seemingly direct recounting on the part of the witness is actually mediated through the *compilador*, and this relationship must be taken into account when considering authorship of auto/biographical plays.

Below I analyze Lagartijas's earliest plays, which contain the kernels of the full-fledged style we see in its more recent works: auto/biographical content and collective creation of documentary plays. I pay particular attention to *Asalto al agua transparente*, which premiered in 2006 and is the first of Lagartijas's plays to remain in its repertoire for a significant number of years. I also refer to the plays *En el mismo barco* (2007) and *Catalina* (2009), which—though not as well-documented or widely performed as *Asalto*—each exhibit, to varying degrees, the characteristics of auto/biography, collective creation, and documentary. In *Asalto* in particular we can observe the beginnings of the commitment to theater of the real that defines Lagartijas's work today.

Asalto al agua transparente is Lagartijas's first documentary play. It traces the history of water in Mexico City. By focusing on two characters, Janet Meléndez and Ixca Cienfuegos, who share an intimate relationship, Luisa Pardo and Gabino Rodríguez create an entrance point for the theme of control of and access to water from precolonial times to the present in the Valley of Mexico. In addition, the concepts of urban migration, environmental responsibility, and romantic love intertwine with the main theme, creating a multifaceted representation of a very real problem. The play was developed collectively by Rodríguez and Pardo, with assistance from Mariana Villegas, and was selected as part of the Muestra Nacional de Teatro 2006 (National Theater Festival 2006). It was also presented as part of Lagartijas's first international tour at the Festival TransAmériques in Montreal in 2010 and the Festival Impatience in 2011 in Paris, where it won the audience prize. Following in Buenaventura and Vidal's footsteps, the pair shared directorial, playwriting, dramaturgical, and acting duties, basing parts of their texts on the classic texts of *Visión de los vencidos* (The broken spears), indigenous accounts of the conquest of Mexico by Spain.

In *En el mismo barco*, a play that attempts to take up the questions that inspired *Asalto al agua transparente*, Pardo and Rodríguez join several other actors onstage to explore, "from a generational perspective, the coexistence of a group of young people and to contrast it with their political ideas and individual desires. This play begins with some questions that have accompanied us since our previous production and that have a direct relation with our everyday life and with us as social beings. How do we humans organize ourselves as a group?" (Lagartijas Tiradas al Sol *En el mismo barco*).[23] The play premiered in 2007, with a cast including Pardo, Rodriguez, Jimena Ayala, Francisco Barreiro , Rocío Bengoal, and Luis Rosales. Certain aesthetic elements of *Asalto al agua transparente* carry over into the follow-up production, such as the messy accumulation of objects, including newspapers, on the stage, and a loud and violent fight that erupts among all characters to the tune of "Imagine" by John Lennon. *En el mismo barco* was later adapted by the company Tristes Tigres in 2013. The fact that adaptation was possible sets the play apart from the rest of Lagartijas's work, which generally includes an auto/biographical element that makes such adaptations impossible or undesirable.

En el mismo barco contains elements that will form the core of Lagartijas's aesthetic: collective creation, minimalist sets built out of found objects, a basis in answering political questions, and a foundation in documentary. Even though this play is among the more traditional, fictionally speaking, of the company's work, it does include the obligatory reference to the Mexican Constitution, in this case Article 20, which guarantees freedom of association, and Article 17, which guarantees the right to property. The play is also deeply concerned with generational issues. In an early scene, Gabino declares, "We were born in the eighties, we are middle-class, we grew up with TV, Nintendo, computers, and the disillusionment of our parents; today we contemplate with discomfort the world that we have inherited" (*En el mismo barco* 1).[24].

The next play in Lagartijas's chronology is *Catalina* (2009). According to Edwin Culp, "When asked to make a work on . . . the Mayan prophesy of the end of the world in 2012, Gabino went back to tell the story of his relationship and further abandonment by his ex-girlfriend Catalina" (2). Indeed, the international obsession with the Mayan calendar, whose cycle ended in 2012 and led to the creation of many Mayan-themed popular culture products, like Mel Gibson's *Apocalypto*, for example, is subverted in *Catalina*. Rather than base the play on the universal concept of time, the national history of Mexico and its relationship to indigenous populations, or the apocalyptic visions of the Earth's ecological future, as the company does in *Asalto al agua transparente*, here Rodríguez turns completely inward. For him, the end of the world is the first heartbreak. Much like Lars von Trier's 2011 film *Melancholia*, in which one character's depression is powerful enough to be linked to the literal end of the world, *Catalina* posits the end of a romantic relationship as the end of the world—or at least a world. The play lets audiences into the intimate world created by a couple, with inside jokes, private messages, and nicknames. The play can only ever be a recap, though—the relationship has ended and all access to it must be mediated through memory. At one point, Rodríguez even applies Vicks VapoRub to his face to bring on tears, as though he were unable to access the emotional response once brought on by the end of his relationship with Catalina. With Catalina, Lagartijas leaps into its obsession with auto/biography, laying bare the most intimate details of an individual life.

Auto/biography and Collective Creation: *Asalto al agua transparente*

In September 2011, I was living in Mexico City and learned that Lagartijas would be putting on a performance of its popular play, *Asalto al agua transparente*. The play had premiered five years before, and Lagartijas had since moved on to other projects, such as *El rumor del incendio*. Thrilled at the chance to time travel and see a play that I had only read about and never expected to see performed live, I made my way to the X Espacio de Arte, an art gallery in the Condesa neighborhood. As in other performances by Lagartijas, the black-box performance space started out fairly sparse, with a backdrop made up entirely of newspapers laid out in a grid. Rows of wooden fruit crates laid out neatly form the basis for the various scene changes that will take place. From the ceiling hang various references to Mexican popular culture: a national flag, a baby doll, and a plastic bag filled with water. While the miniature flag is an obvious reference to the nation, the other two elements are more obscure. The baby doll reminds me of the Isla de las Muñecas (Island of the Dolls) in Xochimilco, in the extreme south of Mexico City. The island, located in the pre-Hispanic canal system, is a *chinampa*, a human-made island developed by the Xochimilcas and Aztecs to create extremely fertile land for agriculture on the lakes of the Valley of Mexico. Today, the Isla de las Muñecas is covered with old, filthy baby dolls, a mysterious and creepy place that attracts tourists who contract colorful boats called *trajineras* to tour the canals in Xochimilco. The plastic baggie is reminiscent of the street vendor's trick of hanging a bag of water to repel flies. The hanging props, then, refer specifically to water in Mexico.

As the play goes on, the orderly, sparse stage becomes more and more chaotic. Janet (Pardo) and Ixca (Rodríguez) interact with the set, tipping the boxes in slow motion, or violently pushing the crates across the stage in a loud domino-effect move. At one point Ixca throws newspapers all over the stage while Janet stands imperviously in the middle of the stage, fenced in by crates, reciting historical facts about water in Mexico. The technique is reminiscent of the historical recitations of *El rumor del incendio*. At one point Ixca breaks the bag of water and allows it to drain into a metal pan. The noise is irritating and loud, competing with the actors' voices, which, in turn, grow louder and more agitated in tone. Later Ixca washes his hair onstage using the water, and the stage ends up covered in trash, water, and upended fruit crates. The effects of human interaction with the environment are made evident—Janet and Ixca wallow in the contamination they have created.

In his reflections on *Asalto al agua transparente*, Rodríguez lays out the company's framework for creating the play. He explains that the company wanted to personalize dramatic discourse, stating: "The process of a show should not start with searching for a play. Rather, [it should start] by recognizing our preoccupations, our questions in that moment and from there adapting the theater to our interests, never adapting our concerns to a preexisting text" (Rodríguez 4).[25] This attitude fits with the concerns of other creators throughout Latin America, perhaps in response to a preponderance of commercial theater, Broadway hits in translation. In his reflection, Rodríguez recounts that in September 2005 he and Pardo began researching the history of Mexico, in particular the Spanish conquest and Mexico City's contemporary history. In addition, they toured the city, collecting materials and objects, often recycled trash. Though the play's story focuses on the history of water in the city, its connection to the creators' real lives is always at the forefront. In this play, as in *Esta es la historia de un niño*, the characters have fictional names unrelated to the those of the actors: Janet and Ixca. They are, however, explicitly linked to Pardo and Rodríguez's real lives in the reflection: "The idea to tell a story parallel to the history of water, that of a girl who arrives (like Luisa in real life) and meets someone who has always been there (like Gabino in real life), was already accepted and in progress" (Rodríguez 9).[26] The idea to tell the story of water in Mexico would be told through the lens of autobiography, albeit obliquely, and the play text was created through research and collaborative creation, as part of the rehearsal process. Rodríguez and Pardo, in *Asalto al agua transparente*, join the collective creation tradition, establishing themselves as equals in a collective and creating their text together by going out into the community rather than imposing a preexisting text onto the performance.

Asalto al agua transparente not only joins the international tradition of documentary theater and collective creation, but also the national inheritance of historical plays and conquest pageants. Much of the play's text comes directly from Miguel León-Portilla's *La vision de los vencidos* (The broken spears, 1962), which also forms the basis for Sabina Berman's 1984 *Aguila o sol* (Heads or tails). Víctor Hugo Rascón Banda, an important practitioner of documentary theater, wrote *La Malinche* (1998), which also refers to León-Portilla. The focus on national history can also be traced back to Emilio Carballido and Rodolfo Usigli, and the idea of commemorating colonial conquest through performance is preserved in pageants and festivals, as Patricia A. Ybarra shows in *Performing Conquest*.

The exceptional contribution of *Asalto al agua transparente* to this tradition of national plays is that it employs the autobiographical and collective modes to draw connections between the national and the personal. Whereas Berman and Rascón Banda are well-known as authors, even auteurs, Lagartijas turns authorship and the authority it implies into a shared, diffuse concept. At the same time, the loose connections between the characters, Janet and Ixca, and the actors Pardo and Rodríguez, bring an intentionally autobiographical aspect to the play that subtly sets national, monolithic narratives atilt. This personal touch keeps the play from being an imitation of traditional pageants that reenact the conquest's encounters between Spaniards and indigenous Aztecs in Tenochtitlán, the Aztec city atop which Mexico City has been built. At the same time, its collective, devised nature makes the play meaningful to local audiences that may identify with Janet's struggle as a newcomer in the massive city.

Indeed, the devised nature of the play, with rehearsals and research blending indistinguishably, is essential to its central message. As the play decries the misuse of water in the Valley of Mexico, citing the long history of drainage, covering rivers, pollution, shortages, and floods, the objects that Pardo and Rodríguez had acquired on their investigative expeditions became part of the scenery. Rodríguez reflects on how the experience of visiting different areas of the city, including the so-called Trash Market (Mercado de la basura) influenced the playtext's development. The uniqueness of the props made the play, like Mexico City and its inhabitants, particularly vulnerable to disaster. One day, as they prepared to move from their rehearsal space to the Teatro Xola, where the play would premiere, they arrived to find their studio empty and painted. No one knew where the props they had painstakingly gathered had disappeared to. They had to begin again, now facing a time crunch (Rodríguez 8–9).

The play opened with a difficult first run in La Madriguera theater, which Timothy Compton describes as "not easy to find and . . . not well-marked. The box office consists of a portable stand placed on the sidewalk in front of the theatre's door about 45 minutes prior to a performance. The theatre has no lobby and does not even have a ground level floor—a long stairway takes spectators directly up to a small, misshapen, bare, second-story apartment" ("Mexico City's Spring 2006 Theatre Season" 153). Though some of the performances were sparsely attended, and others filled only with friends and family members, Lagartijas persisted, as Rodríguez describes in his account of the play: "We suffered a lot through the whole run; our average attendance must have been two or three. Before each performance, after cleaning the space, setting up the chairs, the scenery, and warming up, we would peek through the window to see if any spectator had arrived. Until the fatal day arrived: The World Cup had begun in Germany and the whole world (myself included) was distracted" (Rodríguez 10).[27] When it became clear that not a single soul would come to see the show that day, Pardo and Rodríguez took their play to the streets, screaming their lines in an impromptu performance at a fountain. This commitment to the play and its message shows the urgency of Lagartijas's work. It is an entirely different thing to be snubbed as Hamlet or Ophelia than it is to be ignored as a carefully constructed version of yourself, declaiming the ecological disaster that threatens your home. Fortunately, though the play did not find commercial success in this first run, the right sets of eyes saw it and began to spread the word that Lagartijas had something special to say. The critic Luz Emilia Aguilar Zinser wrote a positive critique of the play, impressed by the "search for the essential in the content, the mastery of the space through the use of minimal elements. This small group of young creators offers an original alternative, inspiring hope through their intuition of theatre, authenticity, and humor, and deserves to be considered in the perspective of national theater" (qtd. in "Montan la premiada").[28] They were invited to a run at the Teatro de la Gruta and then to the prestigious Muestra Nacional de Teatro, where the play was well-received. Through the years, since its premiere in 2006, the play has been presented at various international festivals and residencies, and won the Prix du Public (Audience Award) at the 2011 Festival Impatience in Paris. As would become the norm for Lagartijas, its work received high critical acclaim and international interest, as representative of new Mexican and Latin American theater, but was largely ignored by mainstream Mexican theatergoers and commercial publications.

The play revolves around the story of Janet Meléndez, the one who arrives, and Ixca Cienfuegos, the one who has always been there. Their fictional love story plays out against the background of the history of the Spanish conquest of Mexico as well as major events in the history of water in the Valley of Mexico, the site of the Aztec floating city Tenochtitlán and modern-day Mexico City. Janet and Ixca are at turns replaced by historical figures, like the Spanish conquistador Hernán Cortés, the Aztec emperor Moctezuma, and the controversial figure of La Malinche, a captured woman who served as interpreter between these parties. As these intertwined stories develop, the actors shout information about water in the city, like the fact that major thoroughfares are named for the rivers that were covered in order to build them, or that there used to be a waterfall in the municipality of San Ángel. The pair floats in and out of the different characters and concepts they represent, often within the space of a single conversation, resulting in ambiguity.

As Noé Morales Muñoz suggests in his review of a performance of *Asalto al agua transparente* at La Gruta, there are three analytical streams one can dive into for interpreting the play. The first, the Spanish conquest of Aztec territory; the second, major events in water history in the Valley of Mexico; and the third, the story of Janet and Ixca. As I have argued throughout this chapter and in the introduction, it is the juxtaposition of the personal and the national, the documentary and the fictional, that makes Lagartijas's work special. While I will address each of these streams separately, it is important to keep in mind that they are inseparable in the performance; the play is more of an experienced collage, with the three aspects presented simultaneously and constantly. The scenery itself reflects this fact. The props (which replaced those that disappeared from the rehearsal space) consist of several wooden crates, of the kind used to transport fruit, stacks upon stacks of newspaper, toys suspended from the ceiling, and, of course, water: plastic baggies full of water hang over the stage. As the play progresses the stage becomes more and more chaotic. The actors move the wooden crates around to represent geographic and infrastructural features, like streets, rivers, and beds. They throw props, now garbage, and prick holes in the baggies so that water spurts out of them into tin cans. The sheer accumulation of materials and objects on the stage, and the resulting disorder, echoes the interwoven presentation of the three stories, which surface and disappear seemingly at random, within dialogues. For example, in one scene the two characters take turns with rapid-fire recitations of the history of the conquest:

> IXCA (I): Moctezuma hizo construir una calzada de más de 12000 metros de largo por 20 de ancho para contener las aguas.
>
> JANET (J): Según yo aquí deberían de estar . . .
>
> I: Pues yo que me acuerde aquí no había . . .
>
> J: En la casa donde crecí había un río, en las tardes me sentaba a ver las garzas.
>
> I: Axayácatl, sometió a Tlatelolco por agua dulce. (Lagartijas, *Asalto al agua transparente* 4)
>
> J: In 1446 the city floods almost completely.
>
> I: Moctezuma ordered the construction of an avenue more than 12,000 meters long by 20 meters wide to contain the waters.
>
> J: I thought they were supposed to be here . . .
>
> I: Well as far as I can remember there wasn't anything here . . .
>
> J: In the house where I grew up there was a river. In the evenings I would sit and watch the herons.
>
> I: Axayácatl conquered Tlatelolco for fresh water.

The interruptions of this litany, the expressions of confusion, of searching for something that is not where it was supposed to be, and the non-sequitur nostalgic description of Janet's childhood home, destabilize the familiar historical recitation. Just as the scenic space becomes confused and chaotic, the dialogue echoes this disorder, interweaving distant past, personal memory, and present.

The destabilizing temporal collapse mirrors the interspersing of national history, the documentary mode, and fiction. By presenting the history of the Spanish conquest, the history of water, and fictionalized autobiographical accounts, Lagartijas Tiradas al Sol invites spectators to a new way of being in the city. The play is not a pedagogical public service announcement about the dangers of wasting water. It is, however, sincerely committed to its message of ecological responsibility. The work of socially engaged theater achieves this sincerity without falling into the realm of propaganda because it arises from a collective process of creation and is loosely based on auto/biography.

By this I mean that, because the play was devised through a process of fieldwork, research, and collective creation by workshopping, it aptly makes use of the entire theatrical apparatus to transmit meaning. Rather than applying a prescribed text to the situation, the playtext arises from a particular set of circumstances. The intimacy of the auto/biographical makes the grand discourse of history more human. In the example I gave above, the river and herons Janet remembers are as effectively lost to her as the channels the Aztecs created with their *chinampas*. Janet lives in the city now, with its covered rivers, drought, and floods. By shrinking the distance between contemporary urban and rural spaces and between the present and the past, *Asalto al agua transparente* creates an opportunity for audiences to reflect on history and engage with art. Rodríguez, in his reflections on the play, quotes the Mexican artist Gabriel Orozco: "The important thing isn't so much what people see in the gallery or the museum, but rather what people see after seeing the work; how they confront reality from that point on. Art can regenerate the perception of reality; art can change the world. It isn't a question of better or worse, but of different" (Rodríguez 2).[29] Indeed, *Asalto al agua transparente* asks the theatergoer to look at the city differently; by truly taking in the history of its relationship with water spectators might examine their own relationship with the essential element. As Compton states in his review of the play, "And yet the performance did not feel like a history lesson, but a play focusing primarily on the developing relationship of a young couple in the city" ("Mexico City's Spring 2006 Theatre Season" 153).

The devised theater model, in the case of Lagatijas Tiradas al Sol, leads to the documentary mode. While prior works like *Noviembre* were connected to real experiences, they were not necessarily explicitly engaged with the documentary mode. In *Asalto al agua transparente*, and to some extent *En el mismo barco* and *Catalina*, the troupe joins the tradition of Piscator, Weiss, Leñero, and Rascón Banda, by attempting to stage real historical events as such. Through the recitation of facts, the direct address to the audience, and the socially engaged subject matter, the play takes part in the documentary tradition. Lagartijas itself labels it as a documentary play. The accumulation of newspapers onstage, however, hints at the way the troupe will innovate the genre in future plays. The periodicals are at once evidence of the vast amount of research the troupe has done, a physical manifestation of the credibility it demands, and also a challenge to the dominance of the document as source of truth. The mess the actors make onstage shows the vulner-ability of the newspapers, and the insertion of personal memories and experiences hints at the possibility of other sources of truth.

Asalto, En el mismo barco, and Catalina all display the essential elements that combine to transform the troupe's collective efforts into something more mean-ingful than the sum of its parts. Through collective creation, the company per-forms alchemical experiments in which official documentation combines with lived experience to create another, deeper truth.

Chapter 2

Unfolding Genealogy

When a parent is absent, through death or abandonment, what happens to family stories? Inherited memories, childhood nostalgia, and generational myths are lost to the ages. Lagaritjas Tiradas al Sol, along with several other contemporary theater companies in Latin America, is working to retie those golden threads, reconstructing broken family lines.[1] In chapter 1 I show how Lagartijas works as a collective to create auto/biographical plays that blend individual stories into the fabric of national history. After their first forays into auto/biographical and documentary theater, the company added familial biographies to the mix. Three disparate projects, Lagartijas's *El rumor del incendio* (The rumor of the fire, 2010), Gabino Rodríguez's *Montserrat* (2012), and Mariana Villegas's *Se rompen las olas* (The waves break, 2012) tell the real-life stories of company members' parents, set against the backdrop of Mexican history. While *El rumor del incendio* had a life of its own prior to 2012, the three projects were presented together as part of a series titled *La invención de nuestros padres* (The invention of our parents) in Mexico City's El Milagro theater in early 2012.

Taken together, the three works propose an innovative blend of documentary, autobiography, biography, and fictional drama that transforms the space of the theater into a forum for the ritual revivification of lost loved ones. *El rumor del incendio* focuses on the biography of one central character, director and actor Luisa Pardo's real-life mother, only revealing her relationship to the company in the play's onstage epilogue. *Montserrat*, meanwhile, plays with audiences by attempting to convince them that director/actor/protagonist Gabino Rodríguez's mother, Montserrat Lines Molina, faked her death and was reunited with her son after many years' absence. In *Se rompen las olas*, it is not the death of a parent but rather abandonment through indifference that is mourned in the ritual space of the theater, as Mariana Villegas connects her parents' meeting and her resulting birth to the 1985 earthquake that devastated Mexico City.

It is in this period of 2010–12 that Lagartijas firmly asserts itself as a pracititoner of theater of the real. It publishes the results of exhaustive archival research conducted on its subjects on blogs associated with its plays, gaining extratheatrical credibility. As I mention in the Introduction, Ileana Diéguez cites the inclusion of research as a primary function of artistic creation in contemporary performance practices, observing that the "artists become documentarians and witness-bearers to the pain of others" ("La práctica artística" 77). What is especially interesting in *La invención de nuestros padres* is that the "others" in pain are the company members themselves as well as their family members. Sylvia Molloy praises Spanish American autobiography's tendency to tap into a communal, family memory because it allows the text to "captur[e] a tension between self and other, of generating a reflection on the fluctuating place of the subject within its community, of allowing for other voices, besides that of the 'I,' to be heard in the text" (9). In *La invención de nuestros padres*, this tension expands to include the self against national history, placing official discourses alongside familial and individual voices.

Molloy points out that the difficulty of pinpointing the place where self ends and other begins relates to problems defining one generation's relationship to a previous generation's experience.[2] Marianne Hirsch teases out this intersection between past and present, personal and collective, using the term "postmemory," which "is distinguished from memory by generational distance and from history by deep personal connection" (*Family Frames* 22). Indeed, in *The Generation of Postmemory*, Hirsch highlights the prefix "post-" to define such relationships (3). As Hirsch argues, it is not *remembered* experiences that define postmemory, but rather that "postmemorial work . . . strives to *reactivate* and *re-embody* more distant political and cultural memorial structures by reinvesting them with resonant individual and familial forms of mediation and aesthetic expression" (33).

The memory displayed in plays like Lagartijas's includes both previous generations' experiences and those connections discovered and reconstructed through archival research.[3] In each play analyzed in this chapter, both the loss and the reconstruction of a loved one's life imply a certain violence. In his study on representations of violence in recent Mexican theater, Óscar Armando García writes about the pact between audience and actor: "The [audience's] call is consistent: one attends to see theater, either as a representation of reality or pure fantasy, never reality itself, because in that vein a different kind of performative basis could probably be generated. In the world of theatrical representation, then, one finds the challenge of how to resolve violence starting with the actor's creative body" (179). This same concern applies to the representation of reality. While audiences expect to see not reality but the representation thereof in a scenic documentary, it is in the actor's body that the encounter with the real, a sometimes violent encounter, can occur. Luisa reveals, at the end of the play, that she is genetically related to the historical character she is playing, and this bodily, mother-daughter connection forces a confrontation between audiences and the fact of the histories, national and personal, that the play presents.

These intersecting histories can be conceived of as in the past and therefore abstract. Theater of the real attempts to *re*realize a suspended reality. Offstage reality must enter theater's representational field and be framed as such in order to be understood as real. This mechanism is at the core of these plays' meaning-making structure. All participants willingly suspend disbelief, even as they enter the representational space of the theater, and believe that the material presented and the bodies presenting it are what they purport to be, *really*. As Janelle Reinelt puts it, "Spectators come to a [documentary] theatrical event believing that certain aspects of the performance are directly linked to the reality they are trying to experience or understand. This does not mean they expect unmediated access to the truth in question, but that the documents have something significant to offer" (9). This expectation is important for works like those of Lagartijas, which come with historical and political baggage.

Similarly, it is important to understand that this pact involves an understanding that the audience is not naive, but rather wise to the documentary genre and its problems.[4] Indeed, just as the narrative *testimonio* often, according to John Beverley, "appears . . . as an extraliterary or even antiliterary form of discourse" (*Testimonio* 42), the dramatic documentary, too, can seem antitheatrical, or outside theater. Hans-Thies Lehmann's *Postdramatic Theatre* takes up theater's recent turn toward performance, and the inclusion of the real onstage forms part of the postdramatic tendency he posits. The audience must enter into a new pact with the theater, one that accepts both representation and reality as possible onstage coinhabitants. This understanding includes the difficulties inherent in any auto/biographical project as well, and we can assume these issues are part of the play's draw. If the selves being represented onstage are present, physically in the case of the children and figuratively in the case of the parents, then the "truth" takes on an important if somewhat suspicious significance in the play.

The plays in *La invención de nuestros padres* are significant because facts currently face a precarious situation. The current Mexican president's life is easily confused with that of a telenovela; Mexico is one of the most dangerous places in the world to be a reporter. Lagartijas responds to the need for a space in which to record and share experiences affecting citizens, and the response is the theater. The stage emerges as an alternative source for reality even in the face of diminishing transparency on the part of government officials and threats to a reliable and free press. The inclusion of family narratives in these three plays bridges the divide between the personal and the collective, the individual and the national. The very portrayal of these intensely intimate stories onstage is, in and of itself, a political act.

In this chapter I analyze the three plays in the cycle as artifacts of contemporary Mexican society, reading their portrayals of the relationships between generations as indicative of larger trends. The plays vary in levels of explicit political content, but I find that they all point to the wider context of Mexican politics and history. The focus on the connection between previous generations and the actors' own lives, I argue, inserts the individual auto/biography into a larger collective. In *El rumor del incendio*, the previous generation is cut off from the current one through a lack of transparency on the part of the state and through death; this breach is overcome via historical research and re-creation. In *Montserrat*, there is a similar gap, though the methods for overcoming it lie in accessing internal desire rather than official archives. Finally, in *Se rompen las olas*, the casual disaster of a broken family is related to the natural disaster of the earthquake of 1987. In each case the plays advocate for understanding the individual as part of a larger system, resisting the potential for auto/biography to sacrifice the collective to the individual story.

The Invention of Our Parents

La invención de nuestros padres arose as a cycle after, the company says, "We realized that we were constantly working on the theme of our parents" (Lagartijas Tiradas al Sol, "La invención de nuestros padres").[5] The three independent projects were brought together and presented as a cycle in April 2012. *El rumor del incendio* had already found some acclaim, having premiered in 2010, while *Se rompen las olas* was Villegas's first solo project since joining Lagartijas as a technical assistant years earlier. *Montserrat* was previewed as part of the cycle, and an updated version was presented the following year at Chile's Santiago a Mil festival.

While the plays vary widely in style and content, they all focus on the real-life relationship between onstage actors and their parent/s. *El rumor del incendio*, as I mention above, links the life of Luisa Pardo's mother, Margarita Urías Hermosillo, to the guerrilla movements of the 1960s and 1970s in Mexico. Pardo plays the character Comandante Margarita, among other bit parts, and Rodríguez and Paco Barreiro play supporting characters. The tone is, overall, objective and documentary, insisting on the veracity of the events by providing documentary evidence throughout. In *Se rompen las olas*, meanwhile, the content is distilled to the nucleus of child, mother, father; while documentary evidence does come into play it mainly functions to set the scene in 1980s Mexico with news reports of the earthquake and thematic music. Villegas plays herself, highlighting her relationship with her parents rather than attempting to portray them. *Montserrat*, finally, is about the search for a lost mother; Rodríguez plays himself and, as in *El rumor del incendio*, provides masses of documentary evidence. In this case, however, the evidence supports a fiction—the mother he wishes he still had access to.

The first play I analyze in this chapter, *El rumor del incendio*, premiered at the Universidad Nacional Autónoma de México and is to date regularly presented at festivals in Europe and the Americas, and has won the Audience Award at the Festival Impatience in Paris, as well as the ZKB Förderpreis at the Zürcher Theater Spektakel (in Zurich). It recounts the history of armed resistance movements in Mexico in the 1960s and 1970s, using the life of Comandante Margarita, played by Luisa Pardo, as the narrative thread. Characterized by the company as a "scenic documentary (*documental escénico*), the play presents historical data, video footage, and excerpts from the Mexican constitution alongside re-creations of battles using toy soldiers and torture scenes in which Pardo conspicuously applies makeup to represent wounds, a combination reminiscent of Diana Taylor's archive ("the grisly record of criminal violence—the documents, photographs, and remains that tell of disappearances") and repertoire ("the tales of the survivors, their gestures, the traumatic flashbacks, repeats, and hallucinations—in short, all those acts usually thought of as ephemeral and invalid forms of knowledge and evidence") (*Archive* 192–93).

This juxtaposition of factual information with theatrical elements complicates generic assumptions about both history and theater. In the age of reality television, the memoir boom, and, more recently, fake news, audiences are not so naive as to expect history to be unquestionably, objectively "true" and theater to be purely fictional. It is important to note, however, that Lagartijas works with an archive that had been closed, portraying events that the government had, prior to the twenty-first century, denied; even skeptical spectators are forced to confront the fact of documented massacres and state-sponsored assassinations.

Rodríguez's play *Montserrat*, on the other hand, gives in completely to theater's deceptive reputation, leading audiences to believe in a beautiful impossibility, the reversal of death. While it includes much false information, the play begins and ends with truth. It opens with the fact that Montserrat died when Gabino was a child; it ends with Gabino's description of reuniting with her in his dreams. I analyze how blending documentary and parody broadens the category of the real, inviting us to include desire as a source of truth. While it seems to stray from the bounds of theater of the real by presenting falsehoods, the play actually bolsters the position of theater as an alternate source of knowledge, highlighting the contribution of what Carol Martin calls "theatrical epistemologies" (*Theatre of the Real* 74).

While *Montserrat* previewed in 2012 as part of *La invención de nuestros padres* at the Teatro El Milagro in Mexico City, it officially premiered in its final version in 2013 in Chile at the Santiago a Mil festival, an important forum for innovative theatrical arts in Latin America. The play was also presented at the Festival Temporada Alta in Girona, Spain, at the Centro Cultural España in Guatemala, the Museo de Arte Contemporáneo de Vigo in Spain, the Festival CAIN in Guadalajara, Mexico, at the University of California Institute for Mexico and the United States in Riverside, California, at BAD Festival de Teatro y Danza Contemporánea in Bilbao, Spain, at CASA Latin American Theatre Festival in London, and at the Escena Brasil Internacional festival in Rio de Janeiro. *Montserrat*, by mixing both verifiable, fact-based evidence with invented but credible evidence, offers the audience two possible explanations for the disappearance of Montserrat. Metatheatrical techniques, however, along with common sense, show the audience that the less desirable option, her death to cancer in 1989, is the true one.

Se rompen las olas is Mariana Villegas's first solo project with the company. Villegas joined Lagartijas in 2007 as a production assistant and wrote and starred in *Se rompen las olas* in consultation and collaboration with the rest of the company. The play, like the others it joins in the cycle, reconstructs the actor's parents' lives. In this case, the play revolves around the devastating 1985 earthquake that destroyed much of Mexico City and killed thousands of people. Villegas links her own conception to this destructive event because her parents came together as a result of the earthquake (her father lost his first wife and children in the disaster). Here the focus is much more on Villegas's own childhood and upbringing than on her parents' lives, though the months leading up to her conception and birth loom large in the play's narrative. This gives the play a more intimate, confessional feel than *El rumor del incendio*, with more humor. In addition, it seems more focused on the child role than on the parental one.

The three plays, taken together, indicate a generational view of the nation and the self. The actors insert themselves into history through the family; their role as children and connection to parents anchors them in the flow of history. At the same time, the theatricality of the representations of one's parents calls into question the possibility of ever re-creating a life once it has been lived, of ever knowing another person, even one's own flesh and blood. The cycle's title, *La invención de nuestros padres*, can be taken to refer to something that the parents invented or to the act of inventing one's own parents. The onstage evidence, the body of the child who bears witness to the existence of her parents and the love they once shared, is the child, the parent's invention. At the same time, by reconstructing the biographies of their parents after the fact, the actors have no option but to invent the life stories of their mothers and fathers.

El rumor del incendio

On the vast campus of the Universidad Nacional Autónoma de Mexico (National Autonomous University of Mexico) or UNAM, a secluded collection of theaters, museums, and cafes, the Centro Cultural Universitario (University Cultural Center, CCU) feels as though it is not part of the chaotic capital city. There is very little traffic, save the overflowing, free PUMABUS campus shuttle, and the nature reserve surrounding the center drowns out the noise and rush inherent in city life. I did not know what to expect as I queued up to buy a deeply discounted ticket on Jueves Puma (Puma Thursday), the special-priced Thursdays that almost always sell out at the CCU. I paid for my ticket to see *El rumor del incendio* knowing only that it was billed as a "documental escénico."

The audience was led into the black-box theater, the Foro Sor Juana Inés de la Cruz, which was filling up quickly with a youngish crowd, the kind one might expect at a university theater. A smattering of older but hip-looking spectators, probably professors, and the rest of the crowd negotiated the three rows of chairs set up on risers along two sides of the theater. The floor was covered with green, plastic indoor-outdoor carpeting that looked vaguely like a lawn, the kind that plastic flowers can be snapped into. The tracks of a toy train encircled a dinky Mexican flag. Blown-up, idyllic photographs of meadows and waterfalls formed the backdrop. A fish tank, figurines, and aluminum kitchenware covered the tables, which were pieces of plywood balanced on sawhorses. The lights dimmed and the show began with a reading from the Constitution of 1917. I was dizzied by the rapid-fire crash course on the Partido Revolucionario Institucional (Institutional Revolutionary Party, PRI), the guerrilla movement and teachers' movement of the 1960s and 1970s, the attack on the Madera barracks, Lucio Cabañas, Genaro Vázquez.

Some of the events were reenacted using toy soldiers and a closed-circuit video camera that projected the action onto a screen for all to see; some of it was merely recited quickly, as a child spews a memorized lesson before it is forgotten. Comandante Margarita, the protagonist, held all the disparate parts together. Her life story took her from Chihuahua to Mexico City to Xalapa, and as the play ended the actor portraying her, Luisa Pardo, smoked a cigarette while addressing us directly, recounting Margarita's death from cancer. She announced that Margarita, the character, was her mother in real life, and at once the play's relationship to reality intensified tremendously. I was, in that moment, the unsuspecting spectator, taken in by the fiction of the theater and the promise of truth offered at the play's conclusion.

During the 1970s, Mexico's guerrilla movements usurped the role of family as the fundamental unit of society for their members, asking adherents to give themselves over completely to the cause.[6] These reconstructed families leave the next generation, those children born in the 1970s and early 1980s, with many questions about their origins. By interrogating their parents' biographies, the children construct themselves. In families torn apart by political or domestic violence, a child may access an absent family member through inherited stories. Contemporary theater of the real draws on those stories to re/create lost histories. Lagartijas Tiradas al Sol attempts to make sense of fractured generational stories in its 2010 project, *La rebeldía* (The rebellion). *La rebeldía* is a multigenre work that includes the play *El rumor del incendio*, the blog *El rumor del oleaje* (The sound of waves), and the book *El rumor de este momento* (The sound of this moment).

La rebeldía's creators invert genealogy's top-down hierarchy by giving birth to themselves, creating their own legacy, self-consciously mapping out an image of themselves. In *El rumor del incendio*, as in *Montserrat* and *Se rompen las olas*, self-representation combines with parental biographying to question the generic boundaries between autobiography and biography, documentary and fiction, ultimately redefining drama's social function. It examines the strategies used to convey the family ties between Margarita, the play's protagonist, and Pardo, the actor who plays her, which include documentary evidence, bodily relationships, and genealogical connections.

At the peak of what Mario Vargas Llosa called its "perfect dictatorship" under the PRI, Mexico's perfection did not preclude resistance from student groups, militias, and peasant movements. Decades later, in *El rumor del incendio* and its accompanying publications, director and actor Pardo plays both herself and her real-life mother, Margarita. I argue that theatrical self-representation challenges the auto/biographical genre, blurring lines between biography and autobiography, and redefining drama, asking spectators to consider the stage an alternative source of historical fact. Plays in which an actor plays himself, convincing the audience that the events represented are "real," often hide the mediation of writing, interviewing, researching, and rehearsing as the audience makes a one-to-one equivalence between the character and the historical person.

The actor's body becomes a site of erasure: erasing authorship, erasing theatricality. This elimination, however, is misleading. The mechanism of the theater, with director, actors, and audience cooperating to create meaning, along with the relationship between text and performance, renders autobiographical transmission anything but direct. The play makes historical and political claims about what happened in Mexico in the 1960s and 1970s, but also stakes a claim on the un/truth of the self: the individual is presented as an entity with fluid boundaries, difficult to limit and capable of absorbing other selves. The play's documentary nature emphasizes the concept of "truth." Diana Taylor writes about "theatre of crisis," which "depends on the spectators' ability to accept dramatic conventions and momentarily believe that the unreal is real. . . . Theatre simultaneously allows us to erase, block out, and derealize the real" (*Theatre of Crisis* 11). Even as this suspension of disbelief occurs, its inverse does as well—the real is at the forefront.

El rumor del incendio is an important contribution to a wave of cultural responses to Mexico's so-called dirty war. Because of a lack of transparency and accountability in Mexican government, many citizens turn to cultural means to protest. As Human Rights Watch reported in 2006, "A central obstacle to democratic accountability in Mexico has been the culture of secrecy that has traditionally pervaded all areas of government. . . . This lack of transparency severely undermined [citizens'] ability to counter the abusive practices that state agents and institutions routinely committed against them" (*Lost in Transition* 2). In 2002, under Vicente Fox's presidency, the Mexican Congress passed the Ley Federal de Transparencia y Acceso a la Información Pública Gubernamental (Federal Transparency and Access to Governmental Public Information Act), which established the Instituto Federal de Acceso a la Información y Protección de Datos (Federal Institute for Access to Information and Data Protection), an organ for processing requests for public information.

In 2006 the Fiscalía Especial para Movimientos Sociales y Políticos del Pasado (Special Prosecutor for Social and Political Movements of the Past), Dr. Ignacio Carrillo Prieto, released a report confirming state responsibility for deaths and disappearances during the dirty war of the 1960s–1980s. The *Informe histórico a la Sociedad Mexicana 2006* (Historical report to Mexican society, 2006) includes information on the student movement of 1968 and the Tlatelolco massacre, guerrilla movements, and genocide. Direct access to this report was cancelled in 2015 by the Secretaría de Gobernación (Secretariat of the Interior), without warning, citing the risk that a precedent of allowing direct access to archives would affect research of other historical periods (Martínez). This move was heavily criticized, and the *Informe Histórico* is still available on the National Security Archive's website. The 2010 production of *El rumor del incendio* benefited directly from this period of transparency, 2006–10, in which the archive was open.

The members of Lagartijas Tiradas al Sol used the archive to discover facts about the 1960s–1980s in Mexico and in the life of Margarita Urías Hermosillo, their protagonist and Pardo's mother. The play, then, becomes the permanent record of the time as access to the archive proves to be ephemeral, thus inverting the usual associations of performance versus the archive. In a case like that of Mexico, Hirsch's concept of postmemory can be a useful way to think through the relationship between contemporary youth and the generations that came just before them. Whereas in Argentina and Chile many children were actually born in captivity and kidnapped and raised by agents of the state, and therefore should be considered as direct victims of the dictatorships rather than postgenerations, in the case of Mexico, where getting at the truth of what really happened is clearly such a fraught and difficult task, I find the concept useful.

The same party responsible for the Mexican Miracle, the PRI, also conducted the Dirty War; the same political party that rigged elections, massacred students, and disappeared dissenters was also responsible for nationalized social-welfare and health-care programs. Mexico's twentieth century is complicated and the PRI's dictatorship was perfect, in part, because of its undeniable successes in many areas. These successes in welfare and education overshadowed, for some, the anti-democratic excesses and abuses the party also represented. The facade came crashing down with the massacre in Tlatelolco in 1968, as the world watched. Later, the children of the so-called Lost Decade, beginning with the debt crisis and peso crash of 1982, grew up among the echoes of the heady days of student protests and guerrilla movements. Indeed, the memories portrayed in *El rumor del incendio* are those of another generation, while the history portrayed is anchored in the personal connection between Luisa and Margarita. The facts that the troupe had to do archival research and rely on family lore to re-create Margarita's life and that the enterprise was undertaken so thoroughly, as will be shown, give the story a sense of being anchored in history.

The story is of personal importance at the same time that it is nationally significant. These are memories that cannot be remembered because those who experienced them are no longer around; rather they must be pieced together, as though by a detective or an archaeologist, after the fact. The play's mix of official documentation, such as video footage of presidential speeches and the reading of the constitution, with personal and popular memory, such as music and dance, personal letters, and family lore, provides the next generation with an accumulation of information that, in the end, cannot fill the absence left by Margarita. Her daughter's body, flesh of her flesh, is the true evidence that she lived and that her story continues.

In order to demonstrate the way in which the limits of the self expand to include the collective, I turn to *El rumor del incendio*'s use of evidence, which conveys the reality of the play's historical content and the relationship between the past and the present. As Paola Hernández points out, twenty-first-century Latin American documentary theater questions the validity of the archive itself, fusing the public and the private (115). *El rumor del incendio* follows suit. I examine the play's evidence, dividing it into three categories: documentary, corporeal, and genealogical, analyzing how the play's expanded definition of the self also defies definitions of both autobiography and theater. I will focus mainly on the dramatic production of *El rumor del incendio*, which challenges generic borders, while briefly examining the paratextual world of the play, the blog *El rumor del oleaje*, and the book *El rumor de este momento*, as supports for the theatrical work. Martin affirms that "most contemporary documentary theatre makes the claim that everything presented is part of the archive" and that "more often than not documentary theatre is where 'real people' are absent—unavailable, dead, disappeared—yet reenacted" ("Bodies of Evidence" 18).

In the case I analyze here, however, what the play presents does not come entirely from the archive, but also includes material that originates in memory, specifically the performers/ children's memories of their parents. Similarly, the "real people" are only partially absent—the children, playing themselves, are present. Martin's point that "documentary theatre can directly intervene in the creation of history by unsettling the present by staging a disquieting past" ("Bodies of Evidence" 18) is especially valid here. The play at once creates history, remitting to the parent/past, and unsettles the present, theatricalizing the child/present.

How does representing a supposedly real family member and her life story expand the boundaries of the self? What strategies does the play use to challenge the limits of the self? In this play, and others that incorporate family members' biographies, I find three discrete branches of discursive strategies that question the concept of a self-defined, firsthand experience and memory: documentary, corporeal, and genealogical. The first branch, the documentary, describes the use of documents as evidence of the veracity of the content presented in the play. These documents might take the form of court proceedings, personal writings, and family photographs. Besides extending the bounds of the play to include the real world, these documents also work as extensions of the cast members' memories and selves. The second strategy is the corporeal, which unites past and present. The actors use corporeal practices and physical relics (in the case of the voice) to configure a lived memory, a re/presentation of the parent as part of the actor-child's body. The third strategy is the genealogical, another one in which the play insists on the connections between the actor-characters and the historical. Through the selective presentation of credible, inherited material and an emphasis on proper names, the play extends the reach of the autobiographical self, portrayed to include the biographical self of the parent. The dramatic process, however, both transmits and transforms this information. Lagartijas Tiradas al Sol was no stranger to documentary theater when it produced *El rumor del incendio*. As I show in chapter 1, its earlier plays *Asalto al agua transparente* (2006) and *Catalina* (2009) also show an affinity for staging the real.

In *La rebeldía*, a variety of documents is used to extend the reach of the autobiographical self to include the experiences of family members. Throughout the project, documents form the basis for familial connections. The book *El rumor de este momento*, along with other paratexts like the blog *El rumor del oleaje* or the handbill, clues the audience in to the identities of the represented characters. As Margarita's final monologue ends with the birth of Luisa the alert spectator might wonder whether the actress identified as Luisa Pardo in the program has anything to do with the diminutive name. In this way paratextual documents establish genetic links between the characters and their creators, which challenges the traditional notion of theater as a space of fictional representation. In the scene of Margarita's incarceration, the three actor-characters depend on documentary evidence to reconstruct the situation and to reinforce the reality they present.

The characters "G" (Gabino Rodríguez) and "P" (Paco Barreira) recite the

events of the arrest in a journalistic style, citing court documents. This key moment interweaves documentary evidence with theatricality, thereby merging first-
and secondhand experience. As G and P cite legal documents, Margarita is stylis-
tically tortured. Slowly, deliberately, and openly, she rubs black makeup over her
face to represent wounds, the result of the simulated beating. Her head is placed
in a basin full of water, but the actors do not attempt to re-create the torture in a
realistic way. Hearkening back to Brechtian alienation, the audience is obliged to
watch violence that is clearly a representation. The fact is that the three performers
are incapable of reliving history, no matter how much historical research they do
or how much data they have to support their stories. Here the tension derived from
the habitation of one body by both mother and daughter comes to the forefront.
As much as Luisa would like to transmit her mother, embody her, her actions as
Margarita will always be a copy—theater.

At the same time, however, it is more than just a copy. Rather than simulating
being another character, as she would, say, were she playing Ophelia in *Hamlet*,
Pardo demonstrates her connection to her mother by imperfectly playing her. In
El rumor del incendio, the incompatibility of documentary evidence and the representation of past violence, undertaken and experienced by absent bodies, creates
friction between the reality of the familial connections proposed by the play and
the fictional nature of theatrical representation. The detention scene at once emphasizes the representative nature of theater and reveals the problems inherent in
representing the self. Pardo, attempting to "play" her mother but also herself, as
she does at the end of the play, claims authority over her mother's life, an extension
of her own. Margarita's biography is, in this way, subsumed into Pardo's autobiography, expanding her life beyond its years, experience, and consciousness. While
Margarita is in prison, her family once again plays an important role.

During her incarceration in the women's prison, Margarita addresses the audience, outlining her sister's involvement with prisoners: "My sister visited various
prisoners in different prisons and she helped all of us with legal procedures and
paperwork. She came to see me on Wednesdays and Sundays. Sometimes she cried
a lot; it made her sad to see me there. She told me that she had to cross the city and
then take a bus that traveled far down an unpaved road—at that time Santa Martha Acatitla [women's prison] was on the outskirts of the city. She saw very pretty
sunsets when she came out of the prison after visiting me" (Lagartijas Tiradas al
Sol, *El rumor de este momento* 105–6).[7]

Margarita's sister plays an important role in connecting Margarita with the
greater world. Whereas Margarita is trapped in captivity, her sister moves freely
and attempts to liberate the captives through paperwork. Legal documentation of
detentions and appeals becomes the link between past and present, lending credence to Margarita's claims. While, in this case, the paperwork is never produced,

the mention of it implies officialdom and the metaphorical prison that bureaucracy can represent. Finally, the prisoners' dependence on the sister's help with legal documents reminds the audience of the real-life impact that documents can have.

In *El rumor del incendio*, Luisa's putting on of Margarita is not a manifest act until the end of the play. This results in a series of doublings that emphasizes the hollow where Margarita should be. In her essay on political documentary film "Political Mimesis," Jane M. Gaines asserts that revolutionary documentary films are able to bring about social change through a bodily relationship rather than by relying necessarily on political consciousness-raising. Gaines argues that bodies react identificatorily to sensational or sensual images on the screen, writing that "*political memory* has to do with the production of affect in and through the conventionalized imagery of struggle: bloodied bodies, marching throngs, angry police" (92). This sensuous struggle is also mimeticized in documentary theater. And here, rather than bodies onscreen making the bodies of the spectators (re)act, there is yet another level of obligatory bodily action. As in Ileana Diéguez's "liminal stages, in which "aesthetic elaborations are not distanced from ethical decisions or the motivations behind them" (*Escenarios liminales* 151),[8] *El rumor del incendio* is inseparable from the reality it represents.

Margarita, the character whose body is at the epicenter of the play, is not present for the scenes of torture; there is no film reel of her interrogation and no photograph of her broken body projected onstage. Rather, her daughter stands in for her. Pardo's body must act for Margarita's, in turn making the spectators' bodies do "something." Recorded sound also plays an important part in establishing Margarita as a family member in Lagartijas Tiradas al Sol's play. The recorded sound is the voice of Héctor, who was Margarita's fellow researcher and lover. While his voice is not identified onstage, in the text his interventions are identified as "Fragmento sonoro de Héctor" (Sound clip of Héctor).[9]

During the scene of Margarita's imprisonment, the clip plays Héctor's voice, saying, "I remember that your mother would tell me that in the cell she would imagine that she was a sheet of paper and that way she could escape folded underneath the door" (Lagartijas Tiradas al Sol, *El rumor de este momento* 105).[10] Here the metaphor of transforming the body into a sheet of paper works as the inverse of the theatrical process. Whereas Margarita wishes to disintegrate her physical body and become a two-dimensional blank slate, so to speak, Lagartijas Tiradas al Sol brings the documentary evidence of its archival research—stacks and stacks of papers—to life, reintegrating the historical record in bodily form. Without the paratext of the book, it would be impossible to tell whether the recorded voice belongs to Gabino or Paco, or to a friend or relative of Margarita. The text backs up the recordings' veracity by identifying them as the voice of Héctor, while Margarita provides the backstory for her relationship with this figure.

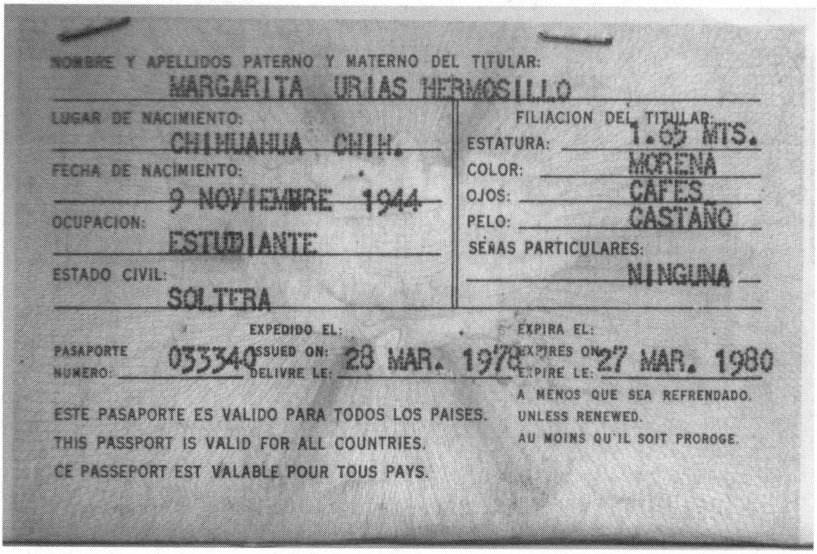

NOMBRE Y APELLIDOS PATERNO Y MATERNO DEL TITULAR: MARGARITA URIAS HERMOSILLO

LUGAR DE NACIMIENTO: CHIHUAHUA CHIH.

FECHA DE NACIMIENTO: 9 NOVIEMBRE 1944

OCUPACION: ESTUDIANTE

ESTADO CIVIL: SOLTERA

FILIACION DEL TITULAR:

ESTATURA: 1.65 MTS.

COLOR: MORENA

OJOS: CAFES

PELO: CASTAÑO

SEÑAS PARTICULARES: NINGUNA

PASAPORTE NUMERO: 033340

EXPEDIDO EL: ISSUED ON: DELIVRE LE: 28 MAR. 1978

EXPIRA EL: EXPIRES ON: EXPIRE LE: 27 MAR. 1980

A MENOS QUE SEA REFRENDADO. UNLESS RENEWED. AU MOINS QU'IL SOIT PROROGE.

ESTE PASAPORTE ES VALIDO PARA TODOS LOS PAISES.
THIS PASSPORT IS VALID FOR ALL COUNTRIES.
CE PASSEPORT EST VALABLE POUR TOUS PAYS.

FIGURE 1. Margarita Urías Hermosillo's passport, as reproduced in the book *El rumor de este momento.*

Genealogy and its emphasis on proper names is another strategy employed in *El rumor del incendio* to expand the definition of autobiography as well as emphasize the reality of the play. Names are important for establishing family connection, in theater as in life. Even if the audience believes Margarita Urías Hermosillo to be a fictional character at the start of the play, her character is rooted in history, given a family tree, and thereby historicized. This genealogy registers her in reality. Margarita introduces herself at the beginning of the play, directly addressing the audience. She shares a photograph of her father, speaking about him and her mother. Margarita also mentions another Luisa, a character her father created for the textbooks he wrote, hinting at a connection to Luisa Pardo, the actor. The image of her 1978 passport in the book *El rumor de este momento* (see figure 1) further supports the naming connection between Margarita and her family members, confirming that her paternal and maternal surnames match up with those she mentions in the play.

During the last scene of the play, Margarita transforms into Luisa, publicly enacting the bloodline that connects them:

MARGARITA: Y seguía trabajando, iba y venía de Xalapa, Df [sic], Hermosillo, Chihuahua, después de tener a Romulito, me embaracé luego luego, porque quería teneruna niña y ya se me estaba pasando el tiempo. En

los ultrasonidos salía que iba a ser niño ... pero yo deseaba la niña y la
deseaba y la deseaba ... en enero del 83 nació la Luisita.

LUISA: Me llamo Luisa. Nací en la ciudad de México el 10 de enero de 1983.
Soy hija de Margarita y Rafael. (Lagartijas Tiradas al Sol *El Rumor De Este Momento* 130–31)

MARGARITA: And I continued working, coming and going from Xalapa, Mexico
City, Hermosillo, Chihuahua; after having Rómulo I got pregnant
right away, because I wanted to have a girl and time was slipping away
from me. In the ultrasounds it came out that it was going to be a boy
... but I wanted a girl and I wanted her and I wanted her ... in
January of '83 la Luisita was born.

LUISA: My name is Luisa. I was born in Mexico City on the 10th of January
1983. I am the daughter of Margarita and Rafael.

In this moment, both Margarita and Luisa are present in one body. The narration
links them together just as their bodies are genetically linked, although Margarita
is absent. Just as her desire created her daughter, her daughter's desire to know her
mother embodies and breathes life into the character of Margarita.

More important than medical science is the desire of the mother in determining the sex of her baby, in an instance of affect winning out over genetics. The idea
of desire trumping reality seems to turn the argument I have been advancing on
its head—the fiction of theater as replaced by reality; the distinction dissolved
between autobiography and biography. However, this instance of the symbolic
winning out over the scientifically real causes the viewer to qualify his or her understanding of truth. The evidence for the heart's desire winning out is right before
the audience's eyes in the body of Pardo. She is, indeed, the hoped-for girl and,
through her mere presence, insists on a truth deeper than what the documentary
evidence can provide.

Montserrat

As is the custom at the Teatro El Milagro in the Colonia Juárez near the historical center of Mexico City, I wait with other audience members in the lobby area,
order a coffee, and wait for the doors to open. When they finally do we climb the
two flights of stairs to the theater entrance and file into our seats. I take notes in
my red notebook, and watch as Rodríguez bares his soul and his search for his
mother before us. Again, the stage is sparse. A white screen dominates the back of
the scenery, where photographs of Rodríguez's parents touring Chichen Itza are
projected. I recognize his father, José Rodríguez, who has appeared in films with

Gabino, as a young man in the photos, but not his companion, who turns out to be Montserrat.

Rodríguez dons a paper children's mask of a stereotypical Native American, complete with feather headdress, and unfolds a piece of paper. He stands before the audience and reads it aloud, a letter to his family apologizing for the collateral damage he has caused through what he calls a betrayal. He nails the letter to a table with the conviction of Martin Luther—his thesis a protest against a story he was told as a child.

The story he rebels against, it turns out, is the story of his mother's death from cancer when Rodríguez was a child. In the play he lays out his argument against this version of events, reading an e-mail from his aunt telling him to go to hell, revealing that his mother's death certificate (produced physically and projected on the screen behind him) was falsified, and claiming to have discovered that she is actually alive and hiding in her home country of Costa Rica. I, along with the rest of the audience, was convinced that once again the Lagartijas players had unearthed the true and hidden history of Mexico by tracing their parents' lives in documents. At the end of the play, however, something curious happens. Gabino claims to have hired a detective in Costa Rica and finally, with the help of a housekeeper, has found his mother. Once again photos are projected on the screen behind him, but now they are of empty rooms. Whereas at the beginning of the play the photographs showed his parents as young, newlywed tourists, these photographs are devoid of human figures. After such careful documentation of his discovery throughout the play, why would Rodríguez leave out pictures of his reunion with his mother? The final line of the play delivers the answer: "This is the only memory I have of my mother, and I am not sure whether I dreamed or lived it." The lights go dim as Willie Nelson's "Always on My Mind" plays. I cry into my notebook, because Willie Nelson always makes me cry and because the weight of the impossibility of the longed-for reunion between mother and child hits me like a ton of bricks. A man in front of me, annoyed by my scribbling, accuses me of being a journalist when the house lights go up. I tell him I am a student, but he does not seem to buy my story.

The death of a parent is an unmooring. With the loss of the life-giving mother, that anchor into time, space, and relationships, the individual casts off alone into a sea of future with no past, a self with no origin. But what of an orphan who fights back? What of memory and desire, forces that undo death and offer communion with that which is lost? The theater is uniquely equipped as the space for such a commemorative ritual, and theater of the real opens up to include affects as "real" alongside documentary evidence and verifiable facts. In this chapter, I turn to an example of Latin American theater of the real that questions what is "real" in theater of the real, proposing the theater as a space for the transmission of affect rather than the staging of verifiable factual scenes.

The play is *Montserrat*, presented in 2013 by Gabino Rodríguez, a founding member of Lagartijas Tiradas al Sol. Rodríguez wrote and directed the play, and is its protagonist in both senses of the word: he is the main character and the actor who plays the main character. The play offers the tantalizing possibility that the main character's mother, Montserrat, did not actually die, as he was told as a child, but rather that she lives in hiding in Costa Rica. *Montserrat* is a detective story in which Gabino follows a trail leading to his mother. The twist (because every detective story needs a twist) lies in the fact that the play is deceptive. Montserrat really did die, and the detective story is a wish for what could be. Audiences, however, have a hard time accepting the fact that they have been deceived; they want Montserrat to be alive, against all odds. In a country like Mexico, the question of whether or not a person has really died has resounding political implications.

The year after *Montserrat*'s debut, in Iguala, Guerrero, six people were killed, forty-three students from the Ayotzinapa Normal School were forcibly disappeared, and thirty-three were wounded ("Estado de la investigación" 4). They were victims of collusion between political authorities, police, and criminal organizations (7), according to the Special Office for the "Iguala Case" of Mexico's National Human Rights Commission. The government later claimed to have found the incinerated bodies of the forty-three students in a garbage dump, though external investigators argue that the evidence does not allow for such a possibility (Valencia Villa et al. 331). This widely publicized—and still unresolved—case is a reflection of the generalized nature of disappearances in Mexico, a critical situation that the Inter-American Commission on Human Rights (IACHR) attributes to "kidnappings at the hands of organized criminal groups" and "a practice of forced disappearances at hands of agents of the State or with their involvement, acquiescence, or tolerance" (*Human Rights* 63) While the more recent Iguala case is emblematic of a systemic problem, the IACHR affirms that forced disappearances are nothing new. Rather, the phenomenon "has occurred in Mexico at different times with varying intensity, such as in the 1960s in the context of the so-called 'Dirty War' up until the 1980s, and currently has spiked dramatically in the country" (*Human Rights* 63).

Considering this context of widespread corruption and impunity and forced disappearance, what is at stake in *Montserrat* comes into sharper focus. Rodríguez's staging of a fiction as fact echoes the abuse of power on the part of the state. He uses the authority of the document to deceive his captive audience, and spectators follow him happily, choosing to believe in his invention rather than face the awful truth that Montserrat is gone forever. His intention, however, is not malevolent; rather, by misusing documentary evidence he goes beyond the archive, offering up bodily experience and dreams as proof of his desire. The play employs the techniques of documentary theater to stage a fiction, thereby transforming the theater into a space for the transmission of "real" affect.

The play is a unique work of documentary theater; it questions the concept of reality within theater of the real by giving audiences documentary evidence for what turns out to be a fiction. Through analysis of the play's use of documentary techniques and parody, in addition to its presentation of desire and dream as verifiable fact, I argue that while Rodríguez subverts the documentary genre by presenting a falsehood as "real," the play ultimately takes documentary to another level. By portraying the impossible desire of a son to see his late mother again, the play elevates subjective experience to the level of verifiable fact, positing desire as real.

The question of what is to be considered "real" in theater of the real is one that concerns almost any scholar who studies the genre. Many plays themselves reveal the cracks in their own claims to truth, thereby questioning the possibility of representing the real in any medium. As Carol Martin asserts, "Complicating and questioning truth claims in order to interrogate the real is indicative of the ways in which what is deemed real can be understood and determined in diverse ways in different historical circumstances" (*Theatre of the Real* 116). In other words, while the idea of representing reality onstage might be questionable and questioned, determining the real to be relative to its context does not mean that there is not a reality outside. Promoting alternative versions of history is one of theater of the real's proposals. Though we live in what Liz Tomlin calls a skeptical age, in which "everything, in this historical period, becomes an equivalent fictional text, a representation without referent, a copy without origin" (30), there is a difference between a fictional play and a play that makes the claim to represent reality. As biased, questionable, or relative as that reality may be, plays that deal with the real do require a different kind of engagement from audiences.

Rather than suspend their disbelief and accept fiction as reality, spectators must, at the very least, respond to the claim to truth, whether or not it is verifiable fact. In *Montserrat*, the fact that the play presents false information as true, and provides documentary evidence supporting its falsehood, troubles this relationship between spectator and play. The play demonstrates the tendency that Tomlin identifies as the "use of personal testimony over 'film clips, photographs, and other documents' in twenty-first century verbatim practice [which] significantly limits the 'truth claims' of the work, as much of its source material is derived from private narratives, as opposed to public documents which are more accessible to verification processes" (116). In Rodríguez's case, however, public documents such as a death certificate are presented as falsified. Likewise, photographs, diary entries, and letters are produced to back up his claims that the official story is untrue.

In a country in which governmental transparency is questionable and unexplained disappearances have become commonplace, the personal testimony can bolster the play's truth claims rather than depending on verifiable public documents. Here, though, I will focus more on what is true in Rodríguez's account than what is not. In her examination of contemporary plastic arts, Lisa Saltzman refers to Pliny the Elder's tale of the origins of sculpture, in which a father and daughter use a projected shadow to create a silhouette, from which a casting is taken to remember the daughter's lover by when he leaves for war. Saltzman reads this "task of remembering an absent and desired body" as presenting "us with a paradigm for theorizing the representational strategies of the present. Projection, silhouettes and casting, such are the representational strategies described in Pliny's tale. And such are the strategies, the techniques and technologies, evinced in the present" (2). As in the plastic arts, many examples of contemporary theater rely on projection and silhouette to evoke that which is absent.

Montserrat is no exception; the one-man show is played against a large screen on which photographs, video clips, and textual slides are projected throughout. The absence and desire Saltzman refers to are central to the play's truth claims. Rodríguez does fool his spectators, but I argue that the real in this play is not to do with dates, facts, and figures; rather, it is the unresolvable desire to undo maternal absence. Saltzman shows that "projection, belatedly and by proxy, offers up, at the same time that it necessarily forecloses, the possibility of bearing witness" (45). Even as the projection supports the play's truth claims with photographs and text, the reliability of the documentary evidence projected pales in comparison to the presence of the body as evidence. In effect, Montserrat has conjured up a ghost. According to Alice Rayner, theater has long been the place where humans confront the dead and their own mortality (xii–xiii).

Martin Welton proposes an understanding of spectatorship in which affective as well as sensory feeling are combined: "The elision of feeling with looking and listening is not accidental here. The division of the sensorium into the five sensory categories is familiar to Western culture since Aristotle obscures the extent to which, in practical terms, activities like looking and listening are frequently bound together" (4–5). Montserrat is an excellent example of the way that the perceptive task of spectating is also necessarily an affective activity. Just as the fourth wall has been destroyed in postdramatic theater, the wall between a spectator's reactions to a fictional play and the spectator's affect has been demolished. As Teresa Brennan argues, "All this means, indeed the transmission of affect means, that we are not self-contained in terms of our energies. There is no secure distinction between the 'individual' and the 'environment'" (6). The theater is an environment in which the individual breaks down. As I will show in this section, Rodríguez's very real desire becomes the spectator's.

It is not empathy but a transmission of that desire that takes place in Montserrat. Brennan's beautiful conception of "the line of the heart" (75) is a perfect way to understand the way that the theater becomes a space of ritual in which individuals are revealed to be a collective with a shared desire. Given the context of contem-

FIGURE 2. Gabino kneels and places flowers in memory of his mother in *Montserrat*.

porary Mexico, and the current debate on affect, I perceive *Montserrat* to be an excellent example of what theater can do in the face of irreparable human loss. Theater can, beyond providing the cleansing of Aristotelian catharsis, provide a forum for performing ritual grief. The play transmits to the audience—itself marked by a context of disappearance—not only the tragic loss of a mother but also the real energetic and material desire and love of her son for her. In this play, documents are not to be trusted. This reflects civil society's mistrust of corrupt political leaders and police forces that collude with criminal organizations and provide false documentation—or none at all—to account for the disappearances of citizens. In *Montserrat*, the gesture of the false documentary serves to transform the theater into a ritual space, requiring audience participation in a funeral rite.

The play represents unreliable authorities, falsified documents, and lost tombs, reflecting the political context in which it is produced. It also, however, finds a way to create its own kind of certainty amid the chaos. Rather than use archival evidence to confirm (or not) the death of Montserrat, Rodríguez creates an altar where he can invite his mother's spirit to visit him and the audience and, simultaneously, mourn her loss along with the spectators (see figure 2). Gabino, the orphaned son, is like an echo of Antigone, finally burying his mother through performance. By affirming the reality of desire, affect and bodily authority are elevated and supersede the importance of an unreliable archive. In the give and take of fact and fiction, claims to truth and accusations of deception, documentary reality is displaced over the course of the play. It does not matter whether Rodríguez has fabricated evidence, whether evidence he calls falsified is real, whether his family members have lied to him.

While these and other representatives of the genre of theater of the real purport to be and are rooted in verifiable fact, and often take ethical, moral, and political stances, they do not pretend to offer an unmediated, direct view of reality. Instead they prioritize the aesthetic, and their success lies in theatrical craft in addition to their claims to truth. *Montserrat* is, more than any other play analyzed here, more intensely concerned with representing real desire than with representing verifiable facts. While audiences expect to see a scenic version of *what really happened*, their expectations are absolutely tempered by centuries of theatrical tradition. These works are theatrical plays, with scripts, rehearsed blocking, production value; they occur at announced times and places, with full cooperation of audiences. Their utmost characteristic is that of a creative work of art; the reality factor is essential but secondary to aesthetics.

The seeming novelty of theater of the real lies in its commitment to reality; what sets it apart, however, is its relationship to and definition of that reality. Drama is capable, unlike any other documentary genre, of transmitting affect through the simultaneous gathering of spectators and actors in the intimate space of the theater. While documentary film and narrative share a commitment to representing reality, and their stark reproduction of testimonies can be extremely moving, it is the simultaneous presence of bodies necessary to the theatrical production that allows for the representation of other realities that go beyond what Diana Taylor calls the archive.

The play uses documentary techniques like presenting letters, diaries, photographs, and official documents to construct its narrative. This evidence, however, is a blend of fabrication and reality; a real death certificate, for example, is presented as falsified, while an invented e-mail is read as factual. There is very little to signal to the audience that they should suspect the play as presenting a falsehood, except for an element of parody. The investigative narrative refers to a Sam-Spadesque detective in a trench coat, surreptitiously passed notes from household servants, and a family conspiracy. The exaggerated nature of the parody, in addition to the play's presentation of Gabino's desires and dreams as verifiable facts, takes the documentary genre to another level. By portraying the impossible desire of a son to see his late mother again, the play elevates subjective experience to the level of verifiable fact. In *Montserrat*, desire is as real as any other source of evidence. In this section, I look at the use of documents, parody, and dreams in *Montserrat* to show how they work together to include desire as a source of truth.

The opening gesture of *Montserrat* situates the play firmly within the world of documentary theater, following the tradition of Lagartijas Tiradas al Sol. The apology letter that Gabino reads at the beginning of the play equates the onstage persona with the historical person of the actor, setting up audiences to give credit to whatever is presented to them: "To my family: I know that I have aired many things, settled many scores through fiction. In a way I am a traitor, but I also know that those very plays, which perhaps hurt, also brought 'the joy of notoriety.' I ask you here, in writing, for forgiveness" (Lagartijas Tiradas al Sol, *Montserrat* 1).[11] This is only the first of several letters to be read aloud during the play, always with the document visible, unfolded, and referred to openly. This letter is written and signed by Rodríguez, while others are letters or e-mails he claims to have received. In every case, the combination of the physical document is used as proof of the veracity of Gabino's claims.

The letters, photographs, certificate, and diary that Gabino presents as evidence throughout the play all serve to establish the fact that Montserrat did, indeed, exist. The written word is, first, a source of credibility. The physical resemblance between the man in the photos and video (José Rodríguez, Gabino's father) and the man onstage (Gabino Rodríguez) indicates that the audience should extend the relationship between them beyond the theater walls, where the connection between Rodríguez and the photographed man exists in reality as well as in the play. The inclusion of hard data, such as the name and location of the street where Gabino lived with his father, stepmother, and half brothers after Montserrat's death, as well as his producing her death certificate (see figure 3), punctuates the real, verifiable nature of the personal history.

FIGURE 3. Gabino presents Montserrat's death certificate in *Montserrat*.

Gabino sums up his childhood by musing that he is sure a large part of who he is has to do with having lost Montserrat and having grown up without her (*Montserrat* 3), a claim that ties the physical body onstage to the idea of Montserrat, reinforcing her life even through her absence. He continues to establish the fact of Montserrat's life, taking the genealogical route to begin reconstructing Montserrat's biography, outlining her relationship to her parents and their own basic biographies. All this documentation, however, only serves to point to the fact that documents are fundamentally unreliable. Right off the bat Rodríguez points to the wider world of his theatrical and cinematic works.

In the apology letter he refers to "'la alegría de la notoriedad'" (the joy of fame) (*Montserrat* 1), perhaps referring to Nicolás Pereda's semidocumentary films that Rodríguez and his father, José Rodríguez, have starred in, playing characters called Gabino or José, or other documentary plays by Lagartijas Tiradas al Sol. He roots himself firmly in the representational world as that most dramatic of actors: the traitor ("De alguna manera soy un traidor" [In a way I am a traitor] (*Montserrat* 1). Pilate and Judas in one, washing hands, kissing lips, flinging ill-gotten coins, Rodríguez wastes no time getting to the drama of betrayal. The audience has been forewarned, then, and should understand that they are in for a betrayal.

First, Rodríguez admits that he has very few memories of childhood, and that those he does have are reconstructed from photographs. Therefore, the memories

that are presented in the play must be approached with suspicion, or at least understood as fallible evidence of reality. Second, the information that Montserrat never
appears in Rodríguez's memories also supports the critique of the representation
of memories implicit in the play. The title character is utterly absent from the primary source of information, that is, Rodríguez's memory. Everything that is presented onstage, even as it insists on its own reality and credibility, must therefore
be understood to be a reconstruction, an intuition, an invention. The fulcrum on
which the balance between reality and fiction rests is a letter that Rodríguez supposedly finds drafted in one of his mother's diaries.

This letter, never revealed or produced for the audience, is the catalyst for the
conspiracy theory. It inspires Gabino to give in to childish hopes that his mother
did not die, that she is alive, somewhere, where he can find her. The play becomes
the reconstruction of such fantasies, presented with the utmost earnestness to an
audience prepped to believe in the reality of the play's events. The magical thinking
is therefore transferred to the audience, while Gabino coldly leads them on. By
positing that he has no memories of his mother, and yet creating and presenting
a play completely based on his relationship to her, Rodríguez also posits the need
for a truth beyond the documentary. When he breaks from documentary style and
goes straight into speculation, Gabino cites neither interviews nor diaries; rather,
he gives verifiable facts such as dates and names of institutions, interspersing them
with completely hypothetical conjectures. He assigns feelings to Montserrat without backing them up. By moving so quickly from extremes of establishing facts to
extreme speculation, Rodríguez weaves a web for his audience members, luring
them into his confusion of fact and fiction.

And if the surreal description of his meeting with Montserrat were not enough
to convince the spectator of the impossibility of the events he describes in the second half of the play, its last line serves as the final nail in the coffin of the illusion.
After showing the projected photographs of the empty rooms, supposedly the site
of his encounter with Montserrat, Gabino addresses the audience directly one
last time: "This is the only memory that I have of my mother, but I don't know if
I lived it or if I dreamed it" (*Montserrat* 18).[12] It might seem, reading about the
performance here, that this is an obvious indication that the meeting did not take
place in the waking plane of reality, but is rather the retelling of a beautiful, tragic
dream. The three audiences I have observed, however, generally retained at least
doubt as to whether Gabino found his mother living in Costa Rica, if not fully
falling for the dream-trick. Gabino feeds the audience the interpretation that it
was all a dream (yet another cliché to go with the detective story), but spectators
prefer to believe in the dream. The deliberate misuse of Montserrat's personal objects, however, is not just a cruel prank or an outright lie. Gabino's misdirecting
the audience not only puts them into the position of the magically thinking son

but also makes a statement about the ethics and possibilities of representing the real on the stage.

This gesture could be related to what Paul Arthur refers to as the "aesthetics of failure" in documentary cinema, in which the "failure to adequately represent the person, event, or social situation stated as the film's explicit task functions as an inverted guarantee of authenticity" (127). By reading his aunt's condemnatory e-mail, Rodríguez demonstrates to his audience his difficulties in securing permission to present his findings. However, there are two glaring differences here. First, Rodríguez does not fail. Unlike the documentary filmmakers who show their equipment malfunctions or film those who would kick them out of the spaces and events they want to record, Rodríguez gets away with it. He presents the letter, while also presenting its fallout. He may have failed to conserve a relationship with his aunt Guadalupe, but he successfully includes the fraught object in his play. Second, this play, as we shall see, does not guarantee its own authenticity. It becomes increasingly fantastical, including documentary evidence all along the way, putting the audience member into the position of judge and in the position of grieving child, fantasizing about the impossibility of a reunion with his dead mother.

Se rompen las olas

In the evening after seeing *Montserrat* for the first time, I return to El Milagro for a new play in Lagartijas's cycle: *Se rompen las olas*. It is my first time seeing a play by Lagartijas that does not star Rodríguez or Pardo; instead, Mariana Villegas wrote and performs the work. Once again I climb the stairs to the theater and settle in to observe the final play in the cycle. The play begins with projected videos of the 1985 earthquake and news reports from the time. As an Oklahoman transplanted first to California and then to Mexico City, my fear of earthquakes was entirely experiential. I had felt the swaying and heard the pops of the San Andreas fault throughout my doctoral work, and the fear it inspired led me to imagine earthquakes when there were none. I had learned to look for hanging light pulls and check them for motion to determine whether an earthquake was really taking place or whether it was just my anxiety playing tricks on me. Stories of the 1985 earthquake, which any Mexico City resident has at the ready either from personal or family experience, only added to my fears. I had heard of people who had lost their entire families, who had been thrown out of windows as buildings twisted in the air, the earth wrung out by angry, enormous forces. *Se rompen las olas* immerses the audience in the terror of such moments, with a video of newscasters experiencing the quake in real time, and then with audio reports of the horrifying aftermath.

The very real danger of earthquakes that permeates life in Mexico City was an intensifier as we watched the play up on the third story of the theater building.

The reminder of and real-life potential for disaster added to the reality effect of the play, which is an auto/biographical re-creation of Villegas's own conception and relationship with her parents. While the play stars Villegas and focuses more on her own experience than that of her parents, it is clearly a Lagartijas production. At one point she burns food on a hot plate; as she collapses onto a sofa sand falls from above onto her head, covering her body and leaving the stage in disarray; toys and an accumulation of little objects, proof of the veracity of her story, litter the scene. All these elements contribute to the sense that what I am witnessing is true (though after seeing *Montserrat* earlier in the day I am more careful to be skeptical of Lagartijas's claims).

As the cycle's title, *La invención de nuestros padres*, indicates (at least in one possible interpretation), a child's version of his parents is a fantasy. In *El rumor del incendio*, the mother is reconstructed based on documentary evidence, while in *Montserrat* the mother is revived through the power of desire. In the last play of the cycle, *Se rompen las olas*, the protagonist longs for a loving father, evoking the Electra myth and Jung's corresponding complex when taken to the extreme. Mariana Villegas's unipersonal play presents the pain of her father's neglect and rejection and her frustrated desire for a family.

The play takes place in a living room set with a futon, a table and chairs, and an assortment of children's toys and furniture, including a miniature table and chairs and a small tent. The juxtaposition of childhood and single adulthood is evident from the start. The moment in time is the earthquake of 1985, a catastrophe that destroyed much of Mexico City and cost tens of thousands of lives. The play opens with television and radio clips reporting on the earthquake; Villegas dances alone, her arms around an imaginary partner, and is suddenly thrown onto the futon. Sand falls on her from above, covering her body and the couch. She runs a knife over her body, miming the knife's penetrating her nostrils, mouth, and vagina in slow motion. She introduces herself as Mariana Silva Villegas, but asks the audience to call her by her maternal last name, forgoing the paternal, "but call me Mariana Villegas—you'll understand why in time" (*pero díganme Mariana Villegas—vámonos entendiendo*) ("Se rompen las olas" 3). She describes how, as a child, she would watch Miss Universe pageants with her mother and then imitate the contestants with the help of a servant. A recording of Villegas reading a segment of José Emilio Pacheco's poem "Miro la tierra" (I look at the earth) plays, praising the generous and damning the looters and thieves who took advantage of the chaos after the earthquake.

From the images of the national tragedy of the earthquake, projected on a screen in the background, the play zooms in on the lives of two individuals, Raúl and María. Villegas announces, "In 1986, María will be my mom. . . . In 1986, Raúl will be my dad" ("Se rompen las olas" 3).[13] She then moves to a table full of artifacts that she holds up and shares with the audience, gifts from her father including a lighter, a set of dominoes, leftover honey, a photo, and 500 pesos. As the unsatisfactory nature of the gifts becomes obvious, Villegas moves into a monologue about meeting "him." The monologue is ambiguous; one could argue that that she is playing the role of her mother, recounting how she met Raúl, or that she is playing herself and recounting a recent encounter. Mariana then recounts her first "arranque violento" (violent outburst), when she attacked a cousin who told her that she did not have a dad. The scene fades out to audio from a 1985 radio report and photos of the earthquake's destruction.

The climaxes of both the earthquake and Mariana's father's absence in her life then come to a head. Villegas narrates how each of her parents experienced the disaster. Her mother, who was told by her supervisor not to come in to work, flew to Acapulco with friends for an impromptu vacation. Her father, on the other hand, returned to where his home had been to find his small son and pregnant wife, dead amid the rubble. As she narrates she laughs incongruously, ending with an exclamation of "Acapulco!" and dancing to the song "¿Dónde te agarró el temblor?" (Where did the earthquake catch you?). After this uncanny display she recounts, as María, how she and Raúl got together after the earthquake and how she became pregnant. Narrating another trip to the beach, Mariana screams her fantasy of having sex with her father on the beach without his realizing it. It is as though she will finally take revenge on her father for having abandoned her by tricking him into her Electra scenario.

The emotional outburst continues, segueing into a lament over the lack of a story. Mariana, still in the throes of her beach fantasy, also desires a family photo, and yells, "Why don't I remember you all and know perfectly well who you are? Why have I had to collect the pieces of my story to see where in the hell I come from? Why didn't you invite me for a coffee at Vips to tell me everything? Why is your dead family still alive while I have always been dead to you?" ("Se rompen las olas" 10).[14] She displays the only photograph she has with both of her parents, and then, suddenly, a bucket of water dumps onto her head. Soaking wet, Villegas blows up a balloon and inserts it into the bathing suit she's wearing, and reenacts her mother telling her father that she is pregnant. The dialogue is one-sided, and obviously does not go well. The lack of paternal input into the conversation about the pregnancy, represented by silences and unanswered questions, sets the tone for the rest of Mariana's life.

Finally, Villegas ties the earthquake to her auto/biography. Though she admits she was not yet alive at the time of the disaster, she explains that if there had not been an earthquake she would not have been born. She shows a photograph of herself with her father's new family, all of whom are much smaller than she is, in Sinaloa. She explains that her father told her to call them her siblings, and that she would love to invite them all to her home for a party. She arranges several stuffed animals around a toy table, posing for the family picture she longs for. Finally, as the stage darkens, a recording of a man's voice reads a letter to Mariana from her father, describing the horrific search for the remains of his deceased wife and son among the improvised morgues set up in the city. It ends with "Ellos Mariana, ellos eran mi familia" (They, Mariana, they were my family) ("Se rompen las olas" 13).

Se rompen las olas is unique in Lagartijas's history, as it is the first play presented under the company's banner that was not created by and starring Pardo or Rodríguez. The inclusion of the play's premiere within the *La invención de nuestros padres* cycle introduced Villegas as part of the collective and, because the other two plays focus on Pardo's and Rodríguez's parents, connected it to their artistic vision. This, however, did not necessarily save it from criticism. Some critics in Mexico latched onto the pieces' visual and technical connections to Lagartijas's previous plays while criticizing Villegas's body and the play's narrative. The petty focus on Villegas's body type belies, for me, the unfairness of these critiques, which do not seem to take a critical distance and instead judge the auto/biographical play as though it were unmediated by the stage.[15] Internationally, however, the piece has been well-received. The Italian critic Alessia Rosa Avallone appraised the play at the Vie Festival as a play that "blends original and dynamic autobiography and history, that tries to stimulate spectators' critical thinking."[16] Presented at the Heidelberg Stückemarkt in 2015, critics called it "a wonderfully unpretentious portrait of society"[17] (Weigel).

The play also, compared to the other two pieces in the cycle, focuses on auto/biographying more than biographying. Putting together the puzzle of her family history is framed as Mariana's odyssey; her parents' lives and brief relationship are explicitly presented from their adult daughter's perspective, in contrast to the objective stances proposed by *El rumor del incendio* and *Montserrat*. This play offers an interesting vision of how family narratives can collapse into the self, and are brought out into the light to explain one's place in the world.

This is not to say that the play is less focused on the national, even if it is from a more subjective perspective. The focus on Villegas's life story and her potential, or her body, in the criticism I mentioned before, seems to point toward an insular, self-absorbed autobiography. The earthquake, however, is presented as an event that touched the entire city and affected families across the nation. Michel Schultheiss argues that the earthquake of 1985 is often connected with "another place in memory, the events of 1968, given that in both occurrences the Plaza de las Tres Culturas functions as a crystalizing point, an historical space where the massacre of Tlatelolco and the destruction of buildings during the earthquake occurred, two events that are associated in the service of critiques against the PRI government" (Schultheiss 67).[18] While there is no overt connection between *Se rompen las olas* and 1968, when we take *La invención de nuestros padres* as a whole we see the events of 1968 in *El ru-*

mor del incendio and the destruction of the natural disaster of 1985 juxtaposed in the cycle. Indeed, the destruction of the earthquake is not, for Mariana, merely a natural disaster; the legacy of the earthquake is her abandonment by her father.

The earthquake is presented, however, as a national historical and political event. Audio played at the beginning of the play gives a rundown of Mexico in 1985, with pop culture references, astrological information, and news items. The contextual audio ends with the following phrase: "After the earthquake and the government's incapacity to resolve its ravages, civil society organized and expressed its great solidarity" ("Se rompen las olas" 2).[19] Mentioned only in passing at this point, the government is presented as a nuisance, whereas the people of Mexico are the agents of change. The government comes up again when Mariana introduces her parents: they both work for the Secretariat of Agrarian Reform in 1985. The entity would be disbanded in 2009, a fact that Villegas does not mention in the play, but would have been pertinent to Mexican audiences.

Raúl and María's love affair is presented as doomed from the start—Villegas explicitly relates her parents' workplace romance and her own birth to the earthquake, while it is implied that their official jobs would disappear years later with the closing of the Secretariat. The quake is, then, a portent of things to come and, like the play, revelatory of paternal abandonment. While the Mexican government is presented as incapable of protecting its citizens or supporting them in the aftermath of the disaster, Villegas's father is presented as neglectful and distant. The individual pain she feels is magnified and projected to the scale of a massive natural disaster.

The play is exemplary of Molloy's proposal that the Latin American autobiography (though the critic was referring to narrative) includes other voices. It recognizes the multiple lives that contribute to the formation of an individual life. Villegas, through her exploration of the time before her conception, of the broken relationship that haunts her, attempts to understand herself in the wider context of her family and her country. The results are, for her, disastrous. She links her own life to a natural catastrophe, and is only able to imagine the longed-for family photo in which she would insert herself. However, the play itself serves as a site of self-actualization. She re-creates the family photo in an absurd way, posing with her stuffed animals. The apparent impossibility of ever repairing the relationship is made evident by the utter insufficiency of the stage, or the inability of the unipersonal play to fully re-create the family. The play points to the limits of recuperating the past, in the theater or otherwise.

Family Histories

Though each of these plays includes fictional aspects, to varying degrees, it would be impossible to fully comprehend their aesthetic value without recognizing their connection to reality. Postdramatic theater in general, and documentary theater in particular, subverts the fictional utopia of the stage. In its place, examples of theater of the real like *El rumor del incendio* shorten the distance between stage and spectator, enveloping audiences, forcing them to consider the reality or fiction of what is represented. Using documentary evidence, such as legal reports and newspapers, corporeal techniques that suggest a biological connection between onstage actors and absent characters, and genealogical links that claim, through proper names and bloodlines, authority over inherited stories, *El rumor del incendio* questions generic limits. The play not only challenges autobiography as a genre, allowing for the inclusion of postmemory, another generation's trauma, in one's own life story but also challenges theater itself. Rather than symbolic representation, the theater becomes an alternative source of truth among more traditional discourses like history and journalism.

Rodríguez, meanwhile, takes an undeniable fact, the death of his mother, and creates an entire reality in which that fact is no longer valid. Using theatrical techniques such as projection of images, music, movement, props, and direct-address monologue, he constructs a parallel universe that replaces the previously established facts with its own version of events. Such a gesture is not without consequence, especially when understood as part of a larger theatrical and cultural context. It is important to note, however, that this action, while pointing to the impossibility of representation, does not render the play a lie, nonsensical, or even deny the value of theater of the real. What it does is force the audience to examine its trust in the plays and their creators, recognize the limitations of any re-creation, and also look for a new meaning. If theater of the real were only designed to re-construct reality, it would be revealed as an impossibility by this play's critique. However, if theater of the real is able to create new meaning by representing past events, then it is empowered and empowering to the audience that engages with it.

Finally, in *Se rompen las olas*, the objective of the play is not only to re-create reality. Rather, it is to connect the present to the past. The play attempts to find meaning in history, both national and personal. It suggests that the traumas of our parents affect us and future generations. The play seeks to explain the unthinkable, a father's rejection, by comparing it to and linking it to a natural disaster. The absence of family is, on a personal level, analogous to the catastrophe of the earthquake to the nation. Villegas engages with the real onstage, sifting through time as though excavating the ruins of her parents' relationship, appealing to the spectator to recognize her deep sense of loss.

In each of these plays, the idea of a deep truth safeguarded in the body, passed down from parent to child, at once affirms and negates the challenge of subverting the theatrical and autobiographical genres. While the bodies onstage are, indeed, those they purport to be—the actors play themselves—they are, of course, participating in the repeated, scripted representation of their parents' lives. The plays are real and also representational. Similarly, the concrete nature of the actor's body displays his or her individual limits. At the same time, though, the claim to inherited truth insists on continuity between the biographical and autobiographical. In *La invención de nuestros padres*, the physicality of absence—whether as the absent parent embodied by the present child, the physical presence of the sound of the absent character's voice, or the use of physical objects as a psychic extension of the absent parent—constantly challenges the limits of the self, especially the limit that is death. Even as the empty center of each play is constantly invoked, the actors make every attempt to fill the emptiness with materiality and, ultimately, the body. This self-sacrifice, an exchange of the "innocent" child for the lost parent, has powerful cultural resonances and insists on a solidarity between spectator and actor, which hearkens back to the very origins of performance and ritual.

═══════════ Chapter 3

Falling Out of History ═══════════

In *La invención de nuestros padres*, Lagartijas Tiradas al Sol uses the family as a portal through which individual and national history fuses. The family is the way into collective identity for the individual child; as the child reconstructs the life of the absent parent, he also finds his place in the grand scheme of history. As each play works through the documentary findings it presents, through the guerrillas and student and peasant movements of the 1960s, the earthquake of 1985, and the possibility of disappearance, the urgencies of national history begin to take the forefront. In the plays that follow the cycle, which I will analyze in this chapter, national history is at the center, while its relationship to the individual experience is never neglected.

The play that followed *La invención de nuestros padres*, *Derretiré con un cerillo la nieve de un volcán* (I shall melt a volcano's snowcap with a match, 2013) proposes no less than to present a theatrical history of the Mexican Partido de la Revolución Institucional (Institutional Revolutionary Party; PRI). In typical Lagartijas style, the play mixes fiction and fact, weaving together documentary, biographical, and dramatic theater. Similar in form to *El rumor del incendio*, the play presents the biography of a teacher who participated in the teachers' union, wrote a history of the PRI, and subsequently disappeared. Additional links to *El rumor* include the publication of her book (authored by Lagartijas but publicized and sold as having been written by the invented character) alongside the production of the play, the concretization of the ephemeral theatrical work. The play's relationship to history is obvious in the sense of its claim to narrate the history of a political party; it also turned out to be eerily, tragically prescient, as the international scandal of the forced disappearance of forty-three students at a teaching college occurred in Ayotzinapa the year following the play's debut, as I discussed in chapter 2.

This interest in contemporary Mexican politics led to the group's next ambitious project: the cycle *La democracia en México* (Democracy in Mexico). This series of plays takes its title from Pablo González Casanova's groundbreaking 1965 sociological study and attempts to examine the fate of democracy in the country fifty years later. The company describes the project on its website, specifically citing Casanova: "Fifty years after the publication of Pablo González Casanova's book *Democracy in Mexico*, we seek to reflect on democracy in light of the analysis of half a century ago" (Lagartijas Tiradas al Sol "La democracia en México").[1] The seamless connection between Casanova's and Lagartijas's projects, in this description, implies that theater can do the work of sociology, at least in some way. The description continues, "This project is an investigation of the ideas that sustain the democratic ideal about the experiences that produce the putting-into-practice of this ideal. . . . More than an explanation of democracy, it is an involvement with democracy" (Lagartijas Tiradas al Sol "La democracia en México").[2] Particularly interesting is that, as Casanova's work represents a watershed empirical investigation into democracy in Mexico, Lagartijas's uses the theater to investigate the putting-into-practice, the *puesta en práctica* of an ideal. The term they use, *puesta en práctica* is reminiscent of the Spanish term for staging in theater: *puesta en escena*. To put democracy onstage is to test it, investigate its practice in society. Like democratic experiments, the project is ambitious, including a projected thirty-two parts, one for each state in the Mexican Republic: "32 visiones de un mismo país" (Thirty-two visions of a single country) (Lagartijas Tiradas al Sol "La Democracia En México"). To date, the project includes four works, which I will analyze here: the theatrical works *Tijuana* (2016), *Santiago Amoukalli* (2016), *Veracruz, nos estamos deforestando o cómo extrañar Xalapa* (Veracruz, we are deforesting ourselves, or how to miss Xalapa, 2016), and the video project *Distrito Federal* (Federal District, 2017) by Juan Leduc.

The book that inspired Lagartijas's theatrical investigations, González Casanova's *La democracia en* México, is considered the first sociological study of Mexican political realities. It asks the questions: "To what degree does the kind of democracy prevalent in Mexico condition and limit economic development? To what degree can the country bring about the kind of democracy that ensures development?" (González Casanova, *Democracy in Mexico* 5).[3] Some of its more sobering conclusions include: "Municipal freedom is virtually nonexistent. . . . The political entity called a free municipality is in effect controlled by state power and the Federation" (González Casanova, *Democracy in Mexico* 30).[4] The study identifies "regional and local *caudillos* and *caciques*, the Army, the clergy, and the latifundists and national and foreign entrepreneurs" (González Casanova *Democracy in Mexico* 32) as the actual factors of power in the country, rather than the government.[5] The study's short, final chapter, titled "El futuro inmediato" (The Immediate Future) is perhaps most pertinent to Lagartijas's cycle on democracy in Mexico. Lagartijas seeks to revisit González Casanova's ideas and the hopes and fears of the 1960s, fifty years on. In his conclusions, the sociologist proposes a national task of constant economic development that consists of the following pressing goals: "To put an end to internal colonialism and semi-capitalist development, to achieve the political rights and liberties of the marginal, semicolonial population, to emphasize civic struggle and political organization in the rural areas and indigenous regions, and to form, in the cities, leading cadres composed of the most aware and radical workers" (González Casanova *Democracy in Mexico* 195).[6] Casanova concludes that because the country is neither fully committed to capitalism nor to socialism, it will never fully develop in either system and will reproduce internal colonialism resulting in drastic inequality.

González Casanova's *La democracia en México* represents a watershed moment for Mexican social sciences (F. Castañeda 420). In a review of González Casanova's contribution to the formation of a critical theory of society in Mexico, Rafael Farfán Hernández acknowledges the importance of *Democracy in Mexico* to its field: "It is the first great book of contemporary Mexican sociology."[7] While Farfán critiques the book's perceived idealization of democracy over the option of a socialist revolution, he recognizes its significance. Cristina Puga categorizes the book as "a point of takeoff for academic work in the social sciences in the country" (118).[8] As director of the Escuela Nacional de Ciencias Políticas y Sociales (National School of Political and Social Sciences), González Casanova expanded the curriculum to include sociology, political science, and public administration, and changed the diplomacy track to international relations. Additionally, the content of the courses began to focus on sociology and political science rather than law and philosophy (Puga 113). González Casanova's mark on the professionalization of the study of society is evidently quite significant. Sociologist Fernando Castañeda affirms that the structural-causal comprehension of the nation's problems, like internal colonialism, is what makes *La democracia en* México the founding work of Mexican academic sociology (F. Castañeda 421). Lagartijas's proposal to take up González Casanova's mantle, then, signals the purported import of their project. They describe the project as looking "at our country from diverse perspectives: social, historical, biographical, fictional" ("Lagartijas Tiradas al Sol presentan").[9] Their project places theater in the realm of groundbreaking academic studies, proposing the stage as a laboratory for sociological research and discovery.

In this chapter I examine the play *Derretiré con un cerillo la nieve de un volcán* as well as the plays that, to date, form part of Lagartijas's project *La democracia en* México, with an eye toward understanding how the plays blend fiction and history to critique the state of democratic representation in Mexico. Even as they reveal the bleak realities of their subject, the plays' aesthetic and social proposals are optimistic calls to action. In *Derretiré* the troupe proposes that young people take an active role in learning the history of their democracy; in *La democracia en*

México they boldly use the stage to renounce corruption and impunity. Each work deals directly with the theme of democracy, criticizing the lack of representation, transparency, and freedom the company observes in modern Mexico. By blending historical facts, documentary evidence, autobiographical experience, literary intertextuality, and invention, Lagartijas makes the stage a forum for identifying problems and proposing solutions, modeling the civic discourse necessary for true democracy.

Lagartijas's approach to research through drama is significant as it is the clearest indication of the theater practitioners' claims to truth. The idea that a play would be the appropriate medium for a follow-up to a political sociology study is audacious and awe-inspiring. Throughout Latin America the stage has become a forum not only for declaring the truth but also for finding it. The stage is a laboratory, and also functions as a microcosm for the nation. In the theater the troupe can test the limits of democracy in Mexico by creating test scenarios and letting them play out. In each of the four theatrical projects examined here, very real political events, situations, and agents are staged: the PRI, and various twentieth-century presidents; the border economy of the maquilas in Tijuana, and its relationship to the center of the country; the corruption of the PRI in Veracruz and the suppression of free speech, in particular of Nadia Vera and Rubén Espinosa; and the buying of elections and the narco state in the sierra.

Each of these situations has relevance and real-life impact on Mexico and Mexicans. The staging of the problems, and the insistence on their reality, even within the confines of the theater's representational apparatus, promotes the possibility of the theater as a space of knowledge creation. The stakes are life and death, as *Veracruz* shows; the scale is international, as we see in the video project *Distrito Federal*. Lagartijas's latest, most ambitious project, combines the theatrical techniques the theater has honed over the past decade or so with the urgency of political consciousness and savvy that spills out beyond the theater walls and into the public space beyond.

A relatively new project, *La democracia en* México has yet to be treated in academic publications, though the plays *Tijuana* and *Santiago Amoukalli* have been featured in international festivals and inspired critical reviews around the world. *Derretiré con un cerillo la nieve de un volcán* received especially high praise from critics within Mexico, who recognized the importance of such a reflection upon the PRI's return to federal power. Hugo Salcedo writes: "*Derretiré con un cerillo la nieve de un volcán* appeals to the reconstruction of memory, the interest in microhistories, ordinary experience, or autobiography, thus marking an extremely outstanding place in the rich portfolio of documentary theater" (115).[10] Meanwhile, a review of *Derretiré* from Puebla calls the play "documentary theater, potent, raw, seditious, committed, Brechtian-ly didactic; tonally tragicomic. With this uncondescending scenic proposal, the Company Lagartijas Tiradas al Sol reveals the brutal corruption of Mexican presidentialism" (Ruiz Vivanco).[11]

Likewise, *Tijuana* inspired trusting praise in Germany: "It could have been a cynical undertaking—an actor looks at the poor. But even the length of his stay indicates sincere interest. And Rodríguez knows, like any good ethnologist, that his results say at least as much about him, the observer, as about the object of observation" (Meiborg).[12] *Veracruz* has also been well-received by European critics. In Spain, where it was first presented, one spectator writes, "The lecture becomes a ceremony in memory of the disappeared compatriots, and also an expression of a painful nostalgia for that exuberant land that in another time fostered the flourishing of art and critical thought" (Prieto Nadal).[13] Pardo herself talks about the difficulty of evoking the difficult memories the lecture brings up: "Actually Veracruz is a performative conference (I say performative to call it something). In the beginning, for Escenas do Cambio, it had been proposed that we do a lecture to explain the murder of Nadia Vera and Rubén Espinosa. Explain, retell, research a topic like that is delicate, because of how painful it is, how recent it is, for the lack of clarity and for the fragile line of opportunism. Put that way, we didn't feel that we had the right" (Gandasegui).[14]

In Switzerland, *Santiago Amoukalli* was praised and its impact on an international scale discussed by Swiss audiences: "'We believe that we help development, but we have no idea what is at play. This has let me understand a side that I had never seen before of development aid.' 'I didn't know about that Mexico, or that a people could be manipulated that way, with gifts like a television,' indicates a university student from Freiburg" (Islas).[15]

Derretiré con un cerillo la nieve de un volcán

After the acclaimed cycle of *La invención de nuestros padres*, discussed in chapter 2, and on the heels of the presidential elections of 2012, Lagartijas premiered its Proyecto PRI (PRI Project). As with *El rumor del incendio*, the project consists of a book and a play. The book *La revolución institucional* (The institutional revolution) was supposedly discovered by Lagaritjas and reedited after the disappearance of its author, Natalia Valdez Tejeda, a teacher and activist. The play documents her life and disappearance alongside the history of the PRI in Mexico. Reminiscent of the style of *El rumor*, the play alternates between scenes from a single protagonist's life and relevant moments of national history from the Revolution of 1910 and the formation of the political party that would become the PRI, to the election of opposition candidate Vicente Fox Quesada in 2000 and the contentious return of the PRI in 2012. In this case, however, the protagonist, Valdez Tejeda, is a fiction, in contrast to *El rumor*'s Comandante Margarita.

Valdez Tejeda's book, *La revolución institucional,* is mentioned in both the company's descriptions of the project and in the play itself. By engaging in the trope of the found manuscript, which goes back at least to Cervantes and books of chivalry in literary history, the troupe not only signals that it is engaging in a fictional game (at least to the most alert spectators),[16] it also takes part in challenging the generic conception of theater. Anthony J. Cascardi argues in a study of *Don Quixote*'s influence that Cervantes breaks with convention by creating a work of "prose fiction that is not associated with any particular subject at all. It is a form that could take up virtually any subject" (131). Lagartijas performs a similar discursive move by creating a work of drama that takes up national history, biography, political science, and sociology—breaking with the norms of the dramatic genre.

Entering into the tradition of the found manuscript, just as for the author of *Don Quixote,* permits Lagartijas "to engage with the topos of the unreliability of . . . historians and with the fluid borders between fiction and history" (Cascardi 131). *Derretiré*'s marriage of these two devices, that of the found manuscript and the challenging of generic borders, exemplifies the way that theater has emerged as an alternative to traditional sources of fact at the same time that it conserves its poetics and reveals truth through fiction. The theatrical work proposes a version of national political history based on verifiable sources, while constructing a fiction of the disappeared activist. I argue in chapter 2 that the disappearance of the eponymous character in *Montserrat* has its echoes in the forced disappearance of activists in Mexico; here the disappearance of the protagonist is directly attributed to her work chronicling the PRI's history and as an activist teacher who clashed with union leaders. The play, when seen as part of a continuum with *El rumor* and *Montserrat,* reveals the shortcomings of democracy in Mexico.

In *Derretiré,* historical fact forms the backbone of the piece. National political history, then, is brought to the stage alongside personal and family histories (albeit fictional ones). The play condenses the history of the PRI into a series of staged vignettes. Quoting presidents and the minutes of conventions, the play follows the documentary tradition of the verbatim use of official transcripts. These scenes emphasize the importance of institution to the postrevolutionary government and the party itself. Officialdom gives at least an illusion of stability.

President Calles, played by Barreira explains, "Perhaps for the first time in its history, Mexico lacks caudillos and must definitively permit the orientation of politics in the country toward directions of a true institutional life, attempting to leave behind, once and for all, the historical condition of a country of one man to that of a nation of institutions and laws" (Lagartijas Tiradas al Sol, *Derretiré* 3).[17] These politico-historical scenes trace the party's evolution from its foundation through Cardenismo and the Milagro Mexicano (Mexican Miracle), the 1968 Olympics and the massacre of student protesters at Tlatelolco, the inauguration of a weeping

President López Portillo, the electoral fraud of 1988, NAFTA and the Zapatista uprising in Chiapas, the assassination of presidential candidate Luis Donaldo Colosio, and finally, the election of National Action Party (PAN) candidate Vicente Fox in 2000. The system of one president designating the next, and his subsequent overwhelming win, is repeatedly described alongside, on one hand, important social contributions, like the foundation of the national university or the social security program, and on the other, party repression of social and labor movements.

The play is full of monologues that directly quote presidential speeches, delivered by three actors (Luisa Pardo, Gabino Rodríguez, and Paco Barreira, in various states of undress), wearing masks representing the presidents that originally gave the speeches. Supertitles projected onto a black screen at the back of the stage provide a crash course in the history of the party now known as the PRI, from its early stages as the Partido Nacional Revolucionario (National Revolutionary Party) through its twentieth-century evolution into a political machine. The use of an objective third-person tone in the supertitles, along with the punctuation of video footage of past presidents' giving speeches (and, frequently, weeping), lend the play authority. While the source material for the facts and figures that appear on the screen is not provided as part of the performance, these are generally well-known facts that follow the lines of accepted national history. The documentary footage supports the claims, as in a documentary film.

At the same time, the live interventions of the performance question the credence of the official story. For example, after the display of supertitles outlining the election and presidency of Miguel Alemán in 1940–46, Barreira announces the designation of Alemán's successor, the elderly Adolfo Ruiz Cortines. The supertitles back him up, stating, "Ruiz Cortines managed to receive 74.31 percent of the votes" (Lagartijas Tiradas al Sol, *Derretiré* 11).[18] At this point Rodríguez, wearing a mask and shuffling as though his legs pained him, asks Pardo and Barreira for the time, repeatedly. Each time they answer in chorus, "Whatever time you say it is, Mr. President" (11).[19] After three repetitions Rodríguez as Ruiz Cortines finally catches their gist and announces the (incorrect) time, and they applaud him with shouts of "bravo." Through the use of the mask and the gestures of senility, the bodily interventions perform the ineptitude and risks inherent to authoritarianism. While the text runs soundlessly on the screen, stating the tired, well-known facts, the performance of their implications forefronts their urgency.

In a particularly poignant moment, which gives the play its title, Barreira narrates how in 1946 the independent Oaxacan representative Jorge Meixueiro committed suicide in the Electoral College after having his win overturned. His dying words pointed to the futility of resisting the PRI (then the Partido de la Revolución Mexicana, or Party of the Mexican Revolution [PRM]): "I know that I am only chipping at a mountain with a nail, or melting a volcano's snowcap with a match"

(10).[20] These vignettes are juxtaposed with scenes in which the family and friends of Natalia Valdez Tejeda, a disappeared teacher who had written a book documenting the history of the PRI, recount their memories of her. The intimacy of these quotidian scenes contrasts with the journalistic reenactments of party history. Natalia's story quickly turns conspiratorial—early in the play her bleeding father forces an eleven-year-old Natalia to promise him never to tell anyone, and leaves a mysterious package with her before being taken as a prisoner to Lecumberri. Later she becomes a teacher in Michoacán and is threatened by the teachers' union after criticizing its policies and proposing democratization. Subtitles at the end of the play inform the audience that Natalia disappeared in 2000, and that her whereabouts are still unknown.

The play's two threads end abruptly then, with the PRI losing to the PAN and Natalia disappearing without a trace. Such an inconclusive finale can be explained by the play's introduction, in which Gabino Rodríguez addresses the audience and explains the rationale for the play. He cites the protests during the 2012 presidential campaigns, punctuated by the unexpected genesis of a youth protest movement, #YoSoy132 (#IAm132), organized on social media and the streets[21]: "G. In the middle of those protests we wondered: What did we know about the party? . . . Why did we young people, who had not lived our entire political lives with the PRI in the presidency, hate it so much? . . . That was when we found a book . . . *The Institutional Revolution* by Natalia Valdez Tejeda. We were surprised that its vision appealed more to the comprehension of a process than to exalt or revile the party" (1).[22]

The play then, is an attempt to understand the party as a historical process, recognizing its conflicting contribution of social goods and infliction of repressive violence.

I see *Derretiré* and the Proyecto PRI as the pilot study providing the foundation for the more ambitious *La democracia en* México. By starting with the questions or hypotheses—What is the PRI? What is its history? Why do Mexican youth perceive it so negatively?—the project joins the work of practitioners of theater as research.[23] The rhetorical gesture of directly addressing the audience and explaining the rationale for the play from within the performance is not new for Lagartijas. Indeed, at the end of *El rumor*, Luisa breaks character and recounts the company's political and personal motivations for creating the play. Here, too, the play explicitly inserts itself into sociological, political, and historical discourse by positing itself as a study. It is in these two projects, *Proyecto PRI* and *La democracia en* México, that Lagartijas's investigative impulses to expand theater's status beyond the aesthetic and offer it up as another source of historical truth come to fruition.

Themes introduced in *Derretiré* will return in the works that compose *La democracia en* México. The play blends historical fact and invention, using documentary footage to bolster its claims to truth even as it peddles a book and biography, created by the company, that was invented from thin air. The company never fully clears up the fact that Valdez Tejeda and her book are inventions. The play gains the public's trust by presenting historical facts even as it pulls the wool over their eyes. The performers actually sell her book, *La revolución institucional* (The institutional revolution) to their spectators, in a beautiful full-color edition. The focus throughout the play on illicit commerce, selling national lands to foreign interests or the mixing of private and public monies, is reflected in the play's function too. The PRI, the idea of a nation marked by institutions and the rule of law, democracy itself—are they the merchandise of a philosophical con artist? The play does not provide a definitive answer, but its inconclusive finale, the disappearance of its main character and the return of the PRI in 2012, imply that the ruling party's history of corruption and authoritarianism does not bode well for the nation's future.

La democracia en México

Tijuana

When I learn that Lagartijas will be presenting in the Fusebox Festival in Austin, Texas, I immediately make plans to drive down from Oklahoma. I walk from my hotel on Austin's noisy Sixth Street to the performance site, which has changed at the last minute. Near the river, the Emma S. Barrientos Mexican American Center rises in concrete glory from the park nearby. Inside, I sit down with the hip Austin crowd to see *Tijuana*, Lagartijas's first installment in its new project. The small, intimate theater seems to inspire more audience interaction than I am used to—laughter is loud and gasps are audible. Rodríguez begins his unipersonal play and tells of his quest to go undercover and find out what it is like to live on the minimum wage in Tijuana. I was interested to see the Texas audience's take on the play. Where I saw glaring clues that Rodríguez had not undertaken any such project, the general response seemed to be total credulity. Afterward, in the outdoor lobby at the cash bar provided by the festival, I listened to audience members retell their own stories of visiting Mexican border towns, the fear they felt for Rodríguez, and their admiration for his bravery.

After the success of *Derretiré*, Lagartijas scattered but continued to work together on creative projects. The core technical group in Mexico City remained, while Rodríguez moved to Europe to complete a master's degree in theater at the Amsterdam University of the Arts and Pardo transitioned to a small town in Oaxaca where she founded the Proyecto Yivi, an arts workshop for children. The first play they produced in this new long-distance mode was Rodríguez's solo project *Tijuana*, the part of the project representing the state of Baja California. In it Rodríguez plays himself, an actor, who decides to embark on a sociological experiment. He leaves everything behind and heads to Tijuana, where he manages to get a job in a maquila and attempts to live on minimum wage.

As in *Montserrat*, in *Tijuana* Rodríguez plays a fictional version of himself, doubly represented. First, the protagonist shares a name and various biographical details, with the actor. Second, the protagonist assumes a false identity, Santiago Ramírez, and travels to Tijuana undercover. The company describes the purpose of the play: "The staging attempts to recount this experience and inquire into the possibilities of representation. To be another, to attempt to live the life of another person. To pass as another. Isn't that acting?" (Lagartijas Tiradas al Sol, "Tijuana").[24] Also echoing the reception of *Montserrat*, it seems that the focus on representation was largely missed by the majority of audiences, who instead focus on the feat he claims to have accomplished.

In Mexico, Patricia Martín writes in *El Financiero* that *Tijuana* makes evident the borders between interpreting oneself and another, fiction and documentary, the actor and the nonactor, and so on. She does not seem to question the idea that Rodríguez undertook the experiment he claims to have in the play. In Spain, Ana Prieto Nadal also buys Rodríguez's story, even mentioning the precise numeric figures that the actor offers in the play as proof of the veracity of his experiment. In the United States, Jeanne Claire Van Ryzin criticizes the undercover project, calling it voyeuristic. The basis of this criticism rests on the belief that Rodríguez actually did what his onstage character claims to have done. While it is important to think through the ethics of representing poverty onstage, I propose that Rodríguez's gesture here shares Van Ryzin's critique of playing at poverty. By creating a false documentary drama he expresses the impossibility of bridging the gap between his comfortable life and the abject poverty so many Mexicans face. In an interview with Lily Kelting, Rodríguez expresses his intentions concerning the piece: "I show a lot of material in the performance which proves I was there. But the spectator has, hopefully, enough material to doubt whether they are seeing truth or fiction. I was worried about a tendency in documentary theater for the truth to take on an almost moral quality. It's suspension of disbelief in the worst way possible: I don't like it. We wanted the audience to have the possibility to doubt the authenticity of these stories on stage, the way they would in real life" (Kelting). Does the fact that various published articles that showed they did not doubt the veracity of the stories, but rather critiqued the morality of the project supposedly undertaken, indicate a failure on the part of *Tijuana*?

If we only focus on Rodríguez's stated intention, to introduce doubt and question the bounds of documentary, the answer may be affirmative. This failure can be productive, however, for thinking through the contributions of theater to discourses on politics and society. I argue throughout this book that Latin American theater is positioning itself as a source of verifiable fact, in contrast to the obscure and corrupt world of officialdom. It would seem, then, that this work is complete; the audiences of *Tijuana* (and *Montserrat*, to an extent) have accepted theater's claim to truth and suspended their disbelief completely. It is as if the urgency of the problems presented in the plays switched off the critical mechanism; the poverty and oppression present in the neoliberal, capitalist factorylands that line the southern side of the US-Mexican border receive all the spectators' critical attention precisely because the problems are real, even if the approach is not.

The play does present documentary evidence of a sort. Throughout *Tijuana* there is a strong focus on photography. Gabino, the character, claims to have worn a hidden camera and audio recorder throughout his time in Tijuana. The photographs projected onto the ubiquitous screen at the back of the stage show Gabino, always alone, dressed in the hoodies of the workers he emulates and looking wistful and cold. This documentary evidence does indicate that he went to Tijuana, but the fact that these are not selfies reveals that he did not take the photographs. The photographic evidence presented to support Gabino's claims directly contradicts his story of solitude. Other video evidence, amateur footage of landslides destroying communities, seem to back his stories about the precariousness of the informal settlement he inhabits. They do not, however, line up with geographical realities— another clue that all is not as it seems.

Gabino also uses his fame to link the character's plot to his real life. He claims to have worn a disguise because he is an actor who has been on television and film, so that no one in the factories would recognize him. Rodríguez's filmography is impressive and critically acclaimed, but he is far from being a household name. The line got laughs with audiences in Mexico City, but in Austin, Texas, for example, audience members took him at his word. The importance of context also came up in international presentations of *Santiago Amoukalli*, discussed below. False auto/biographical evidence works to provoke the desired doubt that Rodríguez mentions above, but when audiences are meeting a character for the first time, auto/biographical evidence is taken at face value, straight from the horse's mouth.

Intertextuality plays an important role in *Tijuana* as in many of Lagartijas's plays. The advance promotional materials for the play reference Arnoldo Gálvez Suárez, whose novel *Los jueces* (The judges) chronicles the vigilante justice meted out by a group of neighbors, a scene that appears in graphic detail in *Tijuana* as an accused rapist is brutally beaten to death by a mob in the neighborhood where Gabino rents a room. The same materials cite Günter Wallraff, a German investigative journalist famous for his controversial undercover reporting, including the famous 1985 book *Ganz Unten* (The lowest of the low) (or *Cabeza de turco* in Spanish), in which he poses as a Turkish guest worker and documents the mistreatment he experienced from landlords, employers, and the general population, and Andrés Felipe Solano, whose book *Salario mínimo* (Minimum wage, 2015) chronicles his project of living on the minimum wage in Colombia for six months. Gabino claims to have undertaken the same type of project, except that clues like the literary references and the untrustworthy photographic and video evidence indicate that he did not.

Finally, some elements of inventiveness and performance communicate that the play functions not merely as a faithful documentation of facts; rather they show that the play is about the possibilities and limits of representation. In particular, the scenes in which Rodríguez pantomimes his repetitive tasks at the maquiladora where he works, folding and boxing articles of clothing, come across like choreographed dance moves. The performance of work, the body of the laborer separated from his materials, becomes a work of art. This transformation is reminiscent of the films *Maquilapolis: City of Factories* by Vicky Funari and Sergio de la Torre (2006) and *Sleep Dealer* by Alex Rivera (2008) , in which workers *perform* performing tasks, through stylized pantomime or virtual reality.

Tijuana, then, uses the language of documentary theater, investigative journalism, and performance to stage the impossibility of experiencing the life of another and subsequently representing that life faithfully. The play is a demonstration of the vast divide between the haves and the have-nots, in Mexico in particular but also on the international stage—the play was created in Amsterdam and has been presented in North America and Europe. The problem of Gabino's difficulties is a red herring; while audiences feel sympathy for the fictional character's troubles, the real issue at hand is the vast inequality present in capitalist society, and the seeming impossibility of bridging the gap.

The play builds sympathy for its character's plight through Gabino's claim to have gone undercover. A fictional play about a poor person might generate some compassion, but the idea of stripping oneself of the trappings of a privileged life (false as it may be) takes audience members one step further toward imagining themselves in the situation of the other. Early in the play, after moving into his small, uncomfortable rented room, he gags and coughs. Afterward he sits down and does some quick calculations of his budget, always converting his pesos into the local currency of the performance site.

The calculations of conversion highlight the schism between audiences seated safely in artsy theaters in cultural capitals and those working to assemble the parts that will go into smart phones, theater projectors, audio speakers, and laptops. At the same time, though, through identification with the character of Gabino, a representative of the privileged first world who goes like a sacrificial lamb into the third world, temporarily and voluntarily, the audiences are asked to imagine not the life of a poor other, but the horror of having to experience that life themselves. That the play is fictional does not change the fact that the inequality it highlights is very real. The play, then, nudges audiences toward a conception of democracy that acknowledges those left out of state narratives of prosperity.

Tijuana's mix of documentary evidence, autobiographical references, literary intertextuality, and performance, turns the stage into a laboratory for democracy. The play asks what happens when a member of the creative class joins the poorest members of society. The answers are that the person is excluded from democratic decision making at all levels. A video voice-over in the play outlines the results of the 1982 economic crisis due to falling oil prices, and the resulting alignment of border cities' economies with the US economy. In the voiceover Rodríguez narrates how migrants from the southern states of Mexico joined the maquiladora industry in the north, whose cities were not ready to accommodate the influx of workers. He concludes the introduction to his new home: "And that is how the large informal settlements began to form. Many dispossessed people united to take territories, wall them off, create neighborhoods, make a life. That is how the neighborhood where I now live was created. That is how the people with whom I share a house moved into it" (Lagartijas Tiradas al Sol, *Tijuana* 2).[25] Because the structures of national democracy failed them, the members of the newly established communities springing up around the border industry created their own accords, outside municipal, state, or federal power.

As in *Derretiré con un cerillo la nieve de un volcán*, in this first installation of *La democracia en* México, reality is approached both directly and indirectly, through documentary and fiction. The blend of literary sources, auto/biographical experience, historical fact, and pure invention suggest that certain realities are only available to those living them. The play, in this way, is a metaphor for democracy, which only represents those with effective access to the decision-making process.

Veracruz

The next installment in the series *La democracia en* México, titled *Veracruz, nos estamos deforestando o cómo extrañar Xalapa*, differs greatly from Rodriguez's project *Tijuana*. This project, directed, written, and performed by Lisa Pardo, is billed not as a play but as a "conferencia," a lecture. The intervention focuses on the brutal killing of Nadia Vera, an activist and public critic of Javier Duarte, then governor of the state of Veracruz, along with four other people in a Mexico City apartment, including photojournalist Rubén Espinosa who had also been a critic of Duarte. The disgraced governor, who was extradited to Mexico from Guatemala in April 2017 after a six-month manhunt, is accused of corruption, graft, and involvement in organized crime. Before his downfall, however, Duarte operated with impunity, threatening and intimidating journalists and other critics. Indeed, Vera and Espinosa had publicly stated that if anything should happen to them, to look to the state. Francisco Goldman writes in *The New Yorker* that "Rubén Espinosa [was] the fourteenth journalist from Veracruz to be murdered since Duarte became governor, in 2010. In his eight years of reporting from Veracruz, . . . he had become accustomed to being roughed-up and harassed by police authorities and receiving threats."

Vera was an anthropology student at the Universidad de Veracruz and an activist who had faced threats for her efforts. Goldman reports that she had been beaten and jailed, her home ransacked. She moved to Mexico City out of fear for her safety, but the distance between the capital and her home state was not insurmountable for the network of corruption that threatens democracy in Mexico, especially the free press considered a basic requirement for democracy. In Susan Rose-Ackerman's 1978 publication *Corruption: A Study in Political Economy*, the political economist and legal scholar concludes that while "an informed electorate is certainly not a sufficient condition for the proper functioning of a representative democracy," neither is it true "that the existence of a comprehensive set of interest groups would be a sufficient condition for an effective democracy. It is only when *both* of these conditions are combined with a political system generating closely contested elections that one can devise a model with strong—if not perfect—protections against corrupt activity" (29). Lagartijas's work examines these conditions. In *Derretiré*, Lagartijas looks at the lack of closely contested elections, and in *Tijuana*, they show the economic exclusion of certain groups from the nation. *Veracruz* demonstrates the state's recognition of the first condition Rose-Ackerman posits: the informed electorate. By brutally and mercilessly silencing journalists and activists, Duarte and his fellows attempt to stifle the flow of information to the electorate.

Veracruz, Pardo insists, is not a dramatic work. In an interview she expressed that she had to stop presenting the *conferencia* because it became like a performance to her, losing its connection to reality.[26] Though Lagartijas deals with the real in all of its work and the personal, the intention of *Veracruz* is to separate itself from the realm of fiction in order to effectively denounce Duarte and his government. The lecture folds in on itself, however, in typical Lagartijas style, and the performance aspect is inescapable.

The first part of *Veracruz* consists of Pardo, wearing an embroidered *huipil* in front of a lectern, accompanied by a slide show flashing photographs of Veracruz, reading a news report. She recounts how a family's pet Labrador carried home a human arm. After the harrowing reading, Pardo welcomes the audience and describes the writing of the lecture: "When, more than eight months ago, I was preparing the text of this lecture for a festival far from here, a festival that asked me to speak about Veracruz, but above all about Nadia Vera, about her murder, there were very difficult moments. In the middle of so much information, so much visual and journalistic material, bad news . . . I got lost, I didn't see the point, the way, sometimes I couldn't find the sense in going there to talk about this"

(Lagartijas Tiradas al Sol, *Veracruz* 1).[27] The lecture, then, is the re-presentation of a lecture given at a faraway festival. The origin story of the play hearkens to so many of the techniques Lagartijas uses in its work to create a motivation for telling the story.

The lecture is structured like an indictment. Charges are brought, evidence is presented, and the audience is asked to judge the guilty and defend the innocent. After the aforementioned introduction, the lecture sounds akin to a school oral report, with an encyclopedic rundown of Veracruz's major exports, geographical features, size, and colonial history. The segments of the lecture are divided and punctuated by multicolored test patterns and static on the screen, and support-ed by audio recordings of interviews with Nadia's acquaintances, who give their testimony of what happened to her, as well as the changes they have observed in their state. Pardo moves into Veracruz's more recent history of producing a large number of presidents affiliated with the PRI, and her personal connections to the state through her paternal family. Finally, Pardo inserts herself fully into the story:

> Some time ago I tried to return to live in Xalapa, after having left to study and work in Mexico City almost nine years before. I found not only a devastated land and a society exponentially more unequal, with a few very rich people and many very poor and hud-dled people, but also an extreme state of violence: gunfights, kidnappings, extortion. The process of decomposition has been long, it's not just the present, but just now is when the problem is revealed to be great. The politicians are very closely tied to orga-nized crime; there is an almost inseparable, codependent relationship between them and the narcos. (Pardo, "Veracruz" 7)[28]

In this moment, after having established her familial ties to the state of Veracruz and remembering her childhood there, Pardo rests on that native authority to give a report on the state of affairs in Veracruz to an audience of outsiders. Unlike Alex-is de Tocqueville, who toured the United States and marveled about its democratic practice in *Democracy in America* (a title that surely influenced the title of González Casanova's *Democracy in Mexico*), Pardo is the native informant who goes out into the world to decry the failures of democracy in her home state. Although she insists that *Veracruz* is a *conferencia* and not a dramatic production, the rhetorical gesture of establishing herself as an eyewitness heir to the disaster is a powerful perfor-mance of testimony.

Pardo includes her own voice, body, and family connections in the audio inter-views, the video reporting, and the photographic evidence presented in *Veracruz* to lend credence to the indictment presented. At the same time, the lecture func-tions as a ritual. While the video footage plays on a large screen behind her, she leaves her lectern to light candles in the middle of the stage, preparing an altar in memory of Nadia Vera and the other victims of the corrupt government's ruthless authoritarianism.

She also shares the stage with Vera herself after reciting the facts of the case, with a measure of poetry: "One year and two days ago. They were murdered with malice, they were tortured. There have been three arrests, one suitcase, and the official investigations that points to a settling of scores, to the recuperation of a suitcase full of drugs."[29] Pardo introduces a video interview of Vera and Espinosa: "The Attorney General of the Federal District went to Veracruz to interrogate Javier Duarte, who denied any involvement whatsoever with the murder, but he can never escape this" (Pardo, "Veracruz." 14).[30] The video projected afterward, an interview with RompevientoTV, shows Vera directly addressing the camera and stating, "We hold Javier Duarte de Ochoa, Governor of the State, and all of his cabinet, totally responsible for anything that might happen to those of us who are involved with and organized in this type of movement, including students, academics, and civil society in general" ("Nadia Vera").[31] Pardo may insist that *Veracruz* is not a play, and it is not; it is, though, an example of how the theater is fully taking its place within society as a forum for justice, in the face of unresponsive tribunals and courts.[32] By providing the space for denouncing those responsible for her murder, even after Vera's death, the theater brings life to the dead and voice to the silenced.

Santiago Amoukalli

I am back at the Teatro El Milagro after many years away from Mexico City. It is where I first saw *Montserrat* and *Se rompen las olas*, and I trudge up the metal stairs with my friend Michael to see Lagartijas's newest play, *Santiago Amoukalli*. We settle into the brightly lit space, and choose the far set of seats flanking the traverse stage below us. A green tarp marks the performance area, which is filled with a wooden model of a town, complete with little cars, houses, trees, and human and animal figurines. The play begins when a disembodied voice thunders out over the crowd, and two characters named Gabino and Luisa wander onto the stage.

The next installment in *La democracia en* México, is decidedly a theatrical production. Indeed, the opening lines are an amplified voice-over stating, "The story we are going to tell you is about a place that doesn't exist, about people that do not exist, and about things that don't happen. It is, as they say, a fictional story" (Lagartijas Tiradas al Sol, *Santiago Amoukalli* 1).[33] Michael whispers that the quote reminds him of Mexican writer Juan Rulfo, whose otherworldly masterpieces *El llano en llamas* (The burning plain) and *Pedro Páramo* propose a vision of the Mexican countryside characterized by death and memory. I murmur my agreement as the onstage fog machines fill the theatrical space with fog, adding to the mysterious, unreal feeling of the play.

FIGURE 4. Luisa takes a tourist photo of Gabino in *Santiago Amoukalli*.

Nevertheless, reality seeps in. The main characters, named Gabino and Luisa, and played by Gabino Rodríguez and Luisa Pardo, are two actors who travel to the high sierra to lead a workshop funded by a Canadian nonprofit that uses theater to teach children about the importance and techniques of proper hand-washing and water sanitation. The town where they are sent, Santiago Amoukalli, is fictional, though statistics are presented about it that could easily describe an impoverished, indigenous town in the mountains of Mexico. When the characters arrive (see figure 4), the town is in full campaign mode before an upcoming election, and the levels of corruption they observe, including vote-buying, disturb them.

The action reaches a crisis when Luisa, who has insisted on a day trip to see the nearby waterfall, only to be constantly put off by locals, finally learns why her attempts have been rebuffed. Upon her return to town, their translator explains to Gabino and Luisa that a group of armed men had come to town and accused its inhabitants of cooperating with another group of narcos, and had massacred many of their neighbors. The bodies were buried at the waterfall. Luisa and Gabino argue, over their complicity with the neocolonial powers that created the situation in Santiago Amoukalli; after all, they are literally washing the hands, and funds, of Coca-Cola and the bottling companies that profit from the lack of accessible potable water in the region. The play is an indictment of the failure of democracy in Mexico's poorest communities, as the election so eagerly and anxiously awaited

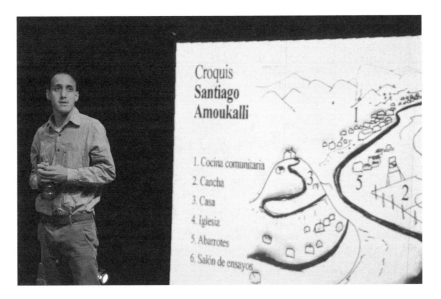

FIGURE 5. Gabino presents a map of the town in *Santiago Amoukalli*.

is bought and sold, and the real powers that be control even the artists who believe themselves to be part of the resistance.

In this case, rather than presenting a fiction as a documentary, the actors announce the fictional status of the play's plot and setting, and yet provide ample documentary evidence to support its existence in reality. Though the existence of Santiago Amoukalli is not verifiable, because it is an invented village, the scenery includes projected maps and photographs of the mountains where it is supposedly located (see figure 5); a topographical map left onstage after the presentation shows spectators exactly where, in the vast, undifferentiated green of the sierra, the play took place. At the same time, the correspondence between the characters' names and those of the actors, who by this point are well-known for presenting auto/biographical plays as themselves, might confuse viewers.[34] The point is, however, that all the play's action *could be* true; it is believable because of the state of democracy in Mexico.

Other dramatic techniques, which hearken back to the company's earlier productions, include the use of water and other natural elements onstage. The two actors spend a few minutes creating a sort of square labyrinth out of river stones on the stage, which later becomes the slippery mountain path that Luisa runs along on her way home from the waterfall. On that day there was a rainstorm, they remember, and the two actors face one another and pour several gallons of water onto their own heads from large buckets, impassively. Soaking wet, they run barefoot on the rocks, slipping painfully and laboriously. Though clearly a dramatic element, the water and the physical responses it causes in the actors' bodies, and in the spectators in the front row who are splashed in the process, are real. I am grateful that we happened to sit farther up the raked seating area. Luisa and Gabino are soaked, just as they are inescapably drowning in complicity as they participate in the nonprofit hand-washing for neocolonial corporations.

At the end of the play, the narrator describes how Gabino and Luisa ended their stay in the sierra: "The election was the next day. Luisa and Gabino never found out who won. Little did it matter. They wanted to cry, to embrace one another, but they never permitted themselves such things. They left Amoukalli, forever" (Lagartijas Tiradas al Sol, *Santiago Amoukalli* 21).[35] And indeed, Rodríguez and Pardo abandon the stage. The lights stay up and the audience is left with the uncomfortable choice of whether to wait for them to go down, so that they may applaud as the actors return for a bow, or to applaud against convention, before any signal that the play has ended. On the two nights I attended the play in the Teatro El Milagro in Mexico City's La Condesa neighborhood in July 2017, after the first show the silence was awkward and long. The complete disappearance of the actors, who never did return to the theater space but did reappear in the lobby after the show, left the audience abandoned—the actors had come, performed, and gone like conquerors, leaving us to pick up the pieces. A metaphor, perhaps, for the way that federal democratic processes buy local municipal elections and disappear, leaving voters with another television in the house or an extra month's worth of groceries in gift cards, but no change or effective power; or how volunteers at nonprofits return to real life after their temporary stints saving the world.

Santiago Amoukalli picks up where González Casanovas left off, examining the state of democracy in Mexico. The corruption and poverty it finds and represents point to the failure of the democratic project in the nation. Where González Casanovas pointed out the complete lack of control at the municipal level in his 1965 study, the play zooms in on the local elections, showing how the federal government and national party officials determine the outcome of the local democratic process. Where González Casanovas decries internal colonialism as an obstacle to overcome on the path to achieving true democracy, Gabino and Luisa are the face of internal neocolonialism, being treated like foreigners. Indeed, they are only able to conduct the workshop with the help of a translator, and seem to have more in common with the French Canadian coordinator of the project than with the inhabitants of the town, their compatriots.

By the same token, the play shows the relationships within plural society, defined by González Casanova as those that "contain two or more socio-cultural aggregates, one which is highly participating and another which is quite marginal; one which is dominant—be it called Spanish, Creole, or Ladino—and another which is dominated—be it called native, Indian, or indigenous" (González Casanova, *Democracy in Mexico* 71).[36] Gabino and Luisa represent the super-participatory group, and the inhabitants of Santiago Amoukalli are the marginalized indigenous. González Casanova immediately links plural society to internal colonialism, "the domination and exploitation of certain groups by others" (González Casanova *Democracy in Mexico* 71).[37]

Gabino and Luisa are complicit participants in the system, as they represent the multinational corporation and, as members of the dominant class, enter the town to, in a sense, wash the hands of Coca-Cola, all while the federal party dominates the election in the marginalized town. Another of González Casanova's conclusions, however, seems to differ with what Lagartijas finds through its performance research. González Casanova writes that after the political crises faced in recent years, both revolutionary and reforming powers have reached a consensus "that they can gain power and lose power. . . . In times of crisis both groups are aware of one fact: that all the economically and politically marginal population can become active and that . . . this makes possible a struggle or brings a real danger, depending on one's perspective" (González Casanova *Democracy in Mexico* 118).[38]

The play, then, uses the tools of documentary and the tradition of fiction to create a story that *could be real* and to denounce a very real situation. The special effects—like the fog machine and the illumination that re-creates a lightning storm—and the use of natural elements—like the water they pour onto themselves, splashing some spectators—literally immerse the bodies of the performers (and some spectators) into the scene. The fog palpably penetrates audience members' respiratory systems and condenses on their skin, sending a chill to their bones. The play itself is inescapable; there is no distance between the spectator and the ethically and politically complex situation being observed. The play is a metaphor for the inescapable corruption, the systemic violence inherent in modern Mexican democracy. The fog, sound, and water call to mind Slavoj Žižek's systemic violence, which he defines as "the often catastrophic consequences of the smooth functioning of our economic and political systems. . . . Systemic violence is . . . the counterpart to an all-too-visible subjective violence" (2). Through the senses and the breath the play's violence violates all who come near. There is no escaping once one has drawn near. In the same way, *Santiago Amoukalli* does not offer a way out to its protagonists or their acquaintances in the town. They escape by walking away; no revolution or call to action concludes this play.

Distrito Federal

The next installment in *La democracia en* México is the 2017 short film *Distrito Federal*, by Juan Leduc and Gabino Rodríguez. The project is based on a text by the political scientist Natalia Verónica Soto Coloballes, "40 años después: Sin soluciones" (40 years later: No solutions), published on Election Day in 2016 in *Nexos*, which decries the inaction on the part of the government in addressing pollution and other ecological problems in the capital. The title refers to the name of the capital city, known as "D.F." for short, which had been controversially changed to Ciudad de México (Mexico City) earlier in 2016. The film is a farewell to a friendship, and a lamentation for the ecological disaster of the city.

The opening shots show footage of high-rises in the Valley of Mexico and aerial footage of freeways crossing the city, as voice-over narration discusses the problem of smog. Some of the shots are blurry, obscured by the aforementioned contamination. Quoting Soto Coloballes, the narration refers to the lack of action on the part of local and federal government to control the levels of pollution that make the city uninhabitable. Rodríguez's voice states, after the ecological, factual introduction, "We were born in Mexico City, in 1983, one month and six days apart" (Lagartijas Tiradas al Sol, *Distrito Federal*).[39] The "we" is never explicitly defined, although through the course of the eleven-minute film, it becomes clear that the collective narration refers to Leduc and Rodríguez. This possibility is backed up with baby pictures of the two together, evidence of their lifelong friendship. Intercalated with the ecological disaster of the city, the film's main focus is a letter. The text is displayed in the frame, with large portions blacked out as though censored for privacy. The letter announces the unhappy end of a lifelong friendship, though the viewer is not given enough information to determine who wronged whom, or how.

The final shots are of Rodríguez, sitting in an apartment with European-style windows, sloped roofs visible outside, and a map of Amsterdam on the wall behind him. As he sits, silently reading a handwritten text, the room fills with fog from an unseen source, finally obscuring him from the camera's view. This setting points to the idea that the breakup is between a city and its native son, though the presence of the mysterious fog indicates that he cannot escape his city's pollution, even across an ocean. The fog and auto/biographical identification of Gabino Rodríguez performing as himself also connects the video to *Santiago Amoukalli* and *Tijuana*. The project represents the treatment of the capital city, and the focus on ecological problems and their relationship to democracy has its roots in Lagartijas's earliest works, such as *Asalto al agua transparente*. The short film is mysterious and quiet, and profoundly sad. The loss it portrays is deep; leaving Mexico City is like losing a lifelong friend, a permanent companion, though the fog at the end suggests that one never really leaves it fully behind.

In the case of *Distrito Federal*, the blend of historical fact and documentary evidence lends particular credence to the film's claims about environmental policy in Mexico's capital city. The narration at the beginning points to the veridical nature of the content. The flyover footage is accompanied by the voice of a reporter, from decades ago, expressing his hope that Mexico will "conquer, with knowledge, this problem of air pollution" (Leduc and Rodríguez).[40] The optimism is immediately answered with video from today, showing a smoggy, blurry city. If knowledge has not conquered this issue, then who has won the battle? According to *Distrito Federal*, special interests and individual politicians have won, at great cost to the rest of society. Rodríguez's narration, which follows immediately, cites Francisco Vizcaíno Murray, then undersecretary of the Subsecretaría de Mejoramiento del Ambiente (Undersecretary of Environmental Improvement, SMA), who in 1973 promised to resolve the problem of pollution *a la mexicana*.

The historical facts, however, are immediately intertwined with auto/biographical accounts. The reference to 1973 is qualified as being ten years before "we" (presumably Leduc and Rodríguez) were born; politics is immanently personal. The frame becomes completely clouded as Rodríguez's narration continues: "Solving the problems *a la mexicana* meant not solving the problems. It meant not making decisions that should have been made. Doing things that can no longer be remedied" (Leduc and Rodríguez).[41] The ominous sense of this statement contrasts painfully with the optimism of the prior narration, which hoped for the triumph of science and knowledge. Here, there is no hope that through the pursuit of knowledge and hard work Mexico will "get ahead" (*salir adelante*). Rather, the film takes as a given that the city it portrays is doomed. This also contrasts with the call to action found in *Asalto al agua transparente*, in which Pardo and Rodríguez put knowledge on the stage, hoping to inspire political and ecological change. In that play, the knowledge was the history of water and its relationship to colonialism; here the knowledge that the first narrator refers to is scientific. In either case, the message of *La democracia en México* once again points to the failure of democracy and knowledge in the face of corruption.

After a title screen, the theme of failure continues through a completely different medium. Now silence reigns, and rather than aerial views of the city the viewer is faced with white text on a black screen. Sections of the text have been blocked out, but the topic is clear. The first line, after a censored greeting, reads, "Writing this letter to your best friend is a defeat" (Leduc and Rodríguez).[42] The letter asks for forgiveness, recalling the letter that Rodríguez reads to his family at the beginning of *Montserrat*, or the e-mails read in *Catalina*. Here, though, it is unclear what the offense that must be pardoned is. What is intriguing is that, while the fate of the city seems sealed, doomed, in the case of the broken friendship some hope is offered: "I think it's the only way that someday the wound that I am opening might heal" (Leduc and Rodríguez).[43]

The soundtrack accompanying the letter is the wind, and it ends reiterating defeat: "I will never stop speaking well of you. I don't expect reciprocity. This letter is a defeat" (Leduc and Rodríguez).[44] After the last words, the soundtrack gives way to the laughing voice of a child, thrilled to be recording himself. Photographs of Rodríguez and Leduc, laughing in the metro, on an airplane, in parties, flash in the frame. The child says, "Friends, this is Gabino and Juan Leduc. We came to record this for you. Ta-da" (Leduc and Rodríguez).[45] The photographs go further back in time, showing the two artists as adolescents; small, naked children at the beach; and finally as infants in a hammock together.

These photographs and the recording are powerfully convincing evidence of the relationship between the two men. If the letter portrayed in the film is real, it would represent be the tragic end of a lifelong friendship. After the photo slideshow the letter itself, handwritten in blue ink on graph paper, with large sections crossed out in the same blue ink, dominates the screen before the camera cuts to Gabino, seated in a wicker chair in the apartment described above, reading. The film likens the destruction of a city by the democratic officials entrusted with its care to the end of a relationship. By replacing the shock and disgust at the ecological state of affairs in Mexico City that the viewer is invited to share in the film's opening shots with sadness and loss over the end of a relationship, the film proposes an intimate, affective response to environmental destruction.

The same fog that penetrates audience members' nasal passages in *Santiago Amoukalli* fills the frame of *Distrito Federal*. Though viewers of a film are not physically affected by the work in the same way that theatergoers are physically assaulted by the fog, sound, lights, and water in *Santiago Amoukalli*, the elements that usually guide a viewer through a film—narrative, sound, light, movement—are only sparsely available in *Distrito Federal* and completely withheld by the end of the film. The letter mentions no names, places, specific behaviors, or events. The windy soundtrack creates a white-noise effect, where no references can be made based on audio clues. The fog in the final scene echoes the smog in the beginning of the film, that totally obscures the visual medium of the film. It also echoes the fog in *Santiago Amoukalli*, and *Distrito Federal*'s ending shares the hopelessness of that play.

The film quietly rejects the city and the lifelong relationship its makers share with the capital. As the city is slowly, silently obliterated by the ecological contamination that, it seems, will be its end, the fog that invades Rodríguez's European studio simultaneously indicates that his rejection is ignored. The artist cannot escape his past, his home. The city follows him like a contaminant—the smog will not leave him alone. The opening remarks on problem-solving *a la mexicana* indicate that the corruption at all levels of government, which leaves millions of people without clean air or water, is an external, evil force that invades citizens' bodies, settling in for good.

The project *La democracia en* México, called "ambitious" by almost every publication that mentions it, is obviously only partially complete. These four works represent only one-eighth of the projected final product, one work for each state in the Mexican union. It is not exactly clear which state *Santiago Amoukalli* represents. Indeed, the company claims that it is about a place and people that do not exist; Santiago Amoukalli is not found on any maps and neither is the district mentioned in the play, Tehuixtintle. With *La democracia en* México Lagartijas has hit its stride. The documentary and auto/biographical techniques it has been honing throughout its career are coming together in an explicit project that uses theater, film, and performance as the ultimate research methodologies.

Lagartijas is creating theater that is also investigation. It is testing democracy through fiction. When Gabino claims that he has gone to Tijuana and lived on the minimum wage, people believe him. The exercise of believing that a middle-class artist has undertaken such a difficult task, and that it worked, does not seem to cause international viewers to stumble. Perhaps the unexamined empathy of the audiences is one of the findings of Lagartijas's investigations. The fact that people think that Gabino's project is possible means they do not realize how vast the breach is between classes, across borders. It is an impossibility that is swallowed without question. Democracy, then, depends on this imperfect empathy, where we see only what we want to see; we imagine that there is democracy because audiences, from our privileged position, are granting the people equality. Claiming that one can live like the poor erases the difference between the poor and the middle and upper classes. And that, in turn, erases their struggle. It also implies that, if Gabino can go down and live like them, they could, if they decided, do the inverse and live as he does. The belief implies that it is not actually all that hard to live on the minimum wage.

This is what the characters Luisa and Gabino are also trying to do in *Santiago Amoukalli*, to convince themselves that it is possible to live ethically, outside of the evils of corporate colonialism. They represent the internal colonialism that González Casanova decried fifty years earlier. But they are blinded by their own goodness and cannot see their complicity until it is too late and they are swimming in Coca-Cola's backwaters. González Casanova's 1965 study shows in Mexico "*caciques* and the Army have lost power and importance," giving way to "native financiers and entrepreneurs . . . along with the large foreign enterprises and the great power that supports them" (*Democracy in Mexico* 67).[46] *Santiago Amoukalli*, fifty years later, investigates the power of the "large foreign enterprises and the great power that supports them" by going undercover. They join the Coca-Cola corporation's artistic collaboration with nonprofits, and then bring the results onstage, performing what they learned. While it is clear that Santiago Amoukalli does not exist and the story is a fiction, as the voice-over claims, the truth rings out that the Mexican highlands are filled with villages and situations just like the one Gabino and Luisa find in the play.

At the same time, with *Veracruz*, Pardo attempts to reveal the unseen, and use the theater as a space for decrying the very corruption that plays a part in maintaining the imbalances of power that *Santiago Amoukalli* and *Tijuana* represent. *Distrito Federal*, too, makes the connection between the personal and the political, personifying the contaminated city and assigning blame for its ecological state to a corrupt government. Fifty years earlier, González Casanovas laid out his themes for analysis, which are echoed in the four works analyzed here: "The relationship between social marginality and political marginality; the relationship between plural society, internal colonialism, and political manipulation; the relationship between social stratification and political nonconformity; the relationship between mobilization, social mobility, and political conformity; and the relationship between the forms assumed by nonconformity and civil struggles" (González Casanova, *Democracy in Mexico* 70).[47] Lagartijas follows in his footsteps, studying "the relationships between the social and political structures of Mexico" (González Casanova, *Democracy in Mexico* 70).[48] While the methodology may be different, focusing on performance as research rather than sociology, the themes Lagartijas focuses on and its conclusions are similar. Lagartijas's *La democracia en* México stages the relationships between political and social marginalization and between a lack of political agency and the extreme social marginalization they face.

Chapter 4

Loosening the Bounds of Theater ===

This chapter focuses on the most recent work of Lagartijas Tiradas al Sol, and puts it into perspective with the wider, Latin American theatrical tradition. In particular, I trace connections between Lagartijas's projects and other examples of theater of the real. The company forms part of a larger cultural tendency, a response, I propose, to unreliable and nontransparent government practices in the late twentieth and early twenty-first centuries. Where national trauma is unresolved legally or politically, art emerges as a possible forum for healing and memorializing. Theater, in particular, is a potent and emergent force for promoting the truth. Lagartijas is at the forefront of this movement.

Throughout this study I have referred to Lagartijas's focus on the real in the theater. It is only one of many theater groups that are participating in the trend Carol Martin calls "theatre of the real," which proposes "a shift in the pattern of understanding the representation of the real as necessarily involving verbatim and documentary sources to one that includes a variety of forms and methods and acknowledges a paradigm, a perspective, a subject, and the development of different methodologies" (*Theatre of the Real* 4). She concludes her study of *Theatre of the Real* with the assertion that theater of the real "stages memory and history to scrutinize and also to invent the people and forces making history.... Staging memory and history has helped create new versions of human experience" (175). Martin's study traces contemporary theater practices to the documentary dramas and autobiographical performances of the 1960s and 1970s.

Hans-Thiess Lehmann posits theories of postdramatic theater, tracing a "path ... from the grand theatre at the end of the nineteenth century, via a multitude of modern theatre forms during the historical avant-garde and then the neo-avant-garde of the 1950s and 1960s, to the postdramatic theatre forms at the end of the twentieth and beginning of the twenty-first centuries" (48). This conception of drama, which can begin with early, medieval examples, according to Lehmann, then hits a crisis wherein theater separates itself from drama. At this point, Lehmann argues, the avant-gardes "each sacrifice certain parts of dramatic representation but in the end preserve the crucial unity: the close connection between the text of an action, report or process and the theatrical representation oriented towards it. This connection ruptures in the postdramatic theatre of the last decades" (56). Finally, in postdramatic theater, the performance text "becomes more presence than representation, more shared than communicated experience, more process than product, more manifestation than signification, more energetic impulse than information" (85). The idea of presence was invoked in the Introduction to this study, as the main source of evidence for the real nature of the subject matter presented in Lagartijas's plays.

Both Martin's and Lehmann's characterizations of contemporary theater are useful for thinking about Lagartijas's work. As we have seen throughout this book, Lagartijas stages memory and history, using the theater as a lens through which to scrutinize history itself, as Martin claims theater of the real does. At the same time, the reality that the theater stages can tend toward the affective rather than the representational; its work is not the pure documentary of the 1960s and 1970s, but rather attempts to communicate an energy in addition to the information being transmitted.

Recent Work

Está escrita en sus campos

Está escrita en sus campos (It is written in their fields, 2014) is a documentary play, characterized as a "scenic essay" (*ensayo escénico*) (Patrón Rivera), in which Francisco Barreiro attempts to understand the history of drug trafficking in Mexico. Barreiro describes the project as "an attempt at generating the map of a territory that I don't recognize, relating a story I don't know, an attempt to reappropriate a country" (Lagartijas Tiradas al Sol, *Está escrita en Sus campos*).[1]

The play premiered in 2014 at La Comuna theater festival in León, Mexico. The unipersonal play stages Barreiro, who plays various characters. One, El Tigre, is a rapper and marijuana farmer, who learned his agricultural trade from his grandfather. At age twenty-three he is father to a toddler. Barreiro performs hip-hop songs, wearing a plaid, hooded jacket and a balaclava, and gives monologues as El Tigre, telling about his life. A screen behind Barreiro and two small monitors at either side of the stage show images of a small boy dressed as a tiger, and maps of Mexican drug cultivation. Another character, who yells menacingly and performs aggressive gestures, narrates the history of drug cultivation in Mexico, tracing it back to the beginning of the opium trade, when the advent of prohibition in the United States pushed the distribution of black-market drugs to Mexico.[2]

In the second half of the play, Barreiro removes the balaclava and introduces himself in familiar Lagartijas style: "My name is Francisco Barreiro. I am 31 years old. I am an actor" (Barreiro, "Está escrita en sus campos" 15).[3] He claims to have met El Tigre through a mutual documentarian friend who was doing a film about Mexican hip-hop. He also announces that El Tigre is dead. The screen behind him then shows a man, wearing the same plaid, hooded jacket and a balaclava, sitting on a couch and introducing himself in the same way that Barreiro does earlier in the play. El Tigre, the play claims, is real. The video evidence for the artist/farmer/drug trafficker's existence supports the claims of the first half of the play, extending credibility not only to the biography of El Tigre but also to the history of drug trafficking in Mexico that has been presented thus far. In a review of the play in the Mexican paper *Vanguardia*, Claudia Luna Fuentes observes, "We will return to the theater—in this case with more sophisticated technological supports—that is becoming the diffusion of information without censorship."[4]

The set in this play is very dark and sparse. The only props are a microphone and a chair. The screens provide most of the visual interest, along with some masks that Barreiro uses in addition to the balaclava. This contrast to the usual accumulation of live plants, furniture, and toys that are characteristic of Lagartijas's productions, points to the antitheatrical gesture of the play. Whereas productions like *El rumor del incendio*, *Derretiré con un cerillo la nieve de un volcán*, or *Santiago Amoukalli* focus on real, pressing political matters, they are all decidedly dramatic works. The re-creations of scenes between characters or invention of characters, the costumes and costume changes, and the set all fit into the theatrical mode. *Está escrita en sus campos*, meanwhile, departs from this mode and is characterized as a scenic essay by the company.

By classifying the play this way, Lagartijas signals that it is participating in theater in a way that Jorge Dubatti calls "matrix-theater" (*teatro-matriz*) defined as "any event in which the simultaneous and combined presence of conviviality, corporal poetry, and spectation. The theater can include technological elements . . . but cannot renounce conviviality, the auratic bodily presence productive of *poíesis*."[5] At the same time that *Está escrita en sus campos* fulfills these basic requirements, it seems to reject Dubatti's all-encompassing gesture through Lagartijas's and Barreiro's insistence on classifying it as a "scenic essay." Dubatti's conceptualization of a "reamplification" of the concept of theater, however, allows us to consider plays like this one, which attempt to direct the spectator's gaze to the reality of the content presented, as theater even if they are not specifically dramatic works.

This, in turn, allows us to see how Lagartijas and other theater practitioners throughout the region are turning the spectator's gaze to the real. The theater, the space of spectation, is presenting the urgent reality of everyday life. This does not ignore theatricality; rather, theatricality is what allows for the projects' success. *Está escrita en sus campos* razes the stage, leaving behind only the bare minimum for theater: bodily creation; simultaneous shared presence; and active spectatorship. The absence of scenery, minimal props and costuming, and low lighting leave only the essence of theatrical creation: the direction of the gaze. The subject matter's urgency is amplified by this single-minded focus on theater, in the original sense of the term.

Yanhuitlán

The film project *7 mono, iya de Yanhuitlán* (Lord 7 monkey of Yanhuitlán, 2016),[6] is realized by Proyecto Yivi (Yivi Project),[7] a collaboration between Lagartijas Tiradas al Sol (mainly Luisa Pardo) and children from Nochixtlán, Oaxaca, a village in the Mixtec highlands. The video, written by and starring the children, recounts the story of the Spanish conquest of their region, and the fall of 7 mono, the Mixtec ruler.

In *7 mono*, children of Yanhuitlán are cast in a pageant-like retelling of a foundational myth of their village. The ruler 7 mono was given to drinking with the Spanish *encomendero* in the community. He did not heed the warnings of his seer, who told him of imminent danger. The arrival of the Inquisition led to the downfall of the Mixtec ruler and the repression of people's religion and culture. The children's performance privileges gesture and pantomime. In one moment, when 7 mono and his Spanish friend are drinking together, they communicate in a sign language that mimics the gestures and postures represented in colonial codices. The video includes some violent moments, such as the removal of a virgin's heart in sacrifice to the gods; the blood spattering from the pumping heart is added in postproduction, in comical animation.

When Pardo presents *7 mono* in international venues, where for financial and political reasons it would be impossible for the children who created the video to visit, she does so within a theatrical framework. She creates an altar before the screen, lighting candles, and reads a text to audiences that explains why the children are unable to travel abroad, and what the presentation represents. While the artifact in question is a video, her presentation of it fits Dubatti's conception of the *teatro-matriz*. Her own corporal poetics, the ritualized offerings she makes at the altar and the reading of the text, along with the conviviality and spectatorship, form a theatrical gesture. She is directing the audiences' attention not only to the work, but to the absence of the children who created it. By standing before the audience, in place of the performers themselves, she becomes a performer. Just as in *El rumor del incendio*, where Pardo's presence emphasizes the absence of her mother, Margarita, here her presence highlights the absence of the children of Yanhuitlán.

In the Emma S. Barrientos Mexican American Cultural Center (MACC) in Austin, Texas, Pardo presented the video in a performance called *Yanhuitlán*, as part of the city's Fusebox Festival. She asked audiences whether they understood Spanish, and took any nod of the head as affirmation for the whole group, reading the text she had prepared in the original language. The text, part of the performance *Yanhuitlán*, mentions the fact that in Yanhuitlán, the small town in Oaxaca where Pardo now lives and works, is a migrant town:

> The majority of those migrants entered this country illegally the first time. Because sometimes it is easier to cross the river and the desert on foot than to get a passport or a visa. I hope that in the future the boys and girls that I teach can be free to come or not to come, that it will be their choice, not a necessity, not an impediment. Today my students, with whom we created this piece, are not here, because there isn't enough money to bring them and because it would be almost impossible to get them a visa, we know why. That's why I brought these objects and they are on these screens, in their stead. (Pardo "Pre-Presentación Austin")[8]

The declaration, given only a few months after the presidential inauguration of Donald Trump amid his calls for a border wall, is an example of the *teatro-matriz*'s ability to direct the spectators' attention. Rather than a cute video made by far-away children about a distant historical event, the performance has now become part of the present-day discourse on human rights, colonialism, and migration.

Este cuerpo mío

Este cuerpo mío (This body of mine, 2016) is Mariana Villega's second solo contribution to Lagartijas's repertoire, following *Se rompen las olas*. Based on Kafka's "Ein Hungerkünstler" (A Hunger Artist), the one-woman auto/biographical show focuses on the process of losing weight and the difficulties Villegas faces as she navigates a society obsessed with body image and women's attractiveness. The play shares many aspects with its predecessor, such as the confessional tone and the uncomfortable display of the body in pain. As usual, the stage is dominated by a large screen on which photographs and video are projected. Similarly to *Se rompen las olas*, the stage is covered with a messy accumulation of objects, in this case articles of clothing (see figure 6).[9]

In addition to Kafka, the play is based on texts by Martín Caparrós, Umberto Eco, Clarice Lispector, Jean-Luc Nancy, and Alejandra Pizarnik. The intertextuality anchors the play in literature, with a particular emphasis on "A Hunger

FIGURE 6. Mariana Villegas in *Este cuerpo mío*.

Artist." Focusing on Villegas's body as larger than the norm, the play situates a topic that could easily turn confessional into art. Just as the hunger artist makes a performance of controlling his bodily functions and necessities, Villegas focuses audiences' attention on art. She abstracts the banal topic from the everyday, with otherworldly choreography, strange movements that do not seem to have a clear reference.

Villegas presents the story explicitly, in relationship to her autobiography: "There are ways to present oneself to the world, to narrate yourself to yourself. I do it through a story, "A Hunger Artist," by Franz Kafka. A story about animals and people, hungry to be seen by you, all of you. Yes, this is my story" (Lagartijas Tiradas al Sol, *Este cuerpo mío*).[10] Although theater, as Dubatti points out, has been reamplified now to include performance and literature, it retains its core characteristics of corporal poetics, spectatorship, and conviviality. Rather than the technological transmission of text present with narrative literature, here the transmission of Kafka's story is corporal, and infused with Villegas's own autobiography and embodiment—a creative act.

Once again, Villegas's piece strays from the norm of Lagartijas's works. As in *Se rompen las olas*, the political themes are subtle, present in subtext, rather than explicit. The politics of the gaze, however, are at the forefront. Kafka's hunger artist represents, for Villegas, the artist's desire to be seen—the desire for spectation. I interpret the play as a commentary on the state of theater itself. The hunger artist agrees to be locked in a cage and deprived of food so that he might be observed by the crowds. In the same way, in Mexico and the world, theater has been locked into the cage of modern drama for more than a century. Dubatti proposes unlocking the cage, allowing the original concept of theater to subsume all spectacle; Villegas uses the metaphor of the cage to free herself from dramatic expectations.

The performer who conforms to the cage is the hunger artist, fasting, denying himself the pleasure of the spectacle. Villegas breaks from the cage; in a series of conditional statements at the play's opening she mentions all the things she *could* talk about: capitalism, classification, beauty standards, growing up in Mexico City, racism, secret sexual relationships, Miss Universe. The emphasis on talking ("I could talk about ..." [*podría hablar de ...*]) points to the primacy of the text in dramatic theater; the terms and concepts she mentions plant the seeds for what the play is about without having to actually flesh them out in language. Rather, Villegas relies on the combination of the spoken literary text and her own body's movements to create meaning in the play.

Pancho Villa from a Safe Distance

Lagartijas, specifically Pardo and Rodríguez, wrote the libretto for *Pancho Villa from a Safe Distance*, an opera by Austin-based composer Graham Reynolds, which premiered in 2016 in Marfa, Texas. The opera opened with Pardo's recorded voice reading an "Auténtica oración al espíritu de Pancho Villa" (Authentic prayer to the spirit of Pancho Villa). The gesture suggests that the historical figure of the Mexican revolutionary has powers that endure even today, one hundred years after his death. The opera is interesting because it illuminates the border space between the United States and Mexico. The opera interacts with the sociopolitical context in which it was produced, proposing the border as a mirage. I approach the opera from a performance studies framework, as a practice, event, and behavior, not as an object. While I do not situate the opera within the Border Art tradition, it does inherit the tradition of the Border Art Workshop/Taller de Arte Fronterizo, with its bilingual character, its focus on performance, emphasis on site-specificity, and the border as a theme.[11]

I understand the opera as a cultural interaction, not only because of the Mexican content presented in Texas but also because of the collaboration between Texan and Mexican artists. I propose that the music, text, video, and acting interact to suggest a porous, dangerous, yet attractive border. The desert town of Marfa in West Texas has had the reputation of an artistic center ever since, in the 1970s, US artist Donald Judd moved from New York to the Chihuahua desert, bought a military base, and turned into a gigantic art exposition that is known today as the Chinati Foundation. The isolation of the site only augments its mythological status.

Marfa is not only an artistic town, it is also a border town. The Chinati Foundation has the Office of Border Control as a neighbor, and the Mexican state of Chihuahua is sixty miles away, between Presidio on the Texas side and Ojinaga on the Chihuahua side. It is in this environment that Reynolds produced his *Marfa Triptych: Three Portraits of West Texas*, a series of site-specific musical compositions.[12] The final entry in the series was the experimental chamber opera *Pancho Villa from a Safe Distance*. The opera features two singers, a tenor representing the revolutionary hero, and a mezzo-soprano, whose role is more diffuse.

As I mentioned, the opera begins with the prayer invoking the spirit of Pancho Villa, and ends with the tenor Paul Sánchez singing that his name is no longer Doroteo (Villa's given name), but rather that he is called Pancho Villa. The opera functions like a spiritist ritual that achieves the embodiment of the figure of the hero Pancho Villa.

The opera premiered three days after the election as US president of Donald Trump, who promised to build a wall between the United States and Mexico. The focus on a figure representing a threat to the state on both sides of the border leads to interesting conclusions about the representation of the border zone in the opera. Just as important as Villa himself is the desert where he was born. It is constantly represented in the lyrics and the slides projected on the big screen that served as a backdrop. Lagartijas's lyrics evoke a mysterious landscape with lines like "This terrible journey / Strange sunset" (*Esta terrible caminata / Extraña puesta del sol*) repeated slowly, chant-like. Some of the songs cite *norteña* music, with the driving beat of tuba and double bass situating the story within the particular space of the desert of northern Mexico.

Pancho Villa from a Safe Distance, through its artistic collaboration of participants from both sides of the river, proposes a vision of the border that recognizes its status as both imaginary and real. It proposes an imaginary border in the sense that it does not represent security, but its opposite. The opera recalls how tourists in El Paso, Texas, would pay to watch the Mexican Revolution from the safety of a hotel roof garden, through opera glasses—the idea that one could observe a war without being affected by it is a sick fantasy. Villa himself demonstrated the porosity of the border by crossing into New Mexico and killing nineteen people; his evasion of US troops, who sought him for a whole year, proved the impossibility of a "safe distance." At the same time the opera does not propose, because of its fantastical nature, that the border does not exist. The mysterious figure of "El Tigre," an adolescent from Oaxaca who walks across Mexico to visit the grave of Pancho Villa in a series of film interludes produced by Lagartijas and scattered throughout the opera, censures the fact that the difference between one side of the border and the other means the difference between life and death for thousands of people (Migrant Death Mapping).

Elisa

Elisa, also by Francisco Barreiro, premiered in 2017 at the Teatro El Milagro in Mexico City. Similar to *Veracruz, nos estamos defrorestando* by Pardo or Barreiro's own *Está escrita en sus campos*, this project is a scenic essay. As in the other two plays, rather than reenacting scenes, the actor takes his place at a lectern and presents, over the course of the performance, the results of an investigation. The project begins with a quote from Tita Gutiérrez, law professor and homicide detective in Coahuila, Mexico. Barreiro says that Gutiérrez gave him her book, *Tres océanos* (Three oceans), with an inscription: "A shared truth, is another kind of justice" (Lagartijas Tiradas al Sol, *Elisa*).[13] The presentation recounts how Gutiérrez's daughter, Elisa Loyo, a bright culinary student with a promising future, took a chef's internship at a resort in the Philippines and was murdered, only to have her death ruled accidental by the authorities there.

The book on which the performance is based recounts Gutiérrez's loss and the facts of her daughter's disappearance. Loyo's death led to street protests in Saltillo, Coahuila, the family hometown, against violence in general. Now funds from the book support the search for the disappeared. Though Loyo was killed in 2008, the story is especially relevant in 2017, when, as I outline in chapter 2 in my discussion of *Montserrat*, uninvestigated disappearances and murder with impunity are widespread problems in Mexico. In contrast to other plays by Lagartijas, this is similar to a prosecutor's presentation of his case. Barreiro lays out the background of Gutiérrez's and Loyo's lives, creating a vivid character study of the mother and daughter. As the narration moves into the fateful final days of Loyo's life, Barreiro presents doubt as to the motivations and credibility of Loyo's associates in the Phililppines. He presents phone records that contest official versions of her time of death. The audience becomes the jury, as Barreiro opts for a shared truth, another kind of justice, where international legal systems have failed.

Elisa, like *Santiago Amoukalli* and *Distrito Federal*, makes heavy use of the fog machine. The fog, present in all three of these indictments of official neglect and ineptitude, might represent a lack of clarity or transparency in official matters. In the case of *Elisa*, the fog blurs the vision of Elisa's grieving mother, who seeks answers about her daughter's death and, eventually, justice. At the performance I attended, a preview presented at the company's 2017 residency at Teatro El Milagro in Mexico City, Gutiérrez was present. Barreiro's teary acknowledgment of her attendance at the end of the show was an extratheatrical, yet powerful piece of evidence supporting the veracity of his claims.

Though Lagartijas characterizes *Elisa*, *Está escrita en sus campos*, and *Veracruz* as something other than theater—Pardo calls *Veracruz* a *conferencia*, or lecture, while Barreiro refers to his plays as *ensayos escénicos*—there is something to be gained by attending to Dubatti's claim that the *teatro-matriz* includes even this sort of performance. Lagartijas's worry is that theater will not be taken seriously because of theatricality's relationship to fiction. Its preoccupation with the real in their its documentary works intensifies in these works that purport to be fully nonfiction.

The distinction between fiction and fact becomes less urgent through the lens of the *teatro-matriz*. Whether or not the play can be considered documentary, scenic essay, or a dramatic production does not affect its status as theater.

Lagartijas in the World

As I have mentioned, Lagartijas is not operating in a vacuum. It is part of a growing movement within Latin American literature toward representing the real onstage. Indeed, theater of the real is a worldwide phenomenon. Within Mexico, Lagartijas joins Mexican playwright and director Conchi León and her company Sa'as Tun, with works like *Del manantial del corazón* (From the heart-spring, 2015), based on Mayan rituals surrounding the birth and death of children. Enrique Mijares characterizes the work as a biodrama, noting that León expresses her solidarity with the parents of children who died in the ABC nursery school fire, a tragedy that has gone unpunished (Mijares, "Las muestras curatoriales 2015" 278). Also in Mexico, David Jiménez Sánchez's 2014 play *Venimos a ver a nuestros amigos ganar* (We came to see our friends win) is a documentary play that details various examples of racial discrimination from all over the world, including Mexico. Another example of collective creation, *Cuando todos pensaban que habíamos desaparecido* (When everyone thought we had disappeared, 2015), directed by Damián Cervantes, includes family stories related to food that is prepared and shared with audience members in the course of the performance. The food theme is also found in *Desvenar: Mole escénico* (2015) by Richard Viqueira, which organizes a theatrical history of Mexico around its relationship to the chili. The play *Dicen que me parezco a Santa Anna . . . ¡y ni guitarra tengo!* (They say I look like Santa Anna . . . and I don't even have a guitar! 2014) by Isaac Pérez Calzada and Paola Izquierdo humorously stages the life of a controversial figure in Mexican history, General López de Santa Anna. Other collectives that work in the same realm of the real as Lagartijas in Mexico include Antonio Zúñiga's company Carretera 45 (Highway 45), located in the Obreros neighborhood of Mexico City, which often draws on residents' life experiences to devise its plays. Teatro Linea de Sombra, too, stages documentaries and representations of real history. A recent example, *Dura66o* focuses on the state of Durango in 1966.

In other countries, theater has been an official tool for dealing with national trauma. For example, in Peru, the Truth and Reconciliation Commission worked with the Grupo Yuyachkani to share its findings. In Brazil, *Lembrar é resistir . . .* the massacre of Afro-Colombians in Bojayá was recounted by the United Nations and the Colombian national government, as well as in journalistic reports.[14] The tragedy also inspired *Bojayá: Los cinco misterios de un genocidio* (Boyjayá: The five mysteries of a genocide) by theater groups Génesis and El Malpensante (Jaramillo 110) and *Kilele: Una epopeya artesanal* (Kilele: A homemade epic) by Felipe Vergara of the Grupo de Teatro Versanta (Jaramillo 111). Also in Colombia, Tramaluna Teatro staged *Antígonas, tribunal de mujeres* (Antigones, women's court) in 2014, a collaboration between theater artists and victims of human rights violations, while Humberto Dorado and Matías Maldonado produced *El deber de Fenster* (Fenster's duty) in Colombia in 2009, a documentary drama about the massacre of Trujillo in that country. In El Salvador, Teatro del Azoro undertook a similar endeavor with *Made in Salvador . . . Y de bordar en bordar se me fue la vida* (Made in El Salvador . . . And stitch by stitch my life left me, 2014). More recently in Bolivia, Percy Jiménez, wrote and directed *Tamayo* (2015), on opposition leaders murdered by President Gualberto Villarroel.

This incomplete sampling of plays from the region demonstrates the proliferation of theatrical works that deal with urgent national issues, often through the auto/biographical and genealogical lens. Rather than staging historical fiction or a dramatized version of events, these plays all attempt to connect the audience with reality. As Martin says, theater of the real scrutinizes the making of history; Lehmann insists on its energetic rather than informational impulses. However, these plays, and those of Lagartijas, not only scrutinize history but also propose to make history. They are the repository of the real stories they re-create; in many cases there are no other archives to access.

Throughout this book I have shown that Lagartijas Tiradas al Sol is exemplary of trends that are occurring throughout Latin America, in particular collective creation and devised theater. This is rooted in the 1960s, as we have seen. Collective creation, in the face of translated, commercial theater, is rooted in the tradition of establishing a national theater in the twentieth century, when Latin American theater broke away from peninsular theater. It eschews even those famous national dramas and moves beyond collective creation's limits to create works where only the artists themselves can present them. Even collective creation might result in a script, such as *Los papeles del infierno*, which someone else may act out, but with Lagartijas's autobiographical works, only the autobiographers themselves may stage the play and retain its autobiographical meaning. Therefore, auto/biographical theater and focus on family stories are two more widespread tendencies that Lagartijas's work exemplifies. Autobiography also has a tradition in Latin America, for example, in the unipersonal works of Argentina's dictatorship and postdictatorship periods. Lagartijas's brand of auto/biography, however, expands to include more than the narrating subject, subsuming the biographies of family members to explain the self. Pardo's auto/biographical works, then, include not only her own life story but also her mother's. In this way, she must be the one acting in the play, starring as herself and claiming authority over her mother's story. Lagartijas members use family stories as well as their own bodies as evidence to expand the concept of autobiography.

Lagartijas's works are localized and individualized, and the company claims authority and ownership over its plays. This possessiveness and uniqueness resists adaptation and, therefore, appropriation. Finally, the company's focus on national history is indicative of a wider interest that can be seen throughout the Latin American region in the theater. The actors insert themselves, by way of the family, into national histories. This again is rooted in the history dramas of the twentieth century. Rodolfo Usigli, of course, is heavily focused on Mexican national history in his plays. He questions the production of history through his metahistorical plays. *El gesticulador*, for example, focuses on the concept that history is an idea that is written, created, and mediated. Another link can be drawn to *testimonio* literature and drama of the twentieth century, where the personal story of an individual or collective is mediated through a "compiler" (*compilador*), as John Beverley puts it (*Testimonio*).

Lagartijas is addressing some of the problems that occur with the narration of history and compilation of *testimonio*. By putting themselves on stage and serving as the voice of their own life story or family story, the performers obscure the role of the theater as mediator from the spectator's view. Obviously, these stories are still being mediated. They must be workshopped, scripted, blocked, directed, staged, and so on. By offering up their own bodies as evidence, however, as the body that lived through the experience and is now reenacting it as a factual representation, they obscure the levels of mediation that occur in history or testimony. The level of self, family, and nation all work together, based in Latin American theater history. Lagartijas's work is one of many examples indicative of what Carol Martin calls theater of the real.

In theater of the real, the theater claims its position as a source for "truth" and "the real." By erasing the mediation or attempting to obscure it, Lagartijas is claiming theater, and perhaps the arts in general, as a reliable source of facts. It is accusing other sources of being unreliable, especially governmental sources. It is almost as though it has found a way to make a postmodern, jaded audience naive again. The body is the key element in this operation. With postmodernism, everyone accepts that documentary is a construction, as is history; everyone knows you cannot trust the news or the government; and yet . . . The theater and theatricality, which is a place of fiction, becomes this space where we want to believe, where audiences return to an innocent and naive space and want to accept the body as evidence. The audience, then, is betrayed. We can see this in many contemporary examples. In Lola Arias's production of *Mi vida después*, when the show travels it cannot often bring the tortoise one actor uses as a demonstration of his father's long life and relatability. They merely replace his father's pet with another, locally available animal, like a rabbit.

Lagartijas and Latin American theater of the real more generally point to the idea that even if the details are not all clear, but instead blurry or modified, there is still an underlying truth. In *Montserrat*, for example, Gabino does not find his mother. She is dead. The story his father and aunts told him as a child was true. But what he is able to communicate by staging his dream of a reunion with his mother, all these years later, is a real and true desire of an orphaned son to see his mother again. In *Santiago Amoukalli*, too, Luisa and Gabino may have had experiences very similar to those portrayed in the play, but the town of Santiago Amoukalli does not exist. It is a fiction, just as the play's narration warns its audiences. And yet, audiences believe it and they want to do something about it. They want to know what Pardo and Rodríguez have done about the massacre they uncovered. The play, then, reveals a deep injustice present in Mexican society; deep racial and ethnic divisions that marginalize indigenous people, economic divisions, divisions between those with and without cultural capital, between urban and rural populations. The play reveals an underlying truth about these differences that are life and death to those experiencing them everyday.

Lagartijas's work tells us that this kind of communication of reality can be done in the theater. Even in an age when digital technology has opened doors for recording, archiving, and sharing information, when facts are constantly challenged even as there is a proliferation of information, getting back to the basics of human communion and ritual is a way to connect with the truth. The presence of the body is a way to find our contact with reality. By positing the theater as a source of truth, Lagartijas is not claiming to be the source of news or history, it is directing spectators back to the body as the source of knowledge and truth.

In this final chapter, where I have reviewed information about Lagartijas's more recent plays, I note an accelerated proliferation of work. What was often a collective effort with multiple actors in the beginning has split into a confederation of actors creating personal projects simultaneously, supporting and cross-pollinating one another. At the same time that the various actors have begun to work on personal projects there is also a renewed interest in telling the stories of others.

Whereas the company's autobiographical focus had taken the forefront earlier in the company's trajectory, now it turns to the other. Plays like *Elisa*, and *Está escrita en sus campos* function more as testimonial plays than autobiographical ones. Even *Veracruz*, which does include Pardo's autobiographical perspective, focuses on the story of the silenced activist Nadia Vera, speaking on her behalf after her brutal assassination. The political turn of *testimonio* and speaking for those who are no longer alive rests on the earlier auto/biographical pieces. The company has gained its audiences trust by sharing its own stories and bodies as credible evidence.

This is indicative of theater trends throughout the Latin American region. In Brazil the Cia. Teatro Documentário, Oficina Teatro, and, of course, August Boal's influence, which remains very present within Brazilian theater. In Argentina creators like Vivi Tellas are working at the vanguard of this kind of production, staging nonactors as themselves, reenacting the lives of parents in light of their relationship to the dictatorship—these techniques are extremely influential, as can be noted in Peru, with Sebastian Rubio and Claudia Tangoa's production of *1980/2000*. This tendency creates a sense of alternatives. I have used the term "alternative" throughout this book to indicate an option other than officialdom. This type of theater is simultaneously challenging the idea of an objective reality, official news sources, government, history, and journalism, and presenting itself as a place where, in the face of censorship and noncredible discourses, there is a source of reality. But it also points to the idea that reality lies in the communion, the ritual, which is also where resistance lives.

The theater has, indeed, escaped some level of censorship because it is not entirely controlled by the government or by Televisa.[15] Theater, then, has more freedom to offer alternative visions of the group to an audience, albeit a select one. In this way, the theater can subvert authoritarian control of the media. Mexico's ruling party, as well as those in power throughout the hemisphere, depend on control or influence over the government for maintaining power. Alternative sources of information, therefore, are available to challenge hegemonic power structures and offer a vision for returning to very basic human technologies such as the projection of voice, gesture, music, images, light, sound, facial expression, and costuming. All these elements of theater are very basic technologies that, interestingly enough, are also the basic ingredients of resistance to hegemony.

Altering one's uniform is a mode of resistance. Using one's voice even as one's body is bound is a mode of resistance. Silence might be imposed, but facial expressions are a mode of expression. Images can be used to signal to others even in the absence of language. Finally, the simultaneous presence of bodies in one space, the gathering, is a form of resistance that contrasts vividly with the model of individuals staring at individual screens, receiving information in isolation. The theater of Lagartijas Tiradas al Sol invites audiences to be present, to gather, and to resist, so that a kind of justice might be achieved.

Appendix A

List of Festival Appearances

2005

Festival de Teatro Universitario, Mexico City, Mexico, *Pía*

2006

Festival Cultural Otoño en Lagos, Lagos de Moreno, Mexico, *Pía*
Muestra Nacional de Teatro, Pachuca, Mexico, *Asalto al agua transparente*

2007

Festival Cultural Otoño en Lagos, Lagos de Moreno, Mexico, *Asalto al agua transparente*
Festival de Teatro de Nuevo León, Monterrey, Mexico, *Asalto al agua transparente*
Festival Nacional de Teatro, Sinaloa, Mexico, *Asalto al agua transparente*
Festival Universitario de Teatro Baja California, Tijuana, Mexico,
Asalto al agua transparente
Fiestas del Pitic, Hermosillo, Mexico, *Asalto al agua transparente*
Muestra Nacional de Teatro, Zacatecas, Mexico, *En el mismo barco*

2008

Encuentro y Festival Teatro y Memoria, Cuernavaca, Mexico, *Asalto al agua transparente*
Festival de Teatro de Nuevo León, Monterrey, Mexico, *Asalto al agua transparente* and
En el mismo barco
Festival Universitario de Teatro Baja California, Tijuana, Mexico, *En el mismo barco*
Fiestas del Pitic, Hermosillo, Mexico, *En el mismo barco*

2010

Festival de Teatro de Nuevo León, Monterrey, Mexico, *Catalina*
Festival TransAmériques de Montreal, Montreal, Canada, *Asalto al agua transparente* and
Catalina

2011

Festival d'Automne à Paris, Paris, France, *El rumor del incêndio* and *Asalto al agua transparente*

Festival Impatience, Paris, France, *Asalto al agua transparente*

Foro Re/Posiciones, Mexico City, Mexico, *El rumor del incendio*

Kunstenfestivaldesarts, Brussels, Belgium, *El rumor del incendio*

Zürcher Theater Spektakel, Zurich, Switzerland, *El rumor del incendio*

2012

Cena Contemporânea, Brasília, Brazil, *El rumor del incendio*

Festival Ambulante, Acapulco and Chilpancingo, Mexico, *El rumor del incendio*

Festival de Teatro de Nuevo León, Monterrey, Mexico, *El rumor del incendio*

Festival Escena Contemporánea, Madrid, Spain, *El rumor del incendio*

Festival Internacional de Artes Cênicas, Salvador da Bahia, Brazil, *Asalto al agua transparente*

Festival Theaterformen, Braunschweig, Germany, *El rumor del incendio*

Festwochen, Vienna, Austria, *El rumor del incendio*

Muestra Nacional de Teatro, San Luis Potosí, Mexico, *El rumor del incendio*

Sibfest, Sibiu, Romania, *El rumor del incendio*

Time-Based Art Festival, Portland, Oregon, US, *El rumor del incendio* and *Asalto al agua transparente*

2013

BAD Bilbao, Festival de Teatro y Danza Contemporánea, Bilbao, Spain, *Montserrat*

Dialog Festival, Wrocław, Poland, *El rumor del incendio*

Encuentro de Teatro de Pequeño Formato Caín, Guadalajara, Spain, *Montserrat*

Encuentro Sacbé, Yucatán, Mexico, *Derretiré con un cerillo la nieve de un volcán*, *Montserrat* and *Se rompen las olas*

Festival de Artes Escénicas, Lima, Peru, *El rumor del incendio*

Festival de México, Mexico City, Mexico, *Derretiré con un cerillo la nieve de un volcán*

Festival de otoño, Madrid, Spain, *Derretiré con un cerillo la nieve de un volcán*

Festival de Otoño a Primavera, Madrid, Spain, *Derretiré con un cerillo la nieve de un volcán*

Festival Intermedio, Xalapa, Mexico, *Está escrito en sus campos*

Festival Internacional de Buenos Aires, Buenos Aires, Argentina, *El rumor del incendio*

Festival of International New Drama, Berlin, Germany *Derretiré con un cerillo la nieve de un volcán*

Festival Temporada Alta, Girona, Spain, *Montserrat*

Fusebox Festival, Austin, Texas, US, *El rumor del incendio*

Kunstenfestivaldesarts, Brussels, Belgium, *Derretiré con un cerillo la nieve de un volcán*

Radar L.A. Festival, Los Angeles, US, *Se rompen las olas*

Santiago a Mil, Santiago, Chile, *Se rompen las olas, Montserrat,* and *El rumor del incendio*

Teatro a una Sola Voz, Various cities, Mexico, *Se rompen las olas*

VIE Scena Contemporanea Festival, Modena, Italy, *Se rompen las olas*

2014

CounterCurrent Festival, Houston, Texas, US, *El rumor del incendio*
Festival de Monólogos Teatro a una Sola Voz, Coahuila, Mexico, *Se rompen las olas*
Festival Temporada Alta, Girona, Spain, *Derretiré con un cerillo la nieve de un volcán*

2015

Ambulante, Xalapa, Mexico, *Montserrat*
CASA Latin American Theatre Festival, London, United Kingdom, *Montserrat*
Cena Contemporânea, Rio de Janeiro, Brazil, *Montserrat*
Encuentro de Teatro de Pequeño Formato Caín, Guadalajara, Mexico, *Está escrito en sus campos*
Festival Cosmicómico de Teatro Alternativo Internacional, Zacatecas, Mexico, *Montserrat*
Festival Internacional de Teatro Carmen, Ciudad del Carmen, Campeche, Mexico, *Derretiré con un cerillo la nieve de un volcán*
Festival Internacional de Teatro de Caracas, Caracas, Venezuela, *Está escrito en sus campos*
Festival Temporada Alta, Girona, Spain, *Está escrito en sus campos*
Heidelberger Stückemarkt, Heidelberg, Germany, *Se rompen las olas*
II Bienal de Teatro da USP, São Paulo, Brazil, *El rumor del incêndio*

2016

BAD Bilbao, Festival de Teatro y Danza Contemporánea, Bilbao, Spain *Veracruz, nos estamos deforestando o como extrañar Xalapa* and *Tijuana*
El lugar sin límites, Madrid, Spain, *Veracruz, nos estamos deforestando o como extrañar Xalapa*
Escenas do Cambio, Santiago de Compostela, Spain, *Veracruz, nos estamos deforestando o como extrañar Xalapa* and *Tijuana*
Estación final: Nostaliga. Teatro en México, Munich, Germany, *Está escrito en sus campos* and *Se rompen las olas*
Festival Belluard Bollwerk International, Fribourg, Switzerland, *Santiago Amoukalli*
Festival de la Joven Dramaturgia, Querétaro, Mexico, *La democracia en México 1965–2015*
Festival Latino-Americano de Teatro da Bahia, Salvador da Bahia, Brazil, *Tijuana*
Festival Temporada Alta, Girona, Spain, *Santiago Amoukalli, Veracruz, nos estamos deforestando o como extrañar Xalapa* and *Tijuana*
Festival TNT, Terrasa, Spain, *Veracruz, nos estamos deforestando o como extrañar Xalapa*
Inteatro Festival, Ancona, Italy, *Tijuana*
International Theater Festival MESS, Sarajevo, Bosnia and Herzegovina, *El rumor del incendio*
La Corunda Escénica: Encuentro de Poéticas Jóvenes en torno a la Teatralidad y la Violencia, Morelia, Mexico, *Está escrito en sus campos*
Le Vie dei Festival, Rome, Italy, *Tijuana*

2017

Festival of International New Drama, Berlin, Germany, *Tijuana*

Festival Temporada Alta, Lima, Peru, *Veracruz, nos estamos deforestando o como extrañar Xalapa*

Fusebox Festival, Austin, Texas, US, *Tijuana, Yanhuitlán* and *Pancho Villa from a Safe Distance*

Kammerspiel Munich, Munich, Germany, *Está escrita en sus campos*

Residencies

2010 Residence and Reflection, Kunstenfestivaldesarts, Brussels, Belgium

2011 Artistic Residency, Festival SISMO, Madrid, Spain

2013 Center for New Performance, Los Angeles, US

2016 Inteatro, Polverigi, Italy

2017 Teatro El Milagro, Mexico City, Mexico

Awards and Honors

Best Direction and Best Play, Festival de Teatro Universitario, Mexico City, Mexico, 2005

Audience Award for Best Play, Festival Impatience, Paris, France, 2011

ZKB Patronage Prize, Theater Spektakel, Zurich, Switzerland, 2011

Appendix B

Interview with Lagartijas Tiradas al Sol

La Rebeldía (Rebellion) is made up of three parts: the blog, the play, and the book, and each one represents an enormous amount of research. What was the process like to produce a project like this one?

Luisa Pardo (LP): In reality it started with a series of interviews—first, the topic was rebellion, before anything else . . . We began to do interviews with active people, in different professions, that we considered to be exercising resistance, rebellion. And we had about ten or fifteen interviews that you don't see directly in the play, but what we discussed was what gives us a certain panorama, fills out a sphere of ideas for us, and gives us clear reference points. Then, after the interviews, the research began. We did research for about a year. First we began with rebellion.

And was the focus always on Mexico?

LP and Gabino Rodríguez (GR): No.

LP: No, it was rebellion in general, and then we realized that we had to cut it down to Mexico. And after Mexico we cut it down to the 60s, the guerrilla, specifically the armed movements. Because we also had peaceful movements, union movements, but with so much it's impossible.

GR: But we started with the idea that artistic creation does not necessarily have to do with the interior of a person who imagines things in solitude . . . nor with our own interiority. For us, our premise was to go out and recover the reality of certain things, and then to withdraw, and afterward to see how to organize it, more than the idea of creating or inventing something that wasn't there before.

LP: And parallel to that, we did the research into my mom's life, about which we didn't know anything. We had ideas—the idea that she was in jail—but then it was a matter of finding her letters, interviewing her friends, family, I don't know. So parallel to that research [on the guerrilla], was the research on Margarita.

Francisco Barreiro (FB): Exactly—the two begin in the same moment. The source for Margarita was the source for many things that occur, documented things.

GR: Yes, that was where the parallel was born, which in the beginning wasn't there. In fact, Luisa had already done a play about her mother some time before.[1]

Was that also an attempt to document her life?

LP: No, in reality . . . who knows what it was? As her death was still very fresh, it was more about pain. It was more sensorial and emotional than documentary.

GR: It was not at all documentary.

So you have always had this interest in putting the personal onstage.

FB, LP, GR: Yes.

And where does this come from? Does it have to do with our generation?

FB: Well, I don't know. There are various factors. It has to do with what we want to say with the theater's own power. I think that at a certain point Gabino told me, many years ago, something like "to tell stories is ingenuous." And I think that telling stories is ingenuous, that we can use our brains for many things, and I think that it's that same maturation—

LP: We were in theater school, and we realized that theater is very distant from *being*. Mexican theater distances itself from the spectator because it seems like it's not talking about anyone, like it's not talking about anything. It's abstractions. And there is a certain type of theater that is like that, that is very well done and serves to entertain you, to understand universalities, no? But, suddenly, we were searching for how to approach ourselves as actors, as creators, and also as spectators, how we approach the theater. How can we make theater have a real connection with individuals?

GR: And also, as we really like theater, we studied it and we liked it, but theater has something in common with the museum, with the idea that there are certain plays written to be staged over and over again, forever and ever. It was difficult to be theater actors, and play characters when, surely, there are other people who do a better job. There is something, yes, a little impersonal in the idea of playing Hamlet; in a way it could be me, it could be another actor, and we liked the idea of doing plays that could only be staged with *those* people. That could not be [played] by other people. . . .

LP: To think that we are indispensable, that it really belongs to us. Right now, currently, a topic I am thinking about is that everything is disposable, and everything is distant, and everything is passing. But we want, or we try to make, theater that comes out naturally, to make theater that is all of our life. Every play is a piece of our life, and we are growing along with the play and the play is always reforming. That is, our company is a process that goes along with our life and shows how we are learning things and with whom we want to work. I think that the theater goes right along with our life and that is the objective. We aren't bureaucrats of theater, we aren't maquiladoras of theater, but rather we are very conscious of the personal part of theater.

There are those that complain that today nothing is private, that everyone is publishing their life on Facebook and Twitter. Is this a parallel tendency, but more polished and made with reflection?

GR: Of course, and it has to do with the fact that yes, we are in the era of the reality show, which didn't exist before. But the idea of responsibility that we feel is that someone could ask us, "Why did you do this?" and we would have to answer them; that is, we are the responsible parties for what we do. So, the idea of responsibility, and the idea that the personal doesn't necessarily have to be . . . how to put it?

LP: Sick?

GR: Sick and stupid, no? Because there is something that is going on, like a generalized idea that is: "Damn, people's lives are shit. You see a reality show, and it's stupidity, you go on Facebook and it's all idiotic comments." And, well, I think that the idea that that is not true might be recovered, that people's lives are awesome, and the media proposes things that, perhaps, aren't so fun, but people's lives are interesting; that is what art is always going to talk about.

LP: And also to recover, in a way, oral history. The recuperation of memory, this very history of the guerrilla hasn't been told. It has been told in different books, and perhaps it is opening up more, but all of our generation, and official history, well, it's an abandoned history—isn't it?—which really contributed to democratic growth in this country. And I think that in this moment it is very important that we reflect: what did our parents do? and what would we have to do in this moment in this country? Or, is there nothing left to do? That is, it isn't just the recuperation of the personal but rather of the collective history, the collective memory.

It was interesting to me how you treated memory in the play *El rumor del incendio*, with the ludic parts using toys to represent battles. One gets the feeling that the children of the people who participated in and lived through these stories, without knowing or wanting to, interpret these stories through play. And also, in the scene of Margarita's torture, you applied makeup very deliberately in front of the audience, Luisa, to represent the wounds, and that emphasizes the theatrical representation of a true story, a received memory—inherited—that is yours at the same time that it isn't. That creates a different kind of distance than the one you mentioned before, a generational distance.

GR: Yes, and it's also always a little difficult to think about how to do those scenes. I think we tried to come in with rifles, and things like that.

LP: Yes, and do battle.

GR: Yes, yes. But it seemed a little stupid to me. And that is one of the things that the theater normally permits, no? like, "Dudududududu! [imitating machine gun] . . . Oh, there they are!" We didn't have a way to approach something that, for us, was as foreign as picking up rifles.

FB: We looked ridiculous.

GR: And the toys, in a way, were cool for that reason. They generated the same sensations that we have. Now there isn't political repression of the Mexican middle class as there was in those days. That is, we can scream, "Damn the President," during the play and nothing happens. In a way [in comparison] it's like child's play, what we are living through. Which is not bad, it's good.

LP: We are appropriating a story that isn't ours, and we are trying to tell it. And how do we make the spectator feel like we don't have the truth either, and we are not representing it? Because the representation, perhaps, would be a little more like pride, because it would say that I have the truth and I am speaking with the truth. Here are the facts, which are also questionable.

So you began with interviews and research, and then chose the character of Margarita as the unifying thread?

LP: We began to research Margarita's history too, and we realized that that could work as the unifying thread. That was when we decided that beginning with Margarita's history, we would tell the other, we would make the parallel . . . We began with the assault on the military headquarters in Madera, and Margarita's story begins there too. And the assault on the Cuartel Madera is a very important model for the armed movements in Mexico, so that was a coincidence.

FB: Although later, yes, if not, we would have connected them in another moment. Because we also could have begun in the 40s, which was also very important for what happened later, to the EZLN [Ejército Zapatista de Liberación Nacional (Zapatista Army of National Liberation)], and it was difficult. But the process itself was asking us: What is it that we have to say, and when, and how?

LP: In reality, with Margarita's story, everything was written in third person, and I narrated it. And it was a lightbulb moment when Gabino said to me, "No, it has to be told in first person, it must be told in first person . . ." And I said, "But I don't know my mom's story." And that I think is something very important that we have been losing, that conversation among family members. I think that is the function of this play, to tell the story of our parents, that no one has told us, not even them. So the recuperation of family history, of generational parents, by which I mean, all of our parents.

. . .

What do you think that theater can do in today's society, with its defects and needs?

LP: I think that the theater is a mode of communication par excellence. And besides that it is an art that goes in a contrary direction to the contemporary. It is what is alive, it is the "I see you," "I'm here, present and you have to listen, and you have to wait."

FB: And you have to behave yourself, too!

GR: It's a little authoritarian.

LP: Much more than solemnities, it is to speak of true communication between human beings, of communication not just verbal but also energetic, and I think that exactly what theater can do is create sensitivity and recover memory and make people reflect.

FB: Yes, I believe that it is a medium that is very powerful in every sense, no? And you have to decide in what way you will exercise that power. . . . And it has to do with that, with generating an impact, in every sense.

GR: Although at the same time it is an impact for very few people, not something like—

LP:—massive. That goes against the contemporary moment, too, that it's the personal, the energetic, the live.

GR: It is something that absolutely doesn't follow any type of rules. Something that costs a lot, commercially speaking, because it costs a lot of money, costs a lot of time. It is difficult, even for big business, to make theater a business; for as much as a Broadway musical is a Broadway musical, it will never be even a third of what a Hollywood movie is. So it is always very expensive to travel, it's tough . . . it's an ancient medium.

FB: I get the sensation sometimes with theater that there is no memory. It isn't like a movie that you can watch anytime you want and refresh your memory and see the scenes; it's something that happens and that in some moment will be forgotten, no?

LP: Or that the memory remains in—

FB:—in the sensorial.

GR: Of some people. That's it . . . its virtue and its defect. Its defect is that it is an art that is very difficult to study, that is, that cannot be studied, and it is difficult to make progress because you can't cite it, no? While you can cite cinema, if you want a certain scene of a particular movie you can watch it. In literature you can read the book. And that allows a lot of depth. In the theater it has to do more with a certain immediacy, and with a personal experience with something, and something that is going to remain with some people and that's it, it will vanish . . .

LP: And, well, in this country, as we have so many social problems, there are few people with access to the theater, very few. The theaters are empty. The theaters—

not the commercial ones, not those belonging to Telmex, and Televisa, which are fine—but the theaters where a reflection is created moderately, those, in general, those are empty. And besides, the people that can access it are of a certain class and so . . . in that sense in this country it is very difficult to create a consistent dialogue. That's why working in a company concerns us and interests us, to create continuity and an audience. And I think that little by little we have managed to generate a consistent audience. Several times we've been told, "I see a continuity between your first play and this one, and when I saw this other one . . ." In this sense it's very enriching, because that's what memory is, no? Memory is the dialogue between the audience and the company. It isn't just an isolated work, but rather this entire process in which we have been involved, that without an audience that has been consistent, would not exist.

Notes

Foreword

1. Lagartijas Tiradas al Sol, "El rumor del incendio, Proyecto La Rebeldía," lagartijastiradasalsol.blogspot.mx/p/el-rumor.html.

Introduction

1. "Fue el narrador y dramaturgo Vicente Leñero (1933–2014), pilar fundamental para la historia del teatro mexicano del siglo veinte, quizá por su oficio y pasión por el periodismo, uno de los que asiduamente utilizaron fuentes documentales en la escritura de algunos de sus dramas" (Salcedo 99).

2. For my analysis of both *Pueblo rechazado* and *La fiera del Ajusco*, see Julie Ann Ward, "Making Reality Sensible."

3. Alison Oddey defines a devised theater performance as "originat[ing] with the group while making the performance, rather than starting from a play text that someone else has written to be interpreted. A devised theatre product is work that has emerged from and been generated by a group of people working in collaboration" (1).

4. In English, Lizards Lounging in the Sun. In this study, I call the company by its full name in Spanish or, for short, Lagartijas (Lizards).

5. See Martin, *Dramaturgy of the Real on the World Stage* and *Theatre of the Real*, and Forsyth and Megson for numerous examples of the genre from North America, Europe, and Africa.

6. See the master's thesis of Lina J. Morales Chacana, and doctoral dissertations by Lilia Adriana Pérez Limón and Julie Ann Ward.

7. See Appendix A: List of Festival Appearances for a history of Lagartijas's festival activity.

8. For an ecocritical reading of *Asalto al agua transparente*, see Compton, "Green/Activist Mexican History." Meanwhile, for discussions of *El rumor del incendio* and its place within Latin American postdramatic and documentary theater, respectively, see Morales Chacana and Sabugal Paz. The growing use of the documentary genre by theater collectives, rather than individual authors is analyzed in Salcedo. Finally, see the excellent essay on how the anthropological concept of liminality can help explain postdramatic works like *Montserrat* by Prieto Stambaugh and Toriz Proenza.

9. For more examples of the tendency toward producing theater of the real in series or cycles, see Vivi Tellas's *Archivos* [Archives] project or the series she curated for the Teatro Sarmiento in Buenos Aires, the *Ciclo Biodrama* [Biodrama cycle].

10. *En el mismo barco*'s presentation in the important annual theater festival the Mues-tra Nacional de Teatro in 2007 received critical acclaim. The writer, scholar, and director Ricard Salvat saw fit to name every member of the group in his review of the marathon of plays at the festival, citing the group's "buena factura y . . . adecuada unidad interpretativa" [good execution and appropriate interpretative unity] (434). (All translations are mine un-less otherwise indicated.) Playwright and author Enrique Mijares, reporting on the Mues-tra Nacional in *Latin American Theatre Review*, judged *En el mismo barco* to be the most outstanding entry ("Muestra Mexicana de Teatro 2007" 135). Though most critics agreed on its relevance and excellence, some did find the collective creation process and the theme of the end of utopias to be tired (see Harmony, "XXVIII Muestra Nacional").

11. See chapter 2 for a discussion of generational themes in Lagartijas's work.

12. I use the slash in auto/biographical following Sidonie Smith and Julia Watson's definition in their helpful list of genres of life narrative: "*Auto/biography, or a/b*. This acro-nym signals the interrelatedness of auto-biographical narrative and biography. Although the slash marks their fluid boundary, they are in several senses different, even opposed, forms. . . . The term also designates a mode of the autobiographical that inserts biography/ies within an autobiography, or the converse, a personal narrative within a biography" (256). The duality of the term is particularly apt when dealing with Lagartijas's theater, which constantly embeds autobiographies within the biographies of family members and within national history. Lagartijas's plays constantly intermingle the biographical and the autobiographical, inviting viewers to question the possibility of ever separating out a life from those it is connected to.

13. "Hay algo, sí, un poco impersonal de la idea de hacer Hamlet, de alguna manera tal vez podría ser yo, podría ser otro actor, y nos gustaba la idea de hacer obras que sólo se podían hacer con esas personas. Que no pudiera ser otras personas."

14. "Pensar que somos indispensables, que realmente es algo propio. Justo en la con-temporaneidad, un tema en que estoy pensando, todo es desechable y todo es ajeno y todo es pasajero. . . . No somos burócratas del teatro, no somos maquiladoras del teatro, sino somos muy conscientes de la parte personal del teatro."

15. An exception to this resistance toward adaptation includes *En el mismo barco*. Lagartijas's text was used as the basis for an adaptation of the play by the company Tristes Tigres.

16. See chapter 2 for a discussion of the use of government archives, which had been sealed, to reconstruct this time in history.

17. For an excellent study of Argentine autobiographical theater, see Beatriz Trastoy.

18. "La presencia de una corporalidad explícita o de una narrativa íntimamente person-al no es garantía de estar ante la 'la verdad.' Más bien, lo que demuestran es que el cuerpo está atravesado por discursos e ideologías, que lo personal es siempre colectivo, que la re-alidad de nuestros cuerpos, de nuestras historias personales y de la historia oficial depende de la interpretación, así como de la re-presentación que se les dé" (Prieto Stambaugh 207).

[The presence of an explicit corporality or an intimately personal narrative is not a guarantee of being before "the truth." Rather, what it demonstrates is that the body is traversed by discourses and ideologies, that the personal is always collective, that the reality of our bodies, of our personal histories and official history depends upon interpretation, as well as on the re-presentation given them.]

19. Taylor explains: "The repertoire requires presence: people participate in the production and reproduction of knowledge by 'being there,' being a part of the transmission" (*Archive* 20).

20. "uma maneira específica de análise das práticas performativas. Esse tipo de análise pretende enfatizar a dimensão de presencialidade, de tangibilidade e de coisidade que tais práticas possuem, na medida em que são práticas corporais por excelência, procurando tirar a ênfase dos significados que atribuímos a elas. Assim, os Estudos da Presença se articulam . . . em torno do objetivo de evitar a interpretação como único e exclusivo acesso à verdade e ao conhecimento."

Chapter 1: Enacting the Collective

1. For a brief account of the rhetoric of a glorious indigenous past in the construction of Mexican national identity, see Héctor Aguilar Camín.

2. It is worth noting that the aforementioned Rubio is the son of two members of Yuyachkani, further extending the theatrical connections between generations.

3. Mexican theater has long been preoccupied with national history. Patricia Ybarra has documented theatrical performances of the Spanish conquest in the eighteenth and nineteenth centuries in the city of Tlaxcala in particular, though many critics focus on the masterpiece of Rodolfo Usigli, *El gesticulador* [The impostor] (1938), as the foundation of modern Mexican drama. Stuart Day shows that this historiographic tendency has been questioned in favor of considering other, prior works as worthy of critical attention ("Performing Mexico" 155–59). *El gesticulador* and Usigli's *Corona de sombra* [Crown of shadows] (1943) each deal explicitly with historical themes: the Mexican Revolution and the Second Mexican Empire, respectively. The playwright himself calls *Corona de sombra* an antihistorical play, meaning that he seeks less to portray verifiable facts than to reflect on history through theater. See the works of Priscilla Meléndez and Kirsten Nigro for excellent commentaries on Usigli's idea of antihistory in *Corona de sombra*. For historical approaches to *El gesticulador*, see works by Pedro Bravo-Elizondo and Mabel Moraña. Mark Frisch compares both plays to historical discourse in Borges's fiction. Sergio Magaña's 1953 historical play *Moctezuma II*, about the last Aztec ruler, is considered by some to be the best piece of theater on the Aztec empire (Serna 87).

4. "Recuerdo en particular las lluvias de la época de la crisis no había nada de dinero pero había mucha lluvia [*sic*]."

5. "Fracasados en época de fracasos."

6. The Mexican peso crisis followed the implementation of the North American Free

Trade Agreement (NAFTA) in January 1994, the Zapatista uprising in the southern state of Chiapas the same month, the assassination of the ruling party's presidential candidate, Luis Donaldo Colosio, mere months before the election, the government's devaluing of the peso, and, finally, severe inflation and recession. The moment is a turning point for Mexicans of Rodríguez's generation, who came of age in a time of great economic stress. For a helpful summary of the economic crisis, see Whitt (1–4). Also see Sabina Berman's theatrical works that explicitly treat the 1994 crisis, like *El gordo, la pájara y el narco* [The fat man, the chick, and the drug dealer] or the aptly named *Krisis* [Crisis] (1996). See Bixler "El teatro de la crisis" and Rojas for excellent studies of Berman's portrayals of the crisis.

7. For further reading on the guerrilla in twentieth-century Mexico, see S. Castañeda, Castellanos, or Glockner (in Spanish) or Aviña, McCormick, or Pensado (in English). For a sampling of Mexican artistic works treating the '68 massacre, see Bixler, "Re-Membering the Past" (121, 124) and Young (73–81).

8. The 2000 cover of the 1978 hit by The Jacksons "Blame It on the Boogie" and its well-known choreography have been staples of Acapulco nightclubs.

9. "El gobierno actual, pero también quienes pretender [*sic*] gobernar en el futuro, deben cargar con las consecuencias de las 1,986 agresiones perpetradas en cinco años; con los estragos de la violencia y de la impunidad imperantes en la mayoría de estas agresiones, que marcan el sexenio más violento, hasta ahora, contra la prensa de la historia reciente de este país."

10. This paragraph appears in Ward "Making Reality Sensible," slightly revised and reprinted with permission.

11. J. Patrice McSherry describes this complex network of terror succinctly: "Operation Condor was a secret intelligence and operations system created in the 1970s through which the South American military states shared intelligence and seized, tortured, and executed political opponents in one another's territory.... The Condor apparatus was a secret component of a larger, U.S.-led counterinsurgency strategy to preempt or reverse social movements demanding political or socioeconomic change" (1).

12. Mario Vargas Llosa famously classified the PRI's reign in Mexico as the "dictadura perfecta." He is quoted in *El País* as stating: "'Mexico is the perfect dictatorship. The perfect dictatorship is not communism. It is not the USSR. It is not Fidel Castro. The perfect dictatorship is Mexico,' said a Vargas Llosa who at this point once again appeared to be the intense politician of a few months ago. Mexico, he continued, 'is the camouflaged dictatorship.' 'It has the characteristics of dictatorship: permanence, not of a man, but of a party. And of a party that is untouchable'" ("Vargas Llosa"). ["'México es la dictadura perfecta. La dictadura perfecta no es el comunismo. No es la URSS. No es Fidel Castro. La dictadura perfecta es México,' dijo un Vargas Llosa que a estas alturas ya parecía de nuevo el político intenso de hace unos meses. México, siguió, 'es la dictadura camuflada.' 'Tiene las características de la dictadura: la permanencia, no de un hombre, pero sí de un partido. Y de un partido que es inamovible.'"]

13. Used to describe a fictionalized autobiographical narrative, the term *autofiction* originates in twentieth-century French literature and has been adopted in English and Spanish as autofiction and *autoficción*, respectively.

14. For a study of commercial theater in Mexico, see Valdés Medellín.

15. "Somos una cuadrilla de artistas convocados por Luisa Pardo y Gabino Rodríguez. Desde 2003 comenzamos a desarrollar proyectos como mecanismo para vincular el trabajo y la vida, para borrar fronteras. Nuestro trabajo busca dotar de sentido, articular, dislocar y desentrañar lo que la práctica cotidiana fusiona y pasa por alto. No tiene que ver con el entretenimiento es un espacio para pensar."

16. Helena Chávez MacGregor provides a helpful review of Teatro Ojo's intervention in a public family housing complex that demonstrates this focus in the company's work. For an analysis of the use of the performer's body in Teatro Ojo's project *Estado Fallido* [Failed state], see Diéguez, "Desmontando escenas." For an analysis of Teatro Ojo's *Atlas Electores* [Electors Atlas] project, which staged real people in the weeks leading to the 2012 elections, see Ward, "Affective Suffrage."

17. "Este sentir que el mundo podía ser cambiable y que el camino a seguir era el del trabajo colectivo, además del afán de subir a la escena una problemática que concerniera a todo el mundo, para establecer una comunicación directa con un público con el que se quiere intercambiar en un sentido dialéctico, aunque en la práctica muchas veces se hizo con intención abiertamente pedagógica, está en la base del éxito que tuvo el método de creación colectiva."

18. "(1) La formación de los miembros del grupo y la elaboración del producto artístico. (2) La relación con el público que ya no puede ser 'libre,' no puede ser una relación de 'oferta y demanda de mercado.'"

19. "El que puede ver la totalidad durante todo el trabajo. Su trabajo no es el de simple coordinador, puesto que la totalidad no es la suma de las partes, no es cuantitativa sin o cualitativa. Su tarea dentro de la nueva división del trabajo, no sólo no ha disminuido, sino que se ha vuelto más rica y más profunda, lo que ha perdido en autoridad lo ha ganado en creatividad."

20. One could argue for the possibility of reading uncorrupted saints' bodies or mass funeral processions as a sort of postmortem performance, but these events lack intentionality on the part of the dead, who, rather than representing themselves, serve more as a prop in the performance.

21. "'Gran escritor' . . . tan evidente por contraste en la narrativa del boom."

22. See *La noche de Tlatelolco* [Massacre in Mexico] by Elena Poniatowska (1971) or *Crónica de una muerte anunciada* [Chronicle of a death foretold] by Gabriel García Márquez (1981), for example.

23. "A partir de una perspectiva generacional, . . . la convivencia de grupo de jóvenes y [contrastarla] con sus ideales políticos y sus anhelos individuales. Esta obra parte de algunas interrogantes que nos han acompañado desde nuestro montaje anterior y que tienen

una relación directa con nuestra vida cotidiana y con nosotros como seres sociales. ¿Cómo nos organizamos en grupo los seres humanos?"

24. "Nosotros nacimos en los 80as, somos de la clase media, crecimos con la televisión, el nintendo, la computadora y las desilusiones de nuestros padres; hoy contemplamos con incomodidad el mundo que heredamos."

25. "El proceso de un espectáculo no debe comenzar por buscar una obra. Sino por reconocer cuáles son nuestras preocupaciones, nuestras preguntas en este momento y de ahí adaptar el teatro a nuestros intereses, nunca adaptar nuestras inquietudes a un texto preexistente."

26. "La idea de contar una historia paralela a la del agua, la de una muchacha que llega (como Luisa en la vida real) y se encuentra con uno que siempre ha estado ahí (como Gabino en la vida real), ya estaba aceptada y en desarrollo."

27. "Durante toda la temporada sufrimos mucho, nuestro promedio de espectadores debió ser 2 o 3. Antes de cada función, después de limpiar el espacio, montar las butacas, la escenografía y calentar, espiábamos por la ventana para ver si había algún espectador; hasta que llegó el día funesto: Había empezado el mundial de Alemania y todo el mundo estaba (mos) pendientes."

28. "Búsqueda de lo esencial en la temática, el manejo del espacio mediante el uso de mínimos elementos. Este pequeño grupo de jóvenes creadores ofrece una alternativa original, esperanzadora por su intuición del teatro, autenticidad y humor, que merece ser tomada en cuenta en la perspectiva del teatro nacional."

29. "Lo importante no es tanto lo que la gente ve en la galería o el museo, sino lo que la gente ve después de mirar la obra; cómo se enfrentan a la realidad a partir de entonces. El arte puede regenerar la percepción de la realidad, el arte puede cambiar al mundo. No es una cuestión de mejor o peor, sino de diferente."

Chapter 2: Unfolding Genealogy

1. In Argentina, see Vivi Tellas's *Archivos* and the series of biodramas she curated, especially Lola Arias's *Mi vida después* [My life after] (2009). Arias's work focuses on such generational issues beyond the biodrama series as well, with *El año en que nací* [The year I was born] (2012) and *Melancolía y manifestaciones* [Melancholy and demonstrations] (2012). In Peru, Claudia Tangoa and Sebastián Rubio adapt Arias's idea to their own national context in *Proyecto 1980/2000: El tiempo que heredé* [Project 1980/2000: The time I inherited] (2012). Please see Julie Ann Ward, "Beside Motherhood: Staging Women's Lives in LAtin American Theatre of the Real," in *The Routledge Companion to Gender, Sex, and LAtin American Culture*. As I discuss in chapter 4, this type of generational work has struck a chord in Latin American theater.

2. Writing about Sarmiento's *Recuerdos*, Molloy posits, "The anxiety of closure that plagues most autobiographers—How to end my life story while still alive? How shall I write down that asymptotic point where my past and my present connect?" (34) It would seem that

including the family in the autobiography is one way to address this anxiety, for Lagartijas and other theater practitioners. By inserting the self into an infinite line of interconnected lives, the end cannot be finite. When one life ends, there are others to carry its memory forward.

3. Pardo states that she did not know much about her mother's life before she did the archival research for the play: "We did the research on my mom's life, about which we didn't know anything, really. We had ideas—the idea that she had been in prison, but then it was a matter of finding her letters, interviewing her friends, her family members" [Se hizo la investigación de la vida de mi mamá, que de tal vida tampoco no sabíamos nada, ¿no? Teníamos ideas—la idea de que estuvo en la cárcel, pero entonces fue sacar sus cartas, entrevistar a sus amigos, a los familiares] (Ward "Entrevista " 139–40).

4. Philippe Lejeune's famous "autobiographical pact" ("Autobiographical Pact") is a useful reference for thinking about the agreement spectators, actors, directors, playwrights, and crew make in theater of the real. Whereas Lejeune's pact has readers agreeing that author, narrator, and historical person are all one and the same, in this pact spectators agree to accept that the actor, portrayed character, and historical person are all one and the same—at least part of the time.

5. "Nos dimos cuenta que estábamos trabajando sobre el tema de nuestros padres de manera constante."

6. For more on Mexican guerrilla movements, see Laura Castellanos, *México armado: 1943–1981*, a journalistic history of armed movements in the country in the twentieth century, or Fernando Herrera Calderón and Adela Cedilla's *Challenging Authoritarianism in Mexico*, which seeks to shed light on Mexico's Dirty War, likening it to other Latin American twentieth-century dictatorships.

7. "Mi hermana visitaba a varios presos en diferentes cárceles y a todos nos ayudaba con trámites legales y papeleo. A mí me iba a ver los miércoles y domingos. A veces lloraba mucho, se ponía triste de verme ahí. Me contaba que tenía que atravesar la ciudad y luego tomar un camión que viajaba lejos por una avenida sin pavimentar, en ese entonces Santa Martha Acatitla estaba en las orillas de la ciudad. Vio atardeceres muy bonitos cuando salía de visitarme en la cárcel."

8. "Escenarios liminales" in which "elaboraciones estéticas no se desmarcan de las decisiones éticas o de los motivos que las generan."

9. This is a reference to Héctor Aguilar Camín, Mexican intellectual and author and Margarita's lover, according to the play.

10. "Recuerdo que tu madre me decía que en la celda se imaginaba que era una hoja de papel y así podía escaparse doblada por debajo de la puerta."

11. "A mi familia: Sé que ya he ventilado muchas cosas, ajustado muchas cuentas a través de la ficción. De alguna manera soy un traidor, pero también sé que esas mismas obras, que quizás dolieron, también trajeron 'la alegría de la notoriedad.' Les pido aquí, por escrito, perdón."

12. "Este es el único recuerdo que tengo de mi madre, no sé si lo viví o lo soñé."

13. "En 1986 María será mi mamá. . . . En 1986 Raúl será mi papa."

14. "¿Por qué no me acuerdo de ustedes y sé perfectamente quiénes son? ¿Por qué he tenido que juntar los pedazos de mi historia para ver de dónde chingados vengo? ¿Por qué no me invitaron un café en el 'Vips' para contármelo todo? ¿Por qué tu familia muerta sigue viva y yo siempre he estado muerta para ti?"

15. See the review in *El Diario de Coahuila*, which categorizes Villegas as a "poor woman, genesis of an earthquake and of a poor existence that she must bear all of her life" ("Se rompen las olas") or Olga Harmony's critique in *La Jornada* ("Se rompen las olas").

16. "è uno spettacolo che riesce a fondere in modo originale e dinamico autobiografia e Storia, che vuole stimolare il pensiero critico dello spettatore."

17. "Ein wunderbar uneitles Gesellschaftsporträt."

18. "Otro lugar de la memoria, los sucesos de 1968, ya que en los dos acontecimientos la Plaza de las Tres Culturas funciona como un punto de cristalización un espacio histórico en que ocurrieron la matanza de Tlatelolco y el derrumbe de los edificios durante el sismo, dos sucesos que se asocian al servicio de la crítica contra el gobierno priísta."

19. "A partir del terremoto y de la incapacidad del gobierno para resolver sus estragos, la sociedad civil se organizó y expresó su gran carácter solidario."

Chapter 3: Falling Out of History

1. "A 50 años de la publicación del libro de Pablo González Casanova *La democracia en México*; buscamos pensar la democracia a la luz del análisis que se hizo hace medio siglo."

2. "Este proyecto es una investigación sobre las ideas que sustentan el ideal democrático y sobre las experiencias que produce la puesta en práctica de ese ideal. . . . Más que una explicación de la democracia es una implicación con la democracia."

3. "¿En qué forma la estructura del poder de un país como México condiciona y limita las decisiones en materia de desarrollo económico, o deriva en decisiones que corresponden propiamente a medidas de simple crecimiento económico? ¿Hasta qué punto es posible modificar la estructura del poder para lograr el desarrollo económico?" (González Casanova, *La democracia en México* 15).

4. "La libertad municipal es una institución que con frecuencia no existe desde su base misma. . . . Y la entidad política que surge y se denomina municipio libre está, en realidad, controlada por el poder estatal y la Federación" (González Casanova, *La democracia en México* 43).

5. "(a) los caudillos y caciques regionales y locales; (b) el ejército; (c) el clero; (d) los latifundistas y los empresarios nacionales y extranjeros" (González Casanova, *La democracia en México* 46).

6. "En acabar con el colonialismo interno y con el desarrollo semi-capitalista, en 'conquistar los derechos políticos y la libertad política' de la población marginal, semicolonial, en acentuar la lucha cívica y la organización política en el campo y en las regiones indígenas, y, en formar, en las ciudades, los cuadros dirigentes con los obreros más conscientes y radicales" (González Casanova, *La Democracia En México* 225–26).

7. "Es el primer gran libro de la sociología mexicana contemporánea."

8. "Un punto de despegue del trabajo académico de las ciencias sociales en el país."

9. "A nuestro país desde diversas perspectivas: sociales, históricas, biográficas, ficcionales."

10. "*Derretiré con un cerillo la nieve de un volcán* [apela] a la reconstrucción de la memoria, el interés por las microhistorias, la experiencia cotidiana o la autobiografía, marcando con ello un lugar por demás destacado en la carpeta enriquecida del teatro documento."

11. "Teatro Documento, potente, crudo, sedicioso, comprometido, brechtianamente didáctico; tonalmente tragicómico. Con esta nada condescendiente propuesta escénica, la agrupación Lagartijas al Sol desnuda las corruptelas brutales del presidencialismo mexicano."

12. "Es hätte ein zynisches Unterfangen werden können—ein Schauspieler schaut sich mal die Armen an. Aber schon die Länge seines Aufenthalts deutet auf aufrichtiges Interesse hin. Und Rodríguez weiß wie jeder gute Ethnologe, dass seine Ergebnisse mindestens so viel über ihn, den Beobachter, aussagen wie über den Gegenstand der Beobachtung."

13. "La conferencia deviene ceremonia en memoria de los compatriotas desaparecidos, y también expresión de una dolorosa nostalgia por aquella tierra exuberante que en otro tiempo propició el florecimiento del arte y el pensamiento crítico."

14. "En realidad Veracruz es una conferencia performativa (digo performativa por llamarla de algún modo). De inicio, para Escenas do Cambio, se nos había planteado hacer una conferencia para explicar el asesinato de Nadia Vera y Rubén Espinosa. Explicar, contar, investigar un asunto así es delicado, por lo doloroso, por lo reciente, por la falta de claridad y por la frágil línea del oportunismo. Dicho así, no nos sentimos con el derecho."

15. "'Creemos que ayudamos al desarrollo, pero no tenemos idea de lo que está en juego. Esto me ha dejado entender un lado que nunca antes vi de la ayuda al desarrollo.' 'No sabía de ese México, ni que se manipulara así a un pueblo, con regalos como una televisión,' indica una universitaria de Friburgo."

16. In an interview, Pardo and Rodríguez related that some astute readers have noticed that *La revolución institucional* cites twenty-first-century sources in its bibliography while the front matter indicates that it was published in 2000 (Pardo and Rodríguez, Personal Interview).

17. "Quizá por primera vez en su historia, México carece de caudillos y debe permitir orientar definitivamente la política del país por rumbos de una verdadera vida institucional, procurando pasar, de una vez por todas, de la condición histórica de país de un hombre a la de nación de instituciones y leyes"

18. "Ruiz Cortines alcanzó 74.31% de los votos"

19. "La hora que usted diga, señor presidente."

20. "Sé que picaré una montaña con un clavo o que derretiré con un cerillo la nieve de un volcán."

21. See Ward, "Affective Suffrage," my article on the #YoSoy132 movement and another example of theater of the real from the Mexican company Teatro Ojo for more information on the performance of democratic representation.

22. "G. En medio de aquellas protestas nos preguntamos: ¿Qué sabíamos nosotros sobre el partido? . . . ¿Por qué jóvenes que no habíamos vivido nuestra vida política con el PRI en la presidencia lo odiábamos tanto? . . . Fue entonces que encontramos un libro . . . *La Revolución Institucional* de Natalia Valdez Tejeda. Nos sorprendió que su visión apelara más a la comprensión de un proceso que a exaltar o denostar al partido."

23. Critics like Michael Anderson and Peter O'Connor point to applied theater as research (ATAR) as one way of conceiving of theater as an investigation. Peter O'Connor and Briar O'Connor define applied theater as "an umbrella term that defines theatre which operates beyond the traditional and limiting scope of conventional Western theatre forms. It is often characterised by work which deliberately engages in spaces or with groups of people where mainstream theatre still fears to tread. . . . Frequently, applied theatre is constructed as a response to social or political challenges and is seen as a process where difference and change can be wrought through its making" (O'Connor and O'Connor 471). While Lagartijas's projects are not generally associated with applied theater, in that they are not community-based, pedagogical, or therapeutic, they do focus on issues of social justice and conceive of the play itself as research.

24. "La puesta en escena busca contar esta experiencia e indagar en las posibilidades de la representación. Ser otro, intentar vivir la vida de otra persona. Hacerse pasar por otro. ¿No es eso la actuación?"

25. "Así comenzaron a formarse grandes asentamientos irregulares. Muchos desposeídos se fueron uniendo para tomar terrenos, bardearlos, hacer colonias, hacer la vida. Así se creó este barrio en el que ahora vivo. Así se instalaron en él las personas con las que comparto la casa."

26. Pardo expresses that after one particular performance of *Veracruz* she thought to herself, "puta, di una mala función" [damn, I gave a bad performance] (Pardo and Rodríguez, Personal Interview), and realized that she could no longer consider *Veracruz* artistic, that it had to be fully grounded in reality.

27. "Cuando, hace más de 8 meses, estaba preparando el texto de esta conferencia para un festival lejos de aquí, un festival que me pidió que hablara de Veracruz, pero sobre todo de Nadia Vera, de su asesinato, hubo momentos muy difíciles. En medio de tanta información, tanto material visual, periodístico, malas noticias . . . me perdí, no encontraba el punto, la forma, a veces no encontraba el sentido de ir ahí a hablar de esto."

28. "Hace un tiempo intenté regresar a vivir a Xalapa, después de casi 9 años de haberme salido para estudiar y trabajar en la ciudad de México. Me encontré no sólo con la tierra devastada y una sociedad exponencialmente más desigual -poca gente muy rica y mucha gente muy pobre y hacinada-, si no [sic] con un estado de violencia extremo: balaceras, secuestros, extorsiones. El proceso de descomposición ha sido largo, no es de hoy, pero justo ahora es

cuando se ve que el problema es grande. Los políticos son muy cercanos al crimen organizado, hay una relación casi inseparable, co-dependiente, entre ellos y los narcos."

29. "Hace un año y dos días. Fueron asesinados con saña, fueron torturados. Hay tres detenidos, una maleta, un auto y la investigación oficial que apunta a una ajuste de cuentas, a la recuperación de una maleta con droga" (Pardo, "Veracruz").

30. "La Procuraduría de Justicia del Distrito Federal fue a Veracruz a interrogar a Javier Duarte quien negó estar implicado de cualquier manera con el asesinato, pero él nunca podrá escapar de esto."

31. "Responsabilizamos totalmente a Javier Duarte de Ochoa, Gobernador del Estado, y a todo su gabinete, sobre cualquier cosa que nos pueda suceder a los que estamos involucrados y organizados en todo este tipo de movimientos, tanto estudiantes, académicos, sociedad civil en general."

32. Whereas in Argentina, public performances serving as extrajudicial trials known as *escraches* took place in the streets to denounce official impunity (Taylor, *Archive* 161–89), here it is the space of the theater that serves as the hall of justice, in the absence of official rulings.

33. "La historia que les vamos a contar es la de un lugar que no existe, de gente que no vive y de cosas que no pasan. Es, como se dice, una historia de ficción."

34. Indeed, especially with audiences outside of Mexico, spectators did occasionally take the play at its documentary word. Pardo and Rodríguez recount the ethical dilemma posed by the consciousness raised in Europe about the problems with international development efforts. In an interview, they told me about an audience member who was deeply affected by the play and asked them how they could have just left, and what they were going to do about the massacre in Santiago Amoukalli. The artists' complicity is an ever-present problem.

35. "Las elecciones fueron al día siguiente. Luisa y Gabino no supieron quién ganó. Poco importaba. Les dieron ganas de llorar, de abrazarse, pero nunca se permitían esas cosas. Se alejaron de Amoukalli, para siempre."

36. "Encierran dos o más conglomerados socio-culturales, uno super-participante y otro supermarginal, uno dominante–llámese español, criado o ladino—y otro dominado–llámese native, indio o indígena" (González Casanova, *La democracia en México* 89).

37. "El dominio y explotación de unos grupos culturales por otros" (González Casanova, *La democracia en México* 89).

38. "En que pueden ganar el poder y pueden perder el poder, respectivamente. . . . En los momentos de crisis ambos partidos politicos perciben un hecho; que toda la población marginal–económica y políticamente marginal—puede entrar en acción y que . . . constituye una indudable posibilidad de lucha o un verdadero peligro, según la perspectiva" (González Casanova, *La democracia en México* 140).

39. "Nacimos en la Ciudad de México, en 1983, con un mes y seis días de diferencia."

40. "[Vencer] con el conocimiento, este problema de contaminación atmosférica."

41. "Resolver los problemas a la mexicana significaba no resolver los problemas. Significó no tomar decisiones que debían ser tomadas. Hacer cosas que ya no se pueden remediar."

42. "Escribirle esta carta a tu mejor amigo es una derrota."

43. "Creo que es el único modo en que algún día sane la herida que estoy abriendo."

44. "Nunca dejaré de hablar bien de ti. No espero reciprocidad. Esta carta es una derrota."

45. "Amigos, somos Gabino y Juan Leduc. Les venimos a grabar esto. Tan tan."

46. "Han perdido fuerza e importancia los caciques y el ejército," giving way to "financieros y emperesarios nativos, . . . al lado de las grandes empresas extranjeras y de la gran potencia que las ampara" (González Casanova, *La democracia en México* 85).

47. "I. Las relaciones entre el marginalismo social y el marginalismo político; II. Las relaciones entre la sociedad plural, el colonialismo interno y la manipulación política; III. Las relaciones entre la estratificación social y la inconformidad política; IV. Las relaciones entre la movilización, la movilización social y el conformismo político; V. Las formas en que se manifiestan la inconformidad y las luchas cívicas" (González Casanova, *La democracia en México* 89).

48. "Las relaciones entre la estructura social y la estructura política de México" (González Casanova, *La democracia en México* 88).

Chapter 4: Loosening the Bounds of Theater

1. "Una tentativa de generar un mapa de un territorio que no reconozco, un relato de una historia que desconozco, un intento por re apropiarme de un país."

2. For more on the fascinating early history of drug trafficking in Mexico, see Recio (2002), Sandos (1984), and Toro (1999).

3. "Mi nombre es Francisco Barreiro. Tengo 31 años. Soy actor."

4. "Volveremos al teatro–en este caso con apoyos tecnológicos más sofisticados-, que se convierte en la difusión de información sin censura."

5. "Todos los acontecimientos en los que se reconoce la presencia conjunta y combinada de convivio, poesía corporal y expectación. El teatro puede incluir elementos tecnológicos . . . pero no puede renunciar al convivio, a la presencia aurática corporal productora de *poíesis*."

6. The work *7 mono, iya de Yanhuitlán* was originally conceived as part of the *Democracia en México* series, treated in chapter 3. It has been disconnected from that project and now stands alone.

7. On the website for the project, Lagartijas explains: "Yivi es una palabra mixteca que se traduce como humano, quiere decir estar vivo, saber pensar, saber hablar, saber razonar, saber respetar, sentir dolor" [Yivi is a Mixtec word that is translated as human, meaning to be alive, to know how to think, to know how to speak, to know how to reason, to know how to respect, to feel pain] (Lagartijas Tiradas al Sol "Proyecto Yivi").

8. "La mayoría de esos migrantes entraron por primera vez a este país de forma ilegal. Porque a veces es más fácil cruzar el río y el desierto a pie que obtener un pasaporte y una visa. Yo espero que en el futuro los niños y las niñas a las que les doy clases puedan ser libres de venir o no venir, que sea su elección, no una necesidad, no un impedimento. Hoy mis alumnos con los que creamos esta pieza no están acá, porque no hay dinero suficiente para traerles y porque sería casi imposible conseguirles una visa, ya sabemos por qué. Por eso, traje estos objetos y están estas pantallas, en su representación."

9. The trope of a stage covered in clothing is often used in theater of the real to evoke the missing, absent, or dead. For example, Argentine theater practitioner Lola Arias's 2009 play *Mi vida después* [My life after] begins with a shower of clothing falling onto the stage from above, from which a character emerges to deliver the first monologue about her parents' lives. Arias's play *El año en que nací* [The year I was born] (2012) also makes use of the empty clothing technique. In Mexico, Mayra Martell documents the rooms of disappeared women from Ciudad Juárez to shed light on the feminicides occurring there; her photographs often feature the clothing of the women, laid out on their beds in place of their bodies. In Villegas's work, the focus is on presence, rather than absence.

10. Hay maneras de mostrarse ante el mundo, de contarse a si mismo. Yo lo hago a través de un cuento, "Un artista del hambre" de Franz Kafka. Un cuento que trata sobre animales y personas hambrientas de ser vistos por ustedes, ustedes. Sí, este es mi cuento."

11. Perhaps the opera forms part of what various authors like Claire Fox and Ila Sheren call the "portable border" (23), which permits the exportation of the border to other regions.

12. The *Marfa Triptych* is defined by its interaction with Marfa. Commissioned by the Ballroom Marfa gallery, the triptych was presented over three years in the high-desert town. The first part, the *Country and Western Big Band Suite*, premiered in the Crowley Theatre in Marfa on November 16, 2013. The instrumental suite for fourteen musicians mixes classic country music with Western soundtracks and jazz ("The Marfa Triptych"). The second entry, *The Desert*, was a concert for solo piano that took place at the Mimms Ranch on the outskirts of Marfa, a live accompaniment to the sunset and the moonrise on October 4, 2014.

13. "Una verdad compartida, es otro tipo de justicia."

14. "*Lembrar é resistir . . .* was written and performed for the express purpose of marking the recovery of a notorious site of repression in the historic center of São Paulo. . . . Prompted by the approaching twentieth anniversary of the controversial Amnesty Law (which was the successful culmination of mass mobilizations united around slogans demanding 'broad, general, and unconditional amnesty' for the politically persecuted, but which also amounted to a self-amnesty for military and police perpetrators), a small group of state government officials and former political detainees with established reputations in theatre obtained authorization to interrupt scheduled renovations of the building in order to stage

a performance that would tell the story of the DOPS and the people imprisoned there" (Atencio 7–8).

15. Studies on the relationship between government funding for artists through programs like the Fondo Nacional para la Cultura y las Artes (FONCA) [National Fund for Arts and Culture] and critical and commercial success are necessary to flesh out this idea. In particular, I wonder whether FONCA grants have been used as a tool for soft censorship.

Appendix B: Interview with Lagartijas Tiradas al Sol

1. The original play on Pardo's mother was *Noviembre*, as discussed in the introduction.

Works Cited

Aguilar Camín, Héctor. "Notas sobre nacionalismo e identidad nacional." *Nexos*, 1 July 1993, https://www.nexos.com.mx/?p=6803.

Aguilar Zínser, Luz Emilia. "México: escenarios de la violencia ¿Qué teatro es necesario?" *Conjunto*, no. 183, 2017, pp. 14–24.

Anderson, Michael, and Peter O'Connor. "Applied Theatre as Research: Provoking the Possibilities." *Applied Theatre Research*, vol. 1, no. 2, 2013, pp. 189–202, https://doi.org/10.1386/atr.1.2.189_1.

Arias, Lola. *El año en que nací* (Subtitled). Vimeo, 2012, http://vimeo.com/39855730.

Arias, Lola. *Mi vida después (My Life After)*. Translated by Ivana Gamarnik and Andrew Haley, Lola Arias, 2009, Buenos Aires.

Arthur, Paul. "Jargons of Authenticity (Three American Moments)." *Theorizing Documentary*, edited by Michael Renov, Routledge, 2012, pp. 108–34.

Atencio, Rebecca J. "Acts of Witnessing: Site-Specific Performance and Transitional Justice in Postdictatorship Brazil." *Latin American Theatre Review*, vol. 46, no. 2, 2013, pp. 7–24. *Project Muse*, https://doi.org/10.1353/ltr.2013.0015.

Avallone, Alessia Rosa. "Storia è autobiografia. *Se rompen las olas* di Mariana Villegas." Altre Velocità, 2013, http://www.altrevelocita.it/incursioni/3/vie-festival/41/2013/150/articoli-e-recensioni/677/storia-e-autobiografia-se-rompen-la-olas-di-mariana-villegas.pdf.

Aviña, Alexander. *Specters of Revolution: Peasant Guerrillas in the Cold War Mexican Countryside*. Oxford UP, 2014.

Beverley, John. "Anatomía del testimonio." *Revista de Crítica Literaria Latinoamericana*, vol. 13, no. 25, 1987, pp. 7–16. *JSTOR*, https://www.jstor.org/stable/4530303.

Beverley, John. *Testimonio: On the Politics of Truth*. U of Minnesota P, 2004.

Bixler, Jacqueline. "El teatro de la crisis: Nueva dramaturgia mexicana." *Tradición, modernidad y posmodernidad (Teatro iberamericano y argentino)*, edited by Osvaldo Pelletieri, Editorial Galerna, 1999, pp. 111–18.

Bixler, Jacqueline. "Re-Membering the Past: Memory-Theatre and Tlatelolco." *Latin American Research Review*, vol. 37, no. 2, 2002, pp. 119–35. *JSTOR*, https://www.jstor.org/stable/26921.

Boal, Augusto. "Teatro Jornal: Primeira Edição." *Latin American Theatre Review*, vol. 4, no. 2, 1971, pp. 57–60. *Journals@KU*, https://journals.ku.edu/latr/article/view/115/90.

Bravo-Elizondo, Pedro. "El concepto de la revolución de lo mexicano en *El gesticulador*." *Texto Crítico*, vol. 10, no. 29, 1984, pp. 197–205. *U Veracruzana Repositorio Institucional*, https://cdigital.uv.mx/handle/123456789/7075.

Brecht, Bertold. "A Short Organum for the Theatre." *Brecht on Theatre: The Development of an Aesthetic.* Translated and edited by John Willett. Hill and Wang, 1964, pp. 179–205.

Brennan, Teresa. *The Transmission of Affect.* Cornell UP, 2004.

Brownell, Pamela. "*Proyecto Archivos*: El teatro documental según Vivi Tellas." *E-misférica,* vol. 9, no. 1–2, 2012, http://hemisphericinstitute.org/hemi/es/e-misferica-91/brownell.

Buenaventura, Enrique, and Jacqueline Vidal. "Esquema general del método de creación colectiva." *Creación Colectiva: El legado de Enrique Buenaventura,* edited by Beatriz Rizk. Atuel, 2008, pp. 127–83.

Carlson, Marvin A. "The Resistance to Theatricality." *SubStance,* vol. 31, no. 98/99, 2002, pp. 238–50. *JSTOR,* https://www.jstor.org/stable/3685489.

Carlson, Marvin A. *Shattering Hamlet's Mirror: Theatre and Reality.* U of Michigan P, 2016.

Cascardi, Anthony J. "Consequences of *Don Quixote*: The Bearable Lightness of Cervantes' Influence." *A History of the Spanish Novel,* edited by J. A. Garrido Ardila, Oxford UP, 2015, pp. 122–41.

Castañeda, Fernando. "La constitución de la sociología en México." *Desarrollo y organización de las ciencias sociales en* México, edited by Francisco José Paoli Bolio, UNAM / Porrúa, 1990, pp. 397–430.

Castañeda, Salvador. *La negación del número: La guerrilla en* México, *1965–1996: Una aproximación crítica.* CONACULTA/Ediciones sin nombre, 2006.

Castellanos, Laura. *México Armado: 1943–1981.* Ediciones Era, 2007.

Castillo, Debra A. "Devising as Pedagogical Practice in Latin American Theatre." *Latin American Theatre Review,* vol. 51, no. 1, 2016, pp. 61–77. *Project Muse,* https://doi.org/10.1353/ltr.2016.0060.

Chávez MacGregor, Helena. "Teatro Ojo, el teatro sin teatro." *Revista Cuadrivio,* 25 Aug. 2013, https://cuadrivio.net/teatro-ojo-el-teatro-sin-teatro/.

Compton, Tim. "Green/Activist Mexican History in *Asalto al agua transparente*." *25 Years Celebrating Hispanic Culture in the United States: The International Hispanic Theatre Festival of Miami,* edited by Beatriz J. Rizk and Nelsy Echávez-Solano, Ediciones Universal, 2013, pp. 295–300.

Compton, Timothy G. "Mexico City's Spring 2006 Theatre Season." *Latin American Theatre Review,* vol. 40, no. 1, 2006, pp. 153–62. *Project Muse,* https://doi.org/10.1353/ltr.2006.0030.

Culp, Edwin. "Rebelliousness Is a Lizard Lying under the Sun." 15 Dec. 2017. *Archivo Virtual Artes Escénicas,* http://artesescenicas.uclm.es/archivos_subidos/companias/306/Rebelliousness-is-a-lizard.pdf.

Davis, Tracy C., and Thomas Postlewait, eds. *Theatricality.* Cambridge UP, 2004.

Day, Stuart A. *Outside Theater: Alliances that Shape Mexico.* U of Arizona P, 2017.

Day, Stuart A. "Performing Mexico." *Writing and Rewriting National Theatre Histories,* edited by S. E. Wilmer, U of Iowa P, 2009, pp. 153–73.

"Democracia simulada, nada que aplaudir." Artículo 19, 20 Mar. 2018, https://articulo19
.org/wp-content/uploads/2018/03/INFORME-A19–2017_v04.pdf.

Diéguez, Ileana. "Desmontando escenas: Estrategias performativas de investigación y creación."
Telón de Fondo: Revista de Teoría y Crítica Teatral, vol. 12, 2010, pp. 1–9, http://www
.telondefondo.org/download.php?f=YXJjMi8zMjUucGRm&tipo=articulo&id=325.

Diéguez, Ileana. *Escenarios liminales*. Atuel, 2007.

Diéguez, Ileana. "La práctica artística en contextos de *dramas sociales.*" *Latin American
Theatre Review*, vol. 45, no. 1, 2007, pp. 75–93. *Project Muse*, https://doi.org/10.1353/
ltr.2011.0027.

Diéguez Caballero, Ileana. *Escenarios Liminales: Teatralidades, Performatividades, Políticas*,
2nd ed. Paso de Gato, 2014.

Dubatti, Jorge. "Teatro-matriz y teatro liminal: La liminalidad constitutiva del aconteci-
miento teatral." *Cena*, vol. 19, 2016, http://dx.doi.org/10.22456/2236-3254.65486."

"Estado de la investigación del 'Caso Iguala.'" Comisión Nacional de los Derechos Humanos,
2015, http://www.cndh.org.mx/sites/all/doc/OtrosDocumentos/Doc_2015_002.pdf.

Farfán Hernández, Rafael. "La contribución de Pablo González Casanova a la formación de
una teoría crítica de la sociedad en México (1966–1970)." *Sociológica*, vol. 9, no. 24, 1994,
http://www.sociologicamexico.azc.uam.mx/index.php/Sociologica/article/down
load/734/707.

Favorini, Attilio. "Collective Creation in Documentary Theatre." *A History of Collective
Creation*, edited by Kathryn Mederos Syssoyeva and Scott Proudfit. Palgrave Macmillan, 2013, pp. 97–112.

Fediuk, Elka, and Antonio Prieto Stambaugh, eds. *Corporalidades escénicas: Representaciones del cuerpo en el teatro, la danza y el performance*. Editorial Argus-a Artes y Humanidades, 2016, http://www.argus-a.com.ar/archivos-ebooks/corporalidades-esce
nicas-representaciones-del-cuerpo-en-el-teatro-la-danza-y-el-performance.pdf.

Forsyth, Alison, and Chris Megson, eds. *Get Real: Documentary Theatre Past and Present*.
Palgrave Macmillan, 2011.

Foster, David William. "Latin American Documentary Narrative." *PMLA*, vol. 99, no. 1,
1984, pp. 41–55. *JSTOR*, https://www.jstor.org/stable/462034.

Fox, Claire F. "The Portable Border: Site-Specificity, Art, and the U. S.-Mexico Frontier."
Social Text, no. 41, 1994, pp. 61–82. *JSTOR*, JSTOR, www.jstor.org/stable/466832.f

Freedom House. "Mexico." *Freedom of the Press 2016*. https://freedomhouse.org/report/
freedom-press/2016/mexico.

Frisch, Mark. "Re-Reading the Past: Fiction and Historical Discourse in Borges and Rodolfo
Usigli's *El gesticulador* and *Corona de sombra.*" *Variaciones Borges*, vol. 32, 2011, pp. 133–
48. Borges Center, https://www.borges.pitt.edu/sites/default/files/Frisch_0.pdf.

Fuchs, Elinor. "Presence and the Revenge of Writing: Re-Thinking Theatre after Derrida."
Performing Arts Journal, vol. 9, no. 2/3, 1985, pp. 163–73. *JSTOR*, https://www.jstor
.org/stable/3245520.

Gaines, Jane M. "Political Mimesis." *Collecting Visible Evidence*, edited by Jane M. Gaines and Michael Renov. U of Minnesota P, 1999, pp. 84–102.

Gálvez Suárez, Arnoldo. *Los jueces*. Letra Negra, 2009.

Gandasegui, Fernando. "Luisa Pardo: 'Hacer historia es construir ficciones.'" *El Lugar Sin Límites*, 29 Sept. 2016, https://ellugarsinlimites.com/2016/09/29/luisa-pardo-hacer-historia-es-construir-ficciones/.

García, Óscar Armando. "Construcciones corporales de la violencia en la escena mexicana: La seducción y sus límites." Prieto Stambaugh and Fediuk, pp. 177–96.

Glockner, Fritz. *Memoria roja: historia de una guerrilla en* México 1943–1968. Grupo Planeta Spain, 2013.

Goldman, Francisco. "Who Killed Rubén Espinosa and Nadia Vera?" *New Yorker*, 14 Aug. 2015. https://www.newyorker.com/news/news-desk/who-killed-ruben-espinosa-and-nadia-vera.

González Casanova, Pablo. *Democracy in Mexico*. Translated by Danielle Salti, Oxford UP, 1970.

González Casanova, Pablo. *La democracia en* México. Ediciones Era, 1965.

Graham-Jones, Jean. *Exorcising History: Argentine Theater under Dictatorship*. Bucknell UP, 2000.

Harmony, Olga. "Se rompen las olas." *La Jornada* 26 Apr. 2012, http://www.jornada.com.mx/2012/04/26/opinion/a08a1cul.

Harmony, Olga. "XXVIII Muestra Nacional De Teatro." *Assaig de teatre: revista de l'Associació d'Investigació i Experimentació Teatral*, vol. 62–64, 2008, pp. 22–24. *RACO*, https://www.raco.cat/index.php/AssaigTeatre/article/view/146330/231400.

Hernández, Paola. "Biografías escénicas: *Mi vida después* de Lola Arias." *Latin American Theatre Review*, vol. 45, no. 1, 2011, pp. 115–28. *Project Muse*, https://doi.org/10.1353/ltr.2011.0033.

Herrera Calderón, Fernando, and Adela Cedillo. *Challenging Authoritarianism in Mexico: Revolutionary Struggles and the Dirty War, 1964–1982*, Routledge, 2012.

Hirsch, Marianne. *Family Frames: Photography, Narrative and Postmemory*. Harvard UP, 1997.

Hirsch, Marianne. *The Generation of Postmemory*. Columbia UP, 2012.

The Human Rights Situation in Mexico, Inter-American Commission on Human Rights. *Organization of American States*, 2015, http://www.oas.org/en/iachr/reports/pdfs/mexico2016-en.pdf.

Icle, Gilberto. "Estudos da Presença: Prolegômenos para a Pesquisa das Práticas Performativas." *Revista Brasileira de Estudos da Presença*, vol. 1, no. 1, 2011, pp. 9–27, http://seer.ufrgs.br/index.php/presenca/article/view/23682/13690.

Informe Histórico a la Sociedad Mexicana 2006. Fiscalía Especial para Movimientos Sociales y Políticos del Pasado. Doyle, Kate. "Official Report Released on Mexico's 'Dirty War.'" *National Security Archive*, 21 Nov. 2006, https://nsarchive2.gwu.edu/NSAEBB/NSAEBB209/index.htm.

Islas, Patricia. "En Suiza, la democracia en México." 17 July 2016, https://www.swissinfo.ch/spa/suiza-m%C3%A9xico_en-suiza-la-democracia-en-m%C3%A9xico-en-escena/42301316.

Jaramillo, María Mercedes. "Bojayá in Colombian Theater. *Kilele: A Drama of Memory and Resistance.*" *Black Writing, Culture, and the State in Latin America*, edited by Jerome C. Branche. Vanderbilt UP, 2015, pp. 103–26.

Kelting, Lily. "Playwright Undercover: Gabino Rodriguez" *Exberliner* 30 Mar. 2017, http://www.exberliner.com/whats-on/stage/gabino-rodriguez-tijuana-find-festival/.

Lagartijas Tiradas al Sol. *Asalto al agua transparente.* Performed by Luisa Pardo and Gabino Rodríguez, X Espacio de Arte, 3 Sept. 2011, Mexico City.

Lagartijas Tiradas al Sol. *Asalto al agua transparente.* Text from Collection of Luisa Pardo, 2012.

Lagartijas Tiradas al Sol. *Derretiré con un cerillo la nieve de un volcán.* Text from Collection of Luisa Pardo, 2014.

Lagartijas Tiradas al Sol. *Derretiré con un cerillo la nieve de un volcán*, Parte 1. Performed by Francisco Barreiro, Luisa Pardo, and Gabino Rodríguez. Vimeo, https://vimeo.com/81829732.

Lagartijas Tiradas al Sol. *Derretiré con un cerillo la nieve de un volcán*, Parte 2. Performed by Francisco Barreiro, Luisa Pardo, and Gabino Rodríguez. Vimeo, https://vimeo.com/82024145.

Lagartijas Tiradas al Sol. *Derretiré con un cerillo la nieve de un volcán*, Parte 3. Performed by Francisco Barreiro, Luisa Pardo, and Gabino Rodríguez. Vimeo, https://vimeo.com/81941711.

Lagartijas Tiradas al Sol. *Derretiré con un cerillo la nieve de un volcán*, Parte 4. Performed by Francisco Barreiro, Luisa Pardo, and Gabino Rodríguez. Vimeo, https://vimeo.com/81920423.

Lagartijas Tiradas al Sol. *Distrito Federal.* Created by Juan Leduc and Gabino Rodríguez. Vimeo, https://vimeo.com/233747746, 2017.

Lagartijas Tiradas al Sol. *El rumor de este momento.* Conejo Blanco, 2010.

Lagartijas Tiradas al Sol. *El rumor del incendio.* Winningstad Theatre, 9 Sept. 2012, Portland, OR. On The Boards, 20 Feb. 2013, https://www.ontheboards.tv/performance/theater/el-rumor.

Lagartijas Tiradas al Sol. *El Rumor del Oleaje.* https://elrumordeloleaje.wordpress.com/.

Lagartijas Tiradas al Sol. *Elisa.* Performed by Francisco Barreiro. 16 July 2017, Teatro El Milagro, Mexico City.

Lagartijas Tiradas al Sol. *En el mismo barco.* Text from Collection of Luisa Pardo, 2007.

Lagartijas Tiradas al Sol. *Esta es la historia de un niño que creció y todavía se acuerda de algunas cosas.* Text from Collection of Luisa Pardo, 2005.

Lagartijas Tiradas al Sol. *Está escrita en sus campos.* Performed by Francisco Barreiro. Vimeo, 2015, https://vimeo.com/115297076.

Lagartijas Tiradas al Sol. *Está escrita en sus campos.* Text from Collection of Luisa Pardo, 2014.

Lagartijas Tiradas al Sol. *Este cuerpo mío.* Performed by Mariana Villegas, Teatro El Milagro, 13 July 2017, Mexico City.

Lagartijas Tiradas al Sol. *Este cuerpo mío.* Text from Collection of Mariana Villegas, 2017.

Lagartijas Tiradas al Sol. "La democracia en México." http://lagartijastiradasalsol.com/en/obra/la-democracia-en-mexico/.

Lagartijas Tiradas al Sol. "La invención de nuestros padres." 28 Feb. 2012, http://lagartijastiradasalsol.blogspot.com/2012/02/la-invencion-de-nuestros-padres.html.

Lagartijas Tiradas al Sol. "Lagartijas Tiradas al Sol." http://lagartijastiradasalsol.com/seccion/.

Lagartijas Tiradas al Sol. *Montserrat.* Performed by Gabino Rodríguez. Teatro El Milagro, 28 July 2007, Mexico City.

Lagartijas Tiradas al Sol. *Montserrat.* Text frrom Collection of Luisa Pardo, 2014.

Lagartijas Tiradas al Sol. "Pre-Presentación Austin." Performed by Luisa Pardo. Text from Collection of Luisa Pardo, 2017.

Lagartijas Tiradas al Sol. "Proyecto Yivi." http://lagartijastiradasalsol.com/proyecto-yivi/.

Lagartijas Tiradas al Sol. *Santiago Amoukalli.* Performed by Luisa Pardo and Gabino Rodríguez, Teatro El Milagro, 15 July 2017, Mexico City.

Lagartijas Tiradas al Sol. *Santiago Amoukalli.* Text from Collection of Luisa Pardo, 2016.

Lagartijas Tiradas al Sol. *Se rompen las olas.* Performed by Mariana Villegas, Teatro El Milagro 21 Apr. 2012, Mexico City.

Lagartijas Tiradas al Sol. *Se rompen las olas.* Text from Collection of Luisa Pardo, 2014.

Lagartijas Tiradas al Sol. "Tijuana." http://lagartijastiradasalsol.com/obra/tijuana/.

Lagartijas Tiradas al Sol. *Tijuana.* Performed by Gabino Rodríguez. Fusebox Festival, Emma S. Barrientos Mexican American Cultural Center, 15 Apr. 2017, Austin.

Lagartijas Tiradas al Sol. *Tijuana.* Text from Collection of Luisa Pardo, 2016.

Lagartijas Tiradas al Sol. *Veracruz, nos estamos deforestando o cómo extrañar Xalapa.* Performed by Luisa Pardo. Agenda Guelatao, 23 July 2017, Oaxaca. Video from Collection of Luisa Pardo, 2017.

Lagartijas Tiradas al Sol. *Veracruz, nos estamos deforestando o cómo extrañar Xalapa.* Text from Collection of Luisa Pardo, 2017.

"Lagartijas Tiradas al Sol presentan: *La democracia en* México." Teatro La Capilla, 2016, http://www.teatrolacapilla.com/lagartijas-tiradas-al-sol-presentan-la-democracia-en-mexico/.

Le Roy, Frederik, and Robrecht Vanderbeeken. "The Documentary Real: Thinking Documentary Aesthetics." *Foundations of Science,* 2016, https://doi.org/10.1007/s10699-016-9513-8.

Lehmann, Hans-Thies. *Postdramatic Theatre.* Translated by Karen Jürs-Munby, Routledge, 2006.

Lejeune, Philippe. "The Autobiographical Pact," edited by Paul John Eakin, translated by Katherine Leary. *On Autobiography.* U of Minnesota P, 1989, pp. 3–30.

Lejeune, Philippe. "Autobiography and New Communication Tools," edited by Anna Poletti and Julie Rak, translated by Katherine Durnin. *Identity Technologies: Constructing the Self Online.* U of Wisconsin P, 2014, pp. 247–58.

León-Portilla, Miguel. *Visión de los vencidos: Relaciones indígenas de la conquista,* 29th ed. Coordinación de Humanidades, UNAM, 2011.

Lost in Transition: Bold Ambitions, Limited Results for Human Rights under Fox. Human Rights Watch, 2006, https://www.hrw.org/reports/2006/mexico0506/.

Luna Fuentes, Claudia. "El Tigre y el rompecabezas de la industria del narco." *Vanguardia,* 16 Mar. 2015, https://www.vanguardia.com.mx/columnas-eltigreyelrompecabezas delaindustriadelnarco-2286362.html.

Lyotard, Jean-François. *The Postmodern Condition: A Report on Knowledge.* Translated by Geoff Bennington and Brian Massumi, U of Minnesota P, 1984.

Magnarelli, Sharon. *Home Is Where the (He)Art Is: The Family Romance in Late Twentieth-Century Mexican and Argentine Theater.* Bucknell UP, 2008.

Maquilapolis. Directed by Vicky Funari and Sergio De La Torre, California Newsreel, 2006.

"The Marfa Triptych: The Country & Western Big Band Suite." *Ballroom Marfa,* 16 Nov. 2013, www.ballroommarfa.org/archive/event/the-marfa-triptych-three-portraits-of -texas/#event-release.

Martell, Mayra. "Habitaciones de las mujeres de Juárez." *Vice,* 24 Nov. 2016, https://www .vice.com/es_mx/article/dpb7mw/habitaciones-de-las-mujeres-de-juarez-0000581-v8n4.

Martin, Carol. "Bodies of Evidence." *Dramaturgy of the Real on the World Stage,* edited by Carol Martin, Palgrave Macmillan, 2010, 17–26.

Martin Carol, ed. *Documentary Theatre.* Special Issue of *TDR: The Drama Review,* Vol. 60, NO. 3, Fall 2006.

Martin Carol, ed. *Dramaturgy of the Real on the World Stage.* Palgrave Macmillan, 2010.

Martin, Carol. *Theatre of the Real.* Palgrave Macmillan, 2013.

Martín, Patricia. "Borrando Fronteras." *El Financiero,* 1 Sept. 2016, http://www.elfinanciero .com.mx/opinion/patricia-martin/borrando-fronteras.

Martínez, Fabiola. "Canceló Gobernación el acceso directo a los archivos sobre la *guerra sucia.*" *La Jornada,* 11 Mar. 2015, http://www.jornada.com.mx/2015/03/11/politica /009n2pol.

Mbembe, Achille. *Necropolítica.* Melusina, 2011.

McCormick, Gladys. "The Last Door: Political Prisoners and the Use of Torture in Mexico's Dirty War." *The Americas,* vol. 74, no. 1, 2017, pp. 57–81. *Project Muse,* muse.jhu .edu/article/647449.

McSherry, J. Patrice. *Predatory States: Operation Condor and Covert War in Latin America.* Rowman and Littlefield, 2012.

Meiborg, Mounia. "Wie geht es dem Rest der Welt." *Süddeutsche Zeitung*, 6 Apr. 2017, https://www.sueddeutsche.de/kultur/theater-wie-geht-es-dem-rest-der-welt-1.3453896.

Meléndez, Priscilla. "La 'antihistoria' y la metaficción en *Corona de sombra* de Rodolfo Usigli." *La Torre*, vol. 4, no. 13, 1990, pp. 49–69.

Migrant Death Mapping. Humane Borders/Fronteras Compasivas, https://humaneborders.org/migrant-death-mapping/.

Mijares, Enrique. "Las muestras curatoriales de Aguascalientes 2015." *Latin American Theatre Review*, vol. 49, no. 2, 2016, pp. 275–79. *Project Muse*, https://doi.org/10.1353/ltr.2016.0023.

Mijares, Enrique. "Muestra Mexicana de Teatro 2007." *Latin American Theatre Review*, vol. 41, no. 2, 2008, pp. 131–36. *Project Muse*, https://doi.org/10.1353/ltr.2008.0009.

Molloy, Sylvia. *At Face Value: Autobiographical Writing in Spanish America*. Palgrave Macmillan, 1991.

"Montan la premiada obra teatral 'Asalto al agua transparente.'" *Globedia*, 3 Nov. 2011, http://es.globedia.com/montan-premiada-obra-teatral-asalto-agua-transparente.

Morales Chacana, Lina J. "Towards Cross-Border Hispanic Theatre: Breaking Barriers of Language, Space and Time Bilingual Website (English-Spanish) www.hispanictheatre.org." University of Maryland, College Park, 2013. ProQuest, https://search-proquest-com.ezproxy.lib.ou.edu/docview/1431455256?accountid=12964.

Morales Muñoz, Noé. "Asalto al agua transparente." *Jornada Semanal*, 24 Sept. 2006, http://criticateatral2021.org/transcripciones/5133_20060924.php.

Moraña, Mabel. "Historicismo y legitimación del poder en *El gesticulador* de Rodolfo Usigli." *Revista Iberoamericana*, vol. 55, no. 148–49, 1989, pp. 1261–75, https://doi.org/10.5195/reviberoamer.1989.4661.

"Nadia Vera responsabiliza al gobernado Javier Duarte, si algo le sucede . . . (A 5 meses del multihomicidio)." Rompeviento TV, 31 Dec. 2015, https://www.rompeviento.tv/?p=5510.

Nigro, Kirsten. "Light and Darkness in Usigli's *Corona de sombra*." *Chasqui*, vol. 17, no. 2, 1988, pp. 27–34. *JSTOR*, https://www.jstor.org/stable/29740082.

Nussbaum, Emily. "My So-Called Blog." *New York Times Magazine*, 11 Jan. 2004, https://www.nytimes.com/2004/01/11/magazine/my-so-called-blog.html.

O'Connor, Peter, and Briar O'Connor. "Editorial." *RiDE: The Journal of Applied Theatre and Performance*, vol. 14, no. 4, 2009, pp. 471–77, https://doi.org/10.1080/13569780903285966.

Oddey, Alison. *Devising Theatre: A Practical and Theoretical Handbook*. Routledge, 1994.

Ortiz, Rubén. *Escena expandida: Teatralidades del siglo XXI*. Conaculta-INBA, 2015.

Pacheco, José Emilio. *Miro la tierra: Poemas 1983–1986*. Ediciones Era, 2003.

Paget, Derek. "Documentary Theatre." *The Continuum Companion to Twentieth Century Theatre*, edited by Colin Chambers, Continuum, 2002. *Drama Online*, www.dramaonlinelibrary.com/genres/documentary-theatre-iid-2482.

Partida Tayzan, Armando. "El teatro épico de Víctor Hugo Rascón Banda." *El teatro de*

Rascón Banda: Voces en el umbral, edited by Jacqueline Bixler and Stuart A. Day, Escenología, 2003, pp. 81–90.

Patrón Rivera, Mauricio. *"Está escrita en sus campos* de Lagartijas Tiradas al Sol." *TimeOut*, 28 Jan. 2015, https://www.timeoutmexico.mx/ciudad-de-mexico/teatro/esta-escrita -en-sus-campos-de-lagartijas-tiradas-al-sol.

Pensado, Jaime M. *Rebel Mexico: Student Unrest and Authoritarian Political Culture during the Long Sixties.* Stanford UP, 2013.

Pérez Limón, Lilia A. "Precarious Attachments to Modernity: Interrogating the Mexican Body Politic through Performative Practices." University of Wisconsin-Madison, Ann Arbor, 2016. ProQuest, https://search-proquest-com.ezproxy.lib.ou.edu/docview /1796990233?accountid=12964.

Prieto Nadal, Ana. "'La Democracia En México, Un proyecto de Lagartijas Tiradas Al Sol." *Culturamas*, 18 Oct. 2016, http://www.culturamas.es/blog/2016/10/18/la-democracia -en-mexico-un-proyecto-de-lagartijas-tiradas-al-sol/.

Prieto Stambaugh, Antonio. "Memorias inquietas: Testimonio y confesión en el teatro performativo de México y Brasil." Prieto Stambaugh and Fediuk, pp. 207–32.

Prieto Stambaugh, Antonio, and Martha Toriz Proenza. "Performance: Entre el teatro y la antropología." *Diario de Campo*, vol. 6–7, 2015, pp. 22–31, http://diariodecampo .mx/2015/04/04/performance-entre-el-teatro-y-la-antropologia/.

Puga, Cristina. "Ciencias sociales: Un nuevo momento." *Revista Mexicana de Sociología*, vol. 71, 2009, pp. 105–31. *JSTOR*, https://www.jstor.org/stable/25677024.

Rayner, Alice. *Ghosts: Death's Double and the Phenomena of Theatre.* U of Minnesota P, 2006.

Recio, Gabriela. "Drugs and Alcohol: US Prohibition and the Origins of the Drug Trade in Mexico, 1910–1930." *Journal of Latin American Studies*, vol. 34, 2002, pp. 21–42, https://doi.org/10.1017/S0022216X01006289.

Reinelt, Janelle. "The Promise of Documentary." *Get Real: Documentary Theatre Past and Present*, edited by Alison Forsyth and Chris Megson, Palgrave Macmillan, 2009, pp. 6–23.

Reynolds, Graham. *Pancho Villa from a Safe Distance.* Libretto by Lagartijas Tiradas al Sol. Ballroom Marfa, 11 Nov. 2016, Marfa, TX.

Rivera, Alex, dir. *Sleep Dealer.* Maya Entertainment, 2008.

Rizk, Beatriz. *Creación colectiva: El legado de Enrique Buenaventura.* Atuel, 2008.

Rodríguez, Gabino. "Proceso *asalto al agua transparente*, Reflexiones." 2014, http://lagarti jastiradasalsol.com/wp-content/uploads/2014/08/proceso-asalto-publicacion.pdf.

Rojas, Mario A. "*Krísis* de Sabina Berman y el escenario político mexicano." *Tradición, modernidad y posmodernidad (Teatro iberoamericano y argentino)*, edited by Osvaldo Pelletieri, Editorial Galerna, 1999, pp. 119–34.

Rose-Ackerman, Susan. *Corruption: A Study in Political Economy.* Academic Press, 1978.

Ruiz Vivanco, Elvira. "Clausura del Festival Internacional de Teatro Puebla Héctor Azar." *e-consulta.com*, 27 Nov. 2013, http://www.e-consulta.com/opinion/2013–11–27/clau sura-del-festival-internacional-de-teatro-puebla-hector-azar.

Sabugal Paz, Paulina. "Teatro documental: Entre la realidad y la ficción." *Investigación Te-atral*, vol. 7, no. 10–11, 2017, pp. 111–29. *U Veracruzana*, http://investigacionteatral .uv.mx/index.php/investigacionteatral/article/view/2533.

Salcedo, Hugo. "El teatro documento en México." *Acotaciones*, vol. 37, 2016, pp. 97–116. *ResearchGate*, https://www.researchgate.net/publication/313874965_El_teatro_docu mento_en_Mexico_by_Hugo_Salcedo_Revista_Acotaciones_RESAD_ Madrid_2016_ISSN_2444-3948.

Saltzman, Lisa. *Making Memory Matter: Strategies of Remembrance in Contemporary Art*. U of Chicago P, 2006.

Salvat, Ricard. "Una aproximación al actual teatro de México." *Assaig de teatre: revista de l'Associació d'Investigació i Experimentació Teatral*, vol. 62–64, 2008, pp. 426–39. *RACO*, https://www.raco.cat/index.php/AssaigTeatre/article/view/182661/235328.

Sánchez, José A. *Prácticas de lo real en la escena contemporánea*. Visor Libros, 2007.

Sandos, James A. "Northern Separatism During the Mexican Revolution: An Inquiry into the Role of Drug Trafficking, 1910–1920." *The Americas*, vol. 41, no. 2, 1984, pp. 191–214. *JSTOR*, https://www.jstor.org/stable/1007456.

Schultheiss, Michel. "Narrar la catástrofe: Las representaciones literarias del terremoto de 1985 en México." *Acontecimientos históricos y su productividad cultural en el mundo his-pánico*, edited by Marco Kunz et al., Lit Verlag, 2016, pp. 51–72.

"'Se rompen las olas,' de Mariana Villegas, terremoto y génesis de existencia." *El Diario de Coahuila*, 24 July 2014, http://www.eldiariodecoahuila.com.mx/sociales/ex-presate/2014/7/24/rompen-olas-mariana-villegas-terremoto-genesis-existencia-446050.html.

Serna, Enrique. "Sergio Magaña: El redentor condenado." *Revista de la Universidad de Méx-ico*, vol. 80, 2010, pp. 86–90, http://132.247.1.5/revista/revistaum/ojs_rum/index .php/rum/article/download/1911/2914.

Sheren, Ila N. *Portable Borders: Performance Art and Politics on the U.S. Frontera since 1984*. U of Texas P, 2015.

Smith, Sidonie, and Julia Watson. *Reading Autobiography: A Guide for Interpreting Life Nar-ratives*, 2nd ed. U of Minnesota P, 2010.

Solano, Andrés Felipe. *Salario Mínimo*. Tusquets, 2015.

Soto Coloballes, Natalia Verónica. "40 años después: Sin soluciones." *Nexos* 1 July 2016, https://www.nexos.com.mx/?p=28768.

Stephenson, Jenn. *Performing Autobiography: Contemporary Canadian Drama*. U of Toron-to P, 2013.

Stephenson, Jenn. "Winning and/or Losing: The Perils and Products of Insecurity in Post-dramatic Autobiographical Performance." *Theatre Journal*, vol. 68, no. 2, 2016, pp. 213–29.

Sutcliffe, Arnold. "Teatro de creación colectiva." *Araucaria de Chile*, vol. 6, 1979. *Centro Documental Blest*, http://www.blest.eu/cultura/teatroC.html.

Taylor, Diana. *The Archive and the Repertoire: Performing Cultural Memory in the Americas.* Duke UP, 2003.

Taylor, Diana. *Theatre of Crisis: Drama and Politics in Latin America.* UP of Kentucky, 1991.

Tomlin, Liz. *Acts and Apparitions: Discourses on the Real in Performance Practice and Theory, 1990–2010.* Manchester UP, 2013.

Toro, María Celia. "The Internationalization of Police: The DEA in Mexico." *Journal of American History*, vol. 86, no. 2, 1999, pp. 623–40. *JSTOR*, https://www.jstor.org/stable /2567049.

Trastoy, Beatriz. *Teatro autobiográfico: Los unipersonales de los 80 y 90 en la escena argentina.* Editorial Nueva Generación, 2002.

Valdés Medellín, Gonzalo. "El show business en el teatro mexicano." *Un siglo de teatro en méxico*, edited by David Olguín, Fondo de Cultura Económica / Conaculta, 2011, pp. 185–209.

Valencia Villa, Alejandro, et al. *Informe Ayotzinapa.* Grupo Interdisciplinario de Expertos Independientes (GIEI), 2015, https://drive.google.com/file/d/0B1ChdondilaHNzF HaEs3azQ4Tm8/view?pli=1.

Vallejo de la Ossa, Ana María. "Reflexiones sobre la relación cuerpo y escritura en el teatro contemporáneo de América Latina." *Revista Corpo-grafías*, vol. 2, no. 2, 2015, pp. 50–63, https://doi.org/10.14483/cp.v2i2.11153.

Van Ryzin, Jeanne Claire. "Lagartijas Tiradas Al Sol's 'Tijuana': Enacting Poverty." *Fusebox Festival Blog*, http://schedule.fuseboxfestival.com/blog/lagartijas-tiradas-al-sols -tijuana-enacting-poverty.

"Vargas Llosa: "México es la dictadura perfecta." *El País*, 1 Sept. 1990, https://elpais.com/ diario/1990/09/01/cultura/652140001_850215.html.

Versényi, Adam. *Theatre in Latin America: Religion, Politics, and Culture from Cortés to the 1980s.* Cambridge UP, 1993.

Wallraff, Günter. *Cabeza De Turco.* Anagrama, 1999.

Ward, Julie Ann. "Affective Suffrage: Social Media, Street Protests, and Theatre as Alternative Spaces for Political Self-Representation in the 2012 Mexican Presidential Elections." *Transmodernity: Journal of Peripheral Cultural Production of the Luso-Hispanic World*, vol. 7, no. 2, pp. 97–118. *eScholarship*, https://escholarship.org/uc/ item/88v6w5c1.

Ward, Julie Ann. "Beside Motherhood: Staging Women's Lives in Latin American Theatre of the Real." *The Routledge Companion to Gender, Sex, and Latin American Culture*, edited by Frederick Luis Aldama. Routledge, 2018, pp. 377–85.

Ward, Julie Ann. "Entrevista con Lagartijas Tiradas Al Sol." *Latin American Theatre Review*, vol. 5, no. 2, 2012, pp. 139–46. *Project Muse*, https://doi.org/10.1353/ltr.2012.0006.

Ward, Julie Ann. "Making Reality Sensible: The Mexican Documentary Theatre Tradition, 1968–2013." *Theatre Journal*, vol. 69, no. 2, 2017. *Project Muse*, https://doi.org/10.1353/ tj.2017.0024.

Ward, Julie Ann. "Self, Esteemed: Contemporary Auto/biographical Theatre in Latin America," University of California, Berkeley, Ann Arbor, 2013. ProQuest, https://search-proquest-com.ezproxy.lib.ou.edu/docview/1439133220?accountid=12964.

Ward, Julie Ann. "Staging Postmemory: Self-representation and Parental Biographying in Lagartijas Tiradas al Sol's *El rumor del incendio.*" *Latin American Theatre Review,* vol. 47, no. 2, 2014, pp. 25–44. *Project Muse,* https://doi.org/10.1353/ltr.2014.0027.

Ward, Julie Ann, and Lola Arias. "Interview with Lola Arias." 4 Oct. 2012.

Ward, Julie Ann, Luisa Pardo, and Gabino Rodríguez. Personal Interview. 16 Apr. 2017.

Weigel, Matthias. "Generation Erdbeben." *nachtkritik.de,* 2 May 2015, http://www.heidel berger-stueckemarkt.nachtkritik.de/2015/index.php/gastland/se-rompen-las-olas -kurzkritik.

Welton, Martin. *Feeling Theatre.* Palgrave Macmillan, 2012.

White, Hayden. *Tropics of Discourse: Essays in Cultural Criticism.* Johns Hopkins UP, 1986.

Whitt, Joseph A. Jr. "The Mexican Peso Crisis." *Economic Review,* vol. 81, no. 1, 1996, pp. 1–20. *Federal Reserve Bank of Atlanta,* https://www.frbatlanta.org/-/media/documents /filelegacydocs/Jwhi811.pdf.

Witchel, Elisabeth. *Getting Away with Murder.* Committee to Protect Journalists, 2016, https://cpj.org/reports/2017/10/impunity-index-getting-away-with-murder -killed-justice.php.

Ybarra, Patricia. *Performing Conquest: Five Centuries of Theater, History, and Identity in Tlaxcala, Mexico.* U of Michigan P, 2009.

Yépez, Gabriel. "La integración de nuevas tecnologías, la escena transversal y los procesos colectivos de creación," edited by Gabriel Yépez. *La escena teatral en México / Diálogos para el Siglo 21,* Instituto Nacional de Bellas Artes y Literatura, 2014, pp. 75–87. *ISSUU,* https://issuu.com/andrescuboalvarado/docs/ebook_35mnt.

Young, Dolly J. "Mexican Literary Reactions to Tlatelolco 1968." *Latin American Research Review,* vol. 20, no. 2, 1985, pp. 71–85. *JSTOR,* https://www.jstor.org/stable/2503521.

Yúdice, George. "Testimonio y concientización." *Revista de Crítica Literaria Latinoamericana.* vol. 18, no. 36, 1992, pp. 211–32. *JSTOR,* https://www.jstor.org/stable/4530631.

Žižek, Slavoj. *Violence.* Picador, 2008.

Note: Page numbers in *italics* indicate illustrative material.